The Essential Guide to Postgraduate Study

DAVID WILKINSON

SAGE Publications

London ● Thousand Oaks ● New Delhi

First published 2005

Apart from any fair dealing for the purposes of research or
private study, or criticism or review, as permitted under
the Copyright, Designs and Patents Act, 1988, this publication
may be reproduced, stored or transmitted in any form, or
by any means, only with the prior permission in writing of
the publishers, or in the case of reprographic reproduction,
in accordance with the terms of licences issued by the
Copyright Licensing Agency. Inquiries concerning
reproduction outside those terms should be sent to
the publishers.

SAGE Publications Ltd
1 Oliver's Yard
55 City Road
London EC1Y 1SP

SAGE Publications Inc.
2455 Teller Road
Thousand Oaks, California 91320

SAGE Publications India Pvt Ltd
B-42, Panchsheel Enclave
Post Box 4109
New Delhi 110 017

British Library Cataloguing in Publication data

A catalogue record for this book is available
from the British Library

ISBN 1 4129 0062 X
ISBN 1 4129 0063 8 (pbk)

Library of Congress Control Number: 2005901454

Typeset by C&M Digitals (P) Ltd., Chennai, India
Printed on paper from sustainable resources
Printed in Great Britain by Athenaeum Press, Gateshead

Contents

Acknowledgements

I am grateful to a sizeable number of people for providing varying levels of assistance to produce this text. The many postgraduate students I spoke to during 2004 offered a wealth of information relating to their own experiences and learning journeys (short summaries of those I spent some time interviewing are provided at the end of this text). A number of my fellow academics also permitted me to steal some of their valuable time to help formulate sections of the book – in particular I am grateful to Professor Richard Thorpe at Leeds University, Alison Price at Leeds Metropolitan University and Peter Birmingham at Oxford University. Thank you also to my initial collaborators on this project, Margaret Gibbons and John Hillard at the University of Leeds, for providing some useful input and suggesting how the text might develop.

The Economic and Social Research Council (ESRC) granted crucial support (Research award number 201 26 1001) during the development phase of this text by providing the financial means to enable the interviews with postgraduate students to take place. In addition, Paul Rouse (ESRC Postgraduate Training Division) provided very welcome guidance and support with the development of lines of enquiry for the interviews conducted.

I would also like to thank Patrick Brindle and Michael Carmichael at Sage for having faith in this work and guiding me through some difficult times during its production.

David Wilkinson

Foreword

The importance and value of research training has never been greater. The Lambert and Roberts reports, together with revisions made to the Research Council's postgraduate training guidelines and the joint statement of the Research Council's skills requirements for research students within postgraduate study, have firmly positioned development opportunity as an essential feature of any university's provision.

For Masters and PhD students, research training ought to be seen as a journey, not an end point. One that provides students and researchers with the development of knowledge, skills and attitudes that will serve them for the rest of their careers.

David Wilkinson's book addresses all the concerns of postgraduate students and provides an invaluable resource for all those considering embarking on postgraduate research. *The Essential Guide to Postgraduate Study* begins with some important context, which will be useful for students of all disciplines; it then starts the journey by guiding students through the questions they might have in relation to such things as: choice of institution, financing your study and seeking support, researching, developing and presenting ideas, managing your time, writing-up your work, how to work with academics including your supervisor (not always as easy as it might at first appear!) as well as offering some understanding of how universities are structured and how to navigate within them.

The style of the book is accessible and offers a host of vignettes and anecdotes that bring to life what to many can be a mysterious process.

I commend the book to those who wish to get underneath what it means to undertake postgraduate study.

Richard Thorpe
Professor of Management Development, University of Leeds
Member of the ESRC Training and Development Board

1 Why read this book? The target audience

Chapter and book overview

This text is targeted at prospective postgraduates, current postgraduates and those interested in better understanding postgraduate study in UK universities and higher education colleges. In essence this guide provides:

- Detailed information relating to recent developments in postgraduate study, its numerous types and forms, and initiatives resourced and favoured by postgraduate funders.
- Summary information collected and collated from influential postgraduate funding organisations in relation to the desirable key skills of an effective postgraduate learner, with guidance on how to develop such skills.
- Guidance on where to apply for postgraduate study (from the thousands of courses and programmes of study available), how to effectively use Research Assessment Exercise (RAE) data, and other performance indicators, and how to obtain other institutional data to assist with institutional and programme/course selection.
- Focused and helpful information exploring postgraduate application processes and procedures, typical information requirements in postgraduate applications, and sample material from previous successful applications.
- Examples of postgraduate research/project proposals, structuring your ideas, and tips for successful proposals.
- Support on how to operate within a university environment, information on roles and responsibilities, and the structure and operation of the typical university.
- Guidance and support for dealing with and managing information and seeking advice, how to get the most out of libraries and electronic information sources.
- Advice on effective academic writing, drafting and structuring written work, and the different types and styles of writing for academic purposes.
- Effective assistance on managing postgraduate work, time management tools and techniques, setting clear goals, and utilising project management ideas.

- Information on how to work effectively with supervisors and postgraduate tutors, the typical roles and responsibilities of the student and the supervisor, and negotiating appropriate input from supervisors and tutors.
- Networking advice, how to develop postgraduate societies and support groups, how to gain the most from working with academics and effectively using conference as developmental events.
- Advice relating to teaching opportunities, how these can aid your research/ project work, and add value to career progression.
- Detailed guidance and support in relation to getting work published, including selecting appropriate publication outlets.

Postgraduates navigating their learning journey

Navigating a learning journey can be a demanding task. There are numerous guides and textbooks available to help support and steer your progress through higher education. Many of these focus upon specific elements or areas of your studies and/or learning; these include excellent expositions on the development of introductory level study skills (Drew and Bingham, 2001; Lashley and Best, 2001; Burns and Sinfield, 2003; McIlroy, 2003). For those engaged in postgraduate study, the above texts (and others like them) may prove useful but they do not unpack some of the unique peculiarities of the typical postgraduate experience. This text seeks to do just that.

In research work conducted whilst preparing this text, a wide range of postgraduates, past and present, were asked about their views, perceptions and experiences of postgraduate study. Short reviews of who they are and the postgraduate work they are involved in are provided in Appendix 1 (Postgraduate Views). Wherever possible direct and attributable quotations have been used throughout to facilitate the provision of more personalised accounts of the points or issues raised in the main body of the text. Occasionally, it has been necessary to preserve the anonymity of postgraduates (either at their own request or as an attempt to save their blushes). Where this is the case, names have been changed and the fictional universities of Northside, Southside, Westside and Eastside have been used.

Peter's personal account, below, presents a common theme for many when discussing their perceptions and experiences of postgraduate study – a need for tailored support and guidance that assists the postgraduate journey. There are hundreds (if not thousands) of generalist (and excellent) texts to support undergraduate study, but only recently have the specific needs of postgraduates been targeted and supported through the study guide literature.

> *Effective postgraduate study demands focus and determination. Undergraduate study is fairly straightforward and structured – at postgraduate level there are far more pitfalls, dangers and potential areas for failure. You need to carefully plan and structure your studies with appropriate support from family, colleagues and fellow academics if you are going to (a) have any chance of success, and (b) an enjoyable experience!*
>
> Peter, PhD student, University of Oxford.

This book has been developed and shaped around a typical postgraduate journey, beginning with an examination of what postgraduate study is, and what it requires from you as a student, through to contemplating and investigating career options post-completion of your studies. For this reason the text follows the format put forward in Figure 1.1 – with indicative chapter issues outlined.

The structure of this text provides that each consecutive chapter develops and builds upon its predecessor. Following an examination of postgraduate learning (in Chapter 2), it is useful to look at the various training guidance material available, before exploring where you might study (in Chapter 3). Once the various options have been investigated, the application and funding process can be assessed, before submitting an application or proposal for research funding (in Chapter 4). In the remaining chapters, coverage is provided that assists postgraduate learners progress successfully through their programme of study and considers options post-graduation. Through this structure and associated analysis of key issues, it is hoped that the text provides useful support to the many postgraduates holding similar views to those put forward by Dan, a current postgraduate student, below.

> *I think it would be useful for postgraduate textbooks to focus on the things that are going to get you through in the longer term – how to get published, what it's like to work in a university, etc. If you want to get into academia these are the kind of things you need to know.*
>
> Dan, ESRC 1 + 3 student, University of Edinburgh.

The following describes a flowchart showing the structure of the book, with linked boxes and arrows.

Why is postgraduate study important? What key skills and attributes are important for postgraduates? What kind of skills do you need to develop? You need to read **Chapter 2: Developments in postgraduate study.**

Which institutions will be best suited to you? What selection criteria might you use? What sources of funding are available and how can you secure them? You need to read **Chapter 3: Where to study and apply for funding.**

How should you frame your project or research ideas for postgraduate study? How can you make sure you meet application requirements? You need to read **Chapter 4: Developing proposals.**

What is it like to operate and work in a university? What are the cultural issues and considerations you should be aware of? You need to read **Chapter 5: Finding your feet – the culture of academia.**

How can you develop key data-gathering skills to support your studies/research? You need to read **Chapter 6: Reading and searching for information and seeking advice.**

How can you effectively manage your studies, time and project/research work? What are the academic standards at postgraduate level? What are the preferred styles of writing? What tools can help present your work? You need to read **Chapter 7: Managing your time, academic writing and presenting your work.**

Why is it important to develop and nurture a good working relationship with your supervisor? You need to read **Chapter 8: Working with your supervisor.**

How can you effectively seek and utilise the views of peers? How important is networking and developing collaborative efforts? You need to read **Chapter 9: Working with other researchers.**

What are the teaching role and duties for postgraduates and how helpful can they be for my postgraduate studies? You need to read **Chapter 10: Career planning.**

What routes and options are available to promote and publicise your work? You need to read **Chapter 11: Publishing opportunities.**

FIGURE 1.1   **The structure of the rest of this book**

In addressing postgraduate needs (as vocally indicated by a variety of post-graduate learners), the entire book methodically tackles the processes, procedures, issues, strategies and requirements of relevance to those wishing to navigate their own postgraduate journey. However, few learning journeys (particularly postgraduate ones) follow what could be described as a methodical and clearly structured path. For this reason (and to appease postgraduates such as Caroline below), the text has been developed for those at various stages in their postgraduate studies – for those who wish to 'dip into' or access specific sections to help resolve a problem or examine an issue of relevance to their own work.

> *Many of the texts to support postgraduate study are quite good, but they do tend to suggest crisply clear models for applying for funding, working with your supervisor, and networking with fellow postgraduates. Reality doesn't always match this guidance. It's for that reason that I'm not really a fan of textbooks that tell you how to do things really. I'm a fan of the pick-and-mix approach – where you take bits from the books as necessary to serve the purpose.*
>
> Caroline, PhD student, University of Westside.

If you are a prospective student, the book should support the personal research that you will need to undertake to identify which postgraduate programme meets your immediate and longer-term academic requirements. For new recruits, and for existing postgraduate students, the book offers an informed insight into the mysteries of the higher education (HE) system, the culture of academia and how best to work with academics and colleague researchers, and it covers practical issues such as academic norms, effective research, academic writing and time management. The book provides a firm foundation for students and sets the context for study at postgraduate level by providing useful information about the academic system that often students do not access until advanced in their studies. The overall aim of the book, therefore, is to enable students to become more strategic and less reactive in their approach to postgraduate learning. This shift in emphasis towards self-management not only involves a greater awareness of the need to develop 'basic' skills, such as time management and being able to set objectives, but also the realisation that learning itself is a skill that needs to be developed. In becoming more self-managed, students will, as emphasised in the book, develop a greater sensitivity of the importance of thinking strategically about longer-term personal goals and career development. The coverage provided of Personal Development Plans (PDPs), an increasingly important area within higher education and beyond, will facilitate the effective assessment, development and coordination of your own personal and professional development.

A central issue for many postgraduate learners is the focused development of transferable skills from general study skills for postgraduates to skills in organising workloads, time management and effective methods of prioritising work so that deadlines are met. At key points in the text, references are made to developing key skills to enable effective collaboration with fellow postgraduates, as well as academic colleagues, enabling you to secure academic and professional success.

This book has been written to inform and support postgraduate students throughout their studies; it also takes the process further by giving advice to new researchers who wish to pursue a research career in higher education or in industry. Teaching and other employment options are covered towards the end of the text, and these should help students to think about the process of structured career planning post-qualification. Throughout, the book emphasises the need to think strategically about longer-term personal and career development.

Academic practitioners and policymakers

This book is also intended to appeal to academic practitioners responsible for postgraduate teaching and research. For taught programmes recent expansion and rapid development of postgraduate provision has created a number of challenges, not least a perceived threat to the quality of postgraduate qualifications. Whilst I cannot pretend to provide solutions to all these challenges, it is important to explore how a 'student-focused' view can help to inform the future development of postgraduate provision. Faced with intensified international competition, quality becomes something more than a mantra reliant upon tradition. Quality relates to the entire student experience from initial enquiry to becoming an alumnus. The approach adopted in this book is primarily intended to provide a prospective student with the knowledge to make an informed choice about postgraduate study but in so doing it will hopefully set a benchmark for improving academic practice.

For those engaged in postgraduate supervision, a major external pressure in the recent past has been to improve completion rates on pain of losing government funding. An underlying theme of the book is to equip students with the skills to navigate through the postgraduate experience. Of necessity, this will create expectations and, for example, our discussion of working with your supervisor is designed to help academics as well as students to maximise the benefits of their relationship.

Reference list and useful reading

Burns, T. and Sinfield, S. (2003) *Essential study skills: the complete guide to success at university.* London: Sage.

Drew, S. and Bingham, R. (2001) *The student skills guide.* Aldershot: Gower.

Lashley, C. and Best, W. (2001) *12 steps to study success.* London: Continuum.

McIlroy, D. (2003) *Studying at university: how to be a successful student.* London: Sage.

2 Developments in postgraduate study

Chapter overview

This chapter provides an overview of the historical developments and potential directions for UK postgraduate study. Specifically, this chapter includes:

- An exploration of historical developments in postgraduate education – which subject or discipline areas are growing in student numbers and which are declining?
- Typical postgraduate provision available in the UK – what are the entry requirements of each, how long are the programmes of study, and indicative examples.
- Reasons for undertaking advanced level, postgraduate study – the benefits for you as a student.
- The growth and impact of postgraduate training guidelines.
- Guidance relating to skills and knowledge at Masters level.
- Guidance relating to skills and knowledge at Doctoral level.

Why undertake postgraduate study?

The reasons for embarking on postgraduate study, whether this be a taught or research Masters, MBA, PhD, or any permutation, are myriad. In the PhD Students' Section of the National Postgraduate Committee (NPC) website, poll results to the question 'why are you looking to do a PhD?' indicate that 48% of respondents answered that it was to improve career prospects (Figure 2.1). Additionally, when exploring the uses and potential benefits of a PhD, a supplementary survey question revealed that the mind was a primary beneficiary of undertaking this type of advanced study. Perhaps surprisingly, perceived financial gain (the wallet) was not an initial reason for study (Figure 2.2).

Many of the postgraduates consulted as part of the development of this text indicated that postgraduate learners are engaged in advanced and focused study around a

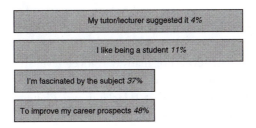

FIGURE 2.1   **Why are you looking to do a PhD?**

Source: FindAPhD.com (http://www.findaphd.com/students/pollresults.asp)
(Accessed: 11/10/04)

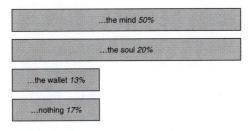

FIGURE 2.2   **A PhD is good for …**

Source: FindAPhD.com (http://www.findaphd.com/students/pollresults.asp)
(Accessed: 11/10/04)

specific discipline area. For some, postgraduate study is the natural continuation of study initiated through a first degree, although, as Anna details below, the work requirement can be considerably more than that required of an undergraduate degree.

> *Some people on my course thought that being a postgraduate was simply a continuation of being an undergraduate, it was just another year. It really is not like that! The amount of work you are required to do, and the limited timeframe you have in which to do it really does apply the pressure. Because most Masters programmes are one year full-time or two years part-time, you really do have to hit the ground running. There's not much time to relax and go drinking (as many undergraduates do)!*
>
> Anna, ESRC 1 + 3 student, University of Manchester.

In their review of a selection of postgraduate education literature, Harland and Plangger (2004) concluded that a central reason for guiding students into studying at advanced (PhD) level was their previous positive experiences gained whilst studying at undergraduate level. For many, advanced level study facilitated a more detailed exploration within their chosen field. Creating or generating 'new' knowledge was an important consideration (Harland and Plangger, 2004: 76). Other typical reasons for undertaking postgraduate study include:

* to increase job prospects;

* to develop skills;

* to work at the cutting edge;

* to train as an academic; and

* to become an expert in a given field.

Postgraduate study has traditionally been a reserved activity of the few – expense, time commitment and specialisation required for the subject have, in the past, successfully kept student numbers low. More recently, however, students, industry, government and other policymakers and beneficiaries have recognised the importance of advanced study. In recent years postgraduate numbers have increased dramatically, as evidenced by review work conducted by the Higher Education Policy Institute. In his examination of UK postgraduate education, Sastry (2004) found that a range of types of postgraduate provision had enjoyed remarkable growth in the seven-year period 1996 to 2003. Through analysing statistical data collected annually by the Higher Education Statistical Agency, Sastry observed that taught Masters programmes had grown by 42% over the period, taught doctorates by 101%, and teacher training programmes (Postgraduate Certificates in Education) by 26% (Sastry, 2004: 6).

Chapter 3 (Where to study and applying for funding) fully utilises a range of data collected by the Higher Education Statistics Agency (HESA) to help inform potential students of the most appropriate place to apply. These data also enable interesting analyses of the changes in postgraduate student numbers across a range of subject or discipline areas. Within many areas, part-time postgraduate student numbers have either fallen (between the period 1995–2002) or they have remained fairly low in terms of any growth achieved. However, the substantive increase in postgraduate numbers has occurred within full-time programmes of study. The largest growth by subject area for full-time programmes of study has been in Biological Sciences (see Figure 2.3 below), Librarianship and Information

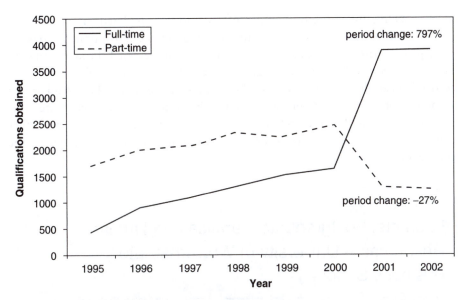

FIGURE 2.3   **Total higher degree qualifications obtained in the UK – Biological Sciences**
Source: Higher Education Statistics Agency (http://www.hesa.ac.uk)

Science, subjects allied to Medicine, Computer Science, Combined Studies, and Humanities. The analyses of HESA data for all subject areas is provided in Appendix 2 (Higher degree qualifications obtained in the UK 1995–2002).

Types of postgraduate study

Postgraduate study, at its simplest, is advanced study that is beyond first degree or undergraduate study. At this level there are a range of qualifications available – all have associated entry requirements, modes of delivery, assessments and costs. Provided here are the most common (and popular) postgraduate programmes of study on offer in UK higher education institutions.

POSTGRADUATE CERTIFICATE (PG CERT.)

The Postgraduate Certificate is a taught programme usually delivered on a part-time basis for up to two years. An increasing number of Certificate programmes are now being delivered through intensive (usually two- to three-day) teaching blocks enabling the entire programme of study to be completed within a shorter period of time. Assessment for Certificate programmes is continuous (report/ essay/project-based), although some elements may be assessed through examination. Postgraduate Certificate programmes can begin at any point during the academic year although popular enrolment periods are September/October and January/February. A number of providing institutions allow Certificate programmes to be used as the preliminary stages of a Masters qualification (further coursework and/or project work providing the required element to enable the conversion).

Example: Postgraduate Certificate in Human Resources – University of Wolverhampton Business School

This Certificate programme is offered part-time or through intensive block release and consists of a number of modules that cover the Chartered Institution of Personnel Development's Core Management, People Management and Development, and Elective fields of study. Applicants are usually expected to have a degree or equivalent plus two years relevant experience.

Source: Prospects (http://www.prospects.ac.uk); University of Wolverhampton (http://www.wlv.ac.uk).

POSTGRADUATE DIPLOMA (PG DIP.)

At many institutions, the Postgraduate Diploma is similar to the PG Cert. It is a taught programme delivered on a full-time basis over six months to a year and on a part-time basis over two years. As with PG Cert. programmes, Postgraduate Diplomas can begin at any point during the academic year although popular enrolment periods are September/October and January/February. The Postgraduate Diploma has a higher taught element than the Certificate and is commonly accepted as a more advanced programme of study. It has secured widespread acceptance among students and funding organisations as providing advanced level study at postgraduate level.

Example: Postgraduate Diploma in Journalism Studies (Newspaper) – Cardiff University

This Diploma programme, offered through the School of Journalism at Cardiff, is a nine-month full-time course which is jointly accredited by the National Council for the Training of Journalists. Programme content includes: newspaper, broadcast and magazine journalism, photo journalism, and public and media relations. Applicants are expected to have a first degree (minimum 2.2 grade) or an equivalent qualification/ professional experience.

Source: Prospects (http://www.prospects.ac.uk); Cardiff University School of Journalism (http://cardiff.ac.uk/jomec/).

MASTER'S DEGREES (MAs, MScs)

Masters degrees are the most popular form of postgraduate study. They are widely recognised as providing academic currency for students and funding organisations alike. Generally, MAs are less quantitative and more qualitative than MScs and some are more general higher degrees than MScs. As a result, background knowledge and/or experience are often prerequisites of MSc programmes. For both programme types, applicants are usually expected to hold a first degree – some funding organisations restrict their funding to those achieving a 2.1 or 2.2 grade. Masters degrees are offered on a one-year full-time basis or a two-year part-time basis and can be undertaken as taught programme or research programmes. The majority of Masters programmes are taught programmes of study consisting of a number of core subject areas or modules and a selection of subjects from a range of electives (modules selected from a range by the student). Research Masters programmes involve much more independent, non-directed study than their taught counterpart. Assessment for Masters programmes can vary but usually includes an examination element and the submission of a dissertation or thesis. Programmes typically begin in September/ October, with submission of final dissertation or thesis work by the following September.

Example: MA British Government and Politics – University of Essex

This Masters course, coordinated through the Department of Government at the University of Essex, is a full-time year-long programme of study. Coverage within the programme includes British political procedures and institutions, governments and parliamentary relations, public administration, policy analysis, and interest groups and local governments. Applicants are required to hold a good first degree or equivalent in relevant subject areas.

Source: Prospects (http://www.prospects.ac.uk); University of Essex (http://www.essex.ac.uk).

Example: MSc Computer Animation – University of Westminster

The MSc in Computer Animation, Department of Computer Science at the University of Westminster, is offered as a full-time (year-long) and part-time (two years and over) programme. Course coverage includes: foundations of animation, computer graphics and modelling, 3D animation, animation for interactive media, post-production techniques, and soundtrack production. The course is taught through teaching blocks of one-week intensive courses every four weeks for full-time learners and every eight weeks for part-time learners. Applicants are expected to hold a relevant first degree or appropriate work experience.

Source: Prospects (http://www.prospects.ac.uk); University of Westminster (http://www.wmin.ac.uk).

MASTERS IN BUSINESS ADMINISTRATION (MBAs)

MBAs are extremely popular higher degree qualifications for business managers and other professionals operating in a management or leadership area. These taught programmes of study are offered by a wide range of higher education institutions on either a part-time (usually two years) or full-time (usually one year) basis. As MBAs are extremely expensive programmes of study (£15,000 isn't unusual for a full-time course), many students are financed through employing organisations or studentships/scholarships. The majority of programmes available are targeted towards business managers/leaders who have several years of work experience to draw upon whilst studying the various elements of the degree. In fact, a number of providers stipulate this as an entry requirement in addition to applicants (usually) holding a first degree.

Example: MBA (IT Management) – Oxford Brookes University

This MBA programme is tailored towards those interested in pursuing IT Management as a subject specialism. It is offered as either a full-time (year-long) or a part-time (two years) programme of study. Applicants are required to hold a minimum of three years' managerial or professional experience and a first degree or equivalent qualification (including substantive management experience in place of formal qualification).

Source: Prospects (http://www.prospects.ac.uk); Oxford Brookes University (http://www.brookes.ac.uk).

MASTERS BY RESEARCH (MRes)

The Masters by Research postgraduate degree is a relatively new programme of study designed to provide students with key skills in research approaches and methods to enable them to operate as effective researchers in an academically focused environment. Such programmes are typically one/two years full-time and up to five years part-time. Learners are usually provided with taught input relating to core elements of research and the research process, and they are expected to undertake substantive independent research (with institutional support provided through academic supervision). Applicants for these Masters programmes are expected to hold a 2.1 grade or above in a relevant subject area and it is less usual for applicants to be accepted on to programmes with other experiences or qualifications. Assessment is via the submission of a thesis and oral examination.

Example: MRes Bioinformatics – University of Leeds

This year-long programme, offered through the University of Leeds, aims to provide scientists with the necessary subject-specific and transferable skills for successful research in Bioinformatics or Computational Biology. Applicants are expected to hold a first degree in a suitable scientific discipline, including Mathematics and Computer Science.

Source: University of Leeds (http://www.leeds.ac.uk).

MASTERS OF PHILOSOPHY (MPhil)

Masters of Philosophy programmes of study tend to be offered in the broadly defined areas of the arts, sciences and social sciences. Applicants are expected to hold a first degree (at grade 2.1 or above), with few deviations from this standard stipulation. They are usually studied for two to three years full-time and up to five or six years part-time. Similar to the MRes, they usually consist of a mixture of taught and research elements. Assessment for programmes is via submission of a thesis and oral examination. Traditionally, MPhil programmes have been the favoured conversion tool for those wishing to progress further to PhD study.

Example: MPhil in Anthropology – University College London

The MPhil in Anthropology at University College London is a three-year programme of study designed for students who wish to follow an advanced research-based degree without intending to enter academic anthropology. Applicants are expected to hold a first degree (at grade 2.1 or above) in a related discipline area. The degree programme consists of a programme of study in which students may follow some graduate coursework in the first year while preparing to complete a thesis, based on non-field reading and research in the second year.

Source: University College London (http://www.ucl.ac.uk).

DOCTOR OF PHILOSOPHY (PhD/DPhil)

These programmes are the highest level qualifications available through university study. They are increasingly viewed as essential qualifications for those interested in pursuing an academic career. Applicants are expected to hold a first degree (at grade 2.1 or above), and an increasing number of PhD programmes prefer applicants to hold a Masters degree. Programmes of study usually span three or four years full-time, or up to six years part-time. Assessment for traditional PhD programmes is through submission of a thesis and an oral examination drawing upon the submitted work. Some universities and funding organisations, such as the Economic and Social Research Council (ESRC), stipulate research training requirements for funded programmes and these can be undertaken at any point during the programme (although they tend to be covered in the early stages of study, such as year 1). Recently, a number of universities have developed variations of the traditional PhD. Some have a substantive taught element and others, such as the New Route PhD, consist of taught elements that are assessed through a mixture of examination, coursework and thesis submission.

Example: ESRC 1 + 3 programme – University of Kent, School of Social Policy, Sociology and Social Research

The Economic and Social Research Council funds a broad range of university-based research activities, including postgraduate studentships/research funding. The 1 + 3 is a funded programme providing training for full- and part-time students who have not previously completed a programme of substantive research training. Students are funded for a one-year research training Masters (two years part-time), and then funded for three years (five years part-time) for a PhD, subject to satisfactory progress. The '1' refers to the one-year Masters and the '3' refers to the three-year PhD. A recognised '1' programme within the School of Social Policy at Kent is the MA in Methods of Social Research. This year-long course provides the ESRC-required research methods training to enable learners to progress to supervised +3 study also at Kent.

Source: University of Kent (http://www.kent.ac.uk).

Example: New Route PhD programme

The New Route PhD is an integrated approach to PhD which coordinates research training alongside the development of traditional PhD project/thesis work. The scheme is recognised by a range of UK universities and has secured the support of the Higher Education Funding Council for England (HEFCE), the British Council and UK government departments. The scheme has an agreed framework of standards and adheres to quality associated processes and procedures as provided by the Quality Assurance Agency (QAA). The New Route programme at the University of Manchester is a three- to four-year programme of study consisting of a range of taught courses and research activities which combine to provide a coherent and structured research-based programme. Programme elements, or modules studied, include research skills and methodology, transferable skills modules covering subjects such as academic writing skills, presentations and time and project management, and developing research project work.

Source: New Route PhD (http://www.newroutephd.ac.uk); University of Manchester (http://www.umist.ac.uk).

Postgraduate training guidelines

The examples of programmes and courses detailed above indicate that there exists a wide variety of provision targeted at the postgraduate learner. All programmes and courses of study have some similarities as well as distinctive features in terms of their content, format, coverage, and the range of skill areas they seek to develop. For many years standards of provision within postgraduate education resided with the providing institution (the university or HE college). It was developed, managed and controlled according to the experiences and understandings of academics charged with developing, directing and teaching such provision. As a result, standards from course to course, and institution to institution, can differ considerably. However, more recently, attempts have been made collectively by universities to develop standards of provision which assure the quality and value of provision.

THE QUALITY ASSURANCE AGENCY FOR HIGHER EDUCATION

The Quality Assurance Agency for Higher Education (QAA) was established in 1997 as an independent organisation with a broad remit to monitor and provide guidance in relation to quality assurance issues in UK institutions of higher education. It is funded through subscription from universities and the various UK university funding councils. The Agency's key role is to provide guidance and supporting material to universities concerning the quality and standard of university-level programmes and the qualifications to which they relate.

A variety of publications have been produced by the QAA that set out subject/discipline benchmarks for programmes offered through UK universities. Most of these are targeted at undergraduate programmes of study and therefore explore the development of skills and knowledge at a first degree level. At postgraduate level, limited subject-specific benchmarking guidance has been produced by the QAA, although more general statements and guidance material have also been produced. However, guidance material of use and relevance to postgraduate learners includes the distinguishing characteristics and associated skill and knowledge areas put forward by the Agency in relation to Masters level and doctoral programmes of study. All UK universities and HE colleges providing higher degree-level programmes of study should seek to ensure that their Masters (and we can include PG Certificate and PG Diploma programmes under this banner) and doctoral programmes observe this guidance. The QAA framework for higher education qualifications indicates that Masters level provision should enable learners to demonstrate the following upon completion of their programme of study.

QAA guidance relating to skills and knowledge at Masters level

Students should be able to:

- deal with complex issues both systematically and creatively, make sound judgements in the absence of complete data, and communicate their conclusions clearly to specialist and non-specialist audiences;
- demonstrate self-direction and originality in tackling and solving problems, and act autonomously in planning and implementing tasks at a professional or equivalent level;
- continue to advance their knowledge and understanding, and to develop new skills to a high level;

(Continued)

(Continued)

and they should have acquired the skills necessary for employment requiring:

- the exercise of initiative and personal responsibility;
- decision-making in complex and unpredictable situations; and
- the independent learning ability required for continuing professional development.

Source: The Quality Assurance Agency for Higher Education, The framework for higher education qualifications in England, Wales and Northern Ireland – January 2001 (http://www.qaa.ac.uk/crntwork/nqf/ewni2001/contents.htm).

Similar ability and skill indicators are also provided for students engaged in doctoral programmes of study. Typical doctoral students would be expected to demonstrate the following upon completion of their advanced programme of study.

QAA guidance relating to skills and knowledge at doctoral level

Students should be able to:

- make informed judgements on complex issues in specialist fields, often in the absence of complete data, and be able to communicate their ideas and conclusions clearly and effectively to specialist and non-specialist audiences;
- continue to undertake pure and/or applied research and development at an advanced level, contributing substantially to the development of new techniques, ideas, or approaches;

and they should have:

- the qualities and transferable skills necessary for employment requiring the exercise of personal responsibility and largely autonomous initiative in complex and unpredictable situations, in professional or equivalent environments.

Source: The Quality Assurance Agency for Higher Education, The framework for higher education qualifications in England, Wales and Northern Ireland – January 2001 (http://www.qaa.ac.uk/crntwork/nqf/ewni2001/contents.htm).

Recently, postgraduate funding bodies have developed training guidelines for institutions to consider when providing postgraduate programmes of study, including the recently revised detailed guidance document issued by the Economic and Social Research Council (ESRC, 2005). This complements guidance issued collectively by UK Research Councils and the Arts and Humanities Research Board (AHRB) (Metcalf et al., 2002). This joint statement identifies crucial skill areas for current and future postgraduate research students – it might be useful to assess your current level of skill in relation to the skill areas identified by the statement. You may already possess some of these skills, some may be taught as you progress through your programme of study, you may undertake specific training to acquire certain skills, and you may obtain skill elements through informal mechanisms (through, for example, working with colleagues, teaching, preparing and presenting work). In which area or areas are you currently strong, and which areas (given your intended career) require additional development or training? It may be useful to use Table 2.1 (detailing all the skill areas identified by the Research Councils/AHRB) to help coordinate, assess and plan areas of your professional development. To assist with this, and to focus developmental activities and actions, you may wish to discuss the results of your analysis with your supervisor/postgraduate tutor. It may be useful to link the results of your analysis within a personal development plan as discussed in Chapter 10 (Career planning).

There is now a widespread recognition that postgraduate study encourages the development of skills that have application and transfer beyond the classroom, lecture theatre or laboratory. Many of the postgraduate learners interviewed as part of the development work for this book highlighted the need for solid, transferable skills that would have a positive impact on their employment prospects upon completion of their studies. Dan's comment, below, was typical.

It's very important, at postgraduate level, to still seek to develop general skills training. For example, skills training in terms of time management is a crucial ingredient of any Masters programme. I procrastinate far too much, so some project management input will be very useful for me. Other generic skills might also include effective ways of writing, not only for advanced level work but also for presentations, etc. All of these are critical transferable skills. If you pick them up or develop them further during your postgraduate study, they will be useful in whatever work you eventually do – be it bricklaying or lecturing.

Dan, ESRC 1 + 3 student, University of Edinburgh.

TABLE 2.1   JOINT STATEMENT OF THE RESEARCH COUNCIL'S AND AHRB'S SKILLS TRAINING REQUIREMENTS FOR RESEARCH STUDENTS

Skill area	Do I already have evidence of these?	How can they be developed?	What is the timescale for developing these skills? (dates)	Who can help me with these skill areas? What are the other resource requirements?
(A) Research skills and techniques – to be able to demonstrate:				
1. the ability to recognise and validate problems				
2. original, independent and critical thinking, and the ability to develop theoretical concepts				
3. a knowledge of recent advances within one's field and in related areas				
4. an understanding of relevant research methodologies and techniques and their appropriate application within one's research field				
5. the ability to critically analyse and evaluate one's findings and those of others				
6. an ability to summarise, document, report and reflect on progress				
(B) Research environment – to be able to:				
1. show a broad understanding of the context, at the national and international level, in which research takes place				
2. demonstrate awareness of issues relating to the rights of other researchers, of research subjects, and of others who may be affected				

(CONTINUED)

by the research, e.g. confidentiality, ethical issues, attribution, copyright, malpractice, ownership of data and the requirements of the Data Protection Act

3. demonstrate appreciation of standards of good research practice in their institution and/or discipline

4. understand relevant health and safety issues and demonstrate responsible working practices

5. understand the processes for funding and evaluation of research

6. justify the principles and experimental techniques used in one's own research

7. understand the process of academic or commercial exploitation of research results

(C) **Research management – to be able to:**

1. apply effective project management through the setting of research goals, intermediate milestones and prioritisation of activities

2. design and execute systems for the acquisition and collation of information through the effective use of appropriate resources and equipment

3. identify and access appropriate bibliographical resources, archives, and other sources of relevant information

(Continued)

TABLE 2.1 (CONTINUED)

Skill area	Do I already have evidence of these?	How can they be developed?	What is the timescale for developing these skills? (dates)	Who can help me with these skill areas? What are the other resource requirements?
4. use information technology appropriately for database management, recording and presenting information				
(D) Personal effectiveness – to be able to:				
1. demonstrate a willingness and ability to learn and acquire knowledge				
2. be creative, innovative and original in one's approach to research				
3. demonstrate flexibility and open-mindedness				
4. demonstrate self-awareness and the ability to identify own training needs				
5. demonstrate self-discipline, motivation, and thoroughness				
6. recognise boundaries and draw upon/use sources of support as appropriate				
7. show initiative, work independently and be self-reliant				
(E) Communication skills – to be able to:				
1. write clearly and in a style appropriate to purpose, e.g. progress reports, published documents, thesis				

(CONTINUED)

2. construct coherent arguments and articulate ideas clearly to a range of audiences, formally and informally through a variety of techniques

3. constructively defend research outcomes at seminars and *viva* examination

4. contribute to promoting the public understanding of one's research field

5. effectively support the learning of others when involved in teaching, mentoring or demonstrating activities

(F) Networking and teamworking – to be able to:

1. develop and maintain cooperative networks and working relationships with supervisors, colleagues and peers, within the institution and the wider research community

2. understand one's behaviours and impact on others when working in and contributing to the success of formal and informal teams

3. listen, give and receive feedback and respond perceptively to others

(Continued)

(CONTINUED)

Skill area	Do I already have evidence of these?	How can they be developed?	What is the timescale for developing these skills? (dates)	Who can help me with these skill areas? What are the other resource requirements?
(G) Career management – to be able to:				
1. appreciate the need for and show commitment to continued professional development				
2. take ownership for and manage one's career progression, set realistic and achievable career goals, and identify and develop ways to improve employability				
3. demonstrate an insight into the transferable nature of research skills to other work environments and the range of career opportunities within and outside academia				
4. present one's skills, personal attributes and experiences through effective CVs, applications and interviews				

ESRC POSTGRADUATE TRAINING GUIDELINES
AND THE POSTGRADUATE RESEARCHER

In recognition of the need to develop a coherent approach to the skill development of trainee academics, the ESRC issued revised training guidelines (in 2005) targeted at postgraduate research students. These guidelines indicate the skills and qualities required of postgraduates seeking to be recognised as professionally trained researchers in their respective fields of study. The training model favoured, and funded, by ESRC requires that research (PhD) students undergo training (usually in their first PhD-funded year of study) that prepares them for research-active academic careers.

At a generic level, ESRC guidelines indicate that funded students are expected to have acquired a range of research-based skills and have the ability to employ them in research work. Specifically, these skill areas include:

- Comprehension of basic principles of research design and strategy, including an understanding of how to formulate researchable problems and an appreciation of alternative approaches to research.

- Competency in understanding and applying a range of research methods and tools.

- Capabilities for managing research, including managing data, and conducting and disseminating research in a way that is consistent with both professional practice and the normal principles of research ethics.

- Understanding the significance of alternative epistemological positions that provide the context for theory construction, research design and the selection of appropriate analytical techniques (ESRC, 2005: 23).

At the discipline or subject level, the ESRC publish guidance material relating to content and skill areas across 18 subject areas. Examples within each of these are provided below. More detailed information, fully describing the subject areas and desirable coverage of programmes within them, are provided on the ESRC website (http://www.esrc.ac.uk). The guidance notes below articulate the general skills required for those wishing to be recognised as professional researchers within specific subject areas. Even for those postgraduate students not funded through ESRC awards, these guidelines provide important 'markers' of skill requirements issued by one of the most influential research funding organisations in the UK. A useful exercise may be to assess your current position in relation to the summary skill areas/issues identified that most closely match your own discipline.

ESRC subject and discipline guidelines

Area and Development Studies

Research in this area is likely to be grounded in at least one social science discipline, but will be informed by an advanced understanding of the theories and methods of related disciplines. Upon completion of their training, a postgraduate researcher in this area will have a sound grasp of:

- at least one social science discipline, including qualitative and quantitative social science research methods and their application to a given area
- when appropriate, a good working knowledge of a relevant language, adequate for at least reading and understanding research materials relating to the chosen geographical area(s)
- the cultural and historical background of an area(s) and relevant knowledge of contemporary economic, social and political developments
- the history and culture of international development cooperation and its institutions, especially as these impact on the area of study.

Demography

Demography is the study of human populations and includes the analysis of characteristics including age, sex, marital and health status and the composition of families and households. This discipline includes social demography which is concerned with the explanations and consequences of population trends and differentials, drawing upon a range of relevant disciplinary perspectives. Postgraduate students in these areas should expect to develop skills and expertise in:

- demographic data sources (such as population registers, censuses, health surveys, historical records)
- analytical methods (including population structures, migration statistics, patterns and trends)
- demographic concepts and models
- theoretical developments in population studies
- analytical tools and approaches drawn from relevant social science discipline areas.

Economic and Social History

Research programmes in this area will build on the particular strengths of each institution, some specialising in Economic History, some in Social History, and others

(Continued)

may cover both. Upon completion of their research training it is expected that students will have acquired:

- an ability to identify, initiate and complete a substantial piece of research in Economic or Social History
- an ability to draw on key concepts from one or more of the social science disciplines
- an appreciation of the advanced literature in one or more areas of economic and social history
- a familiarity with historiography, historical explanation and research methods in history
- an understanding of appropriate statistical, computing and other techniques relevant to data collection and analysis.

Economics

Economics research draws upon a range of methodological approaches but typically it involves observation, abstraction, the construction of models and the testing of the hypotheses to which these give rise. Data and data collection can play a central role in the process of assessing, refining and validating analysis and the development of techniques for analysing data is a key feature of the subject. A key part of initial training should focus upon developing skills and knowledge in:

- microeconomic theory and analysis
- macroeconomic theory and analysis
- quantitative methods
- econometric theory and methods.

Education

Educational research may include any enquiry which promotes theoretical and/or empirical social science understanding of educational and/or learning processes and settings, or which informs judgements and decisions about educational policy and practice. Research may be conducted in any social context including formal educational settings, and industrial, commercial and professional situations or informal contexts (such as parent–child interaction, self-help groups or local communities). Postgraduate research students in Education should have training in philosophical issues in educational research including an introduction to:

(Continued)

(Continued)

- epistemological and ontological issues in the philosophy of social science and the philosophical underpinnings of educational theories
- the nature of theory and explanation in education
- the philosophical assumptions underlying different methods of empirical enquiry, e.g. evaluation and action research
- the use of a range of concepts such as objectivity, subjectivity and reflexivity in educational research
- the relationship of the researcher to the researched and connections between theory and educational practice, including the nature of professional knowledge
- interpretations of the concept of education and their implications for research and the role of values in educational theory and research methodologies.

Human Geography

This area is fundamentally an interdisciplinary endeavour, with research links stretching from the arts and humanities through the social sciences to the natural sciences and technology. Human Geography deals with a diverse range of subject matter and it necessarily engages with a broad spectrum of philosophies, epistemologies, theories and methods. It emphasises that different theoretical and epistemological positions require different forms of evidence and methods of analysis. Professional researchers in this area are expected to:

- understand relations between physical and human aspects of environments and landscapes
- recognise that spatial relations are inherent to human activity, and that they reflect and re-make social relationships
- understand how the distinctiveness of place is constituted and continually re-made by the interaction of natural and social processes, and how places influence the constitution and unfolding of such processes
- be aware of the significance of spatial and temporal scales for social and natural processes and their interactions
- appreciate the plural character of the discipline
- exhibit knowledge of a range of theoretical and methodological approaches appropriate to the definition, collection, analysis and interpretation of evidence.

(Continued)

Science and Technology Studies

This is a wide-ranging field which examines the social, economic, historical, managerial and/or political dimensions of science, technology and innovation. The field seeks to recruit students who combine strong academic ability in their original disciplines with critical and flexible intellectual abilities and an enthusiastic interest in the issues confronted in the field. As a result of the diverse nature of this area, and the wide-range of experiences of postgraduates associated with it, research training is expected to include:

- an in-depth and critically analytical grasp of key literature in some domain of the subject area
- practical experience in the successful design and management of a research project
- competence in the operational use of at least one systematic method in both data collection (or compiling data sets from existing sources) and data analysis
- effective integration of empirical material and conceptual argument
- an enthusiasm for pursuing further research in the field.

Linguistics

Linguistics is concerned with the description, analysis and theorising of language in all its forms. Postgraduate researchers operating within this area will require further training, usually in the form of deepening knowledge acquired in their first degree (and also professional) work. Students trained in linguistics would normally be expected to have knowledge of a substantial subset of the following issues in the first year of their research training:

- knowledge of standard descriptive terminology
- theory construction, problem formulation and explanation
- the nature and status of linguistic data; the role of formalisation
- linguistic argumentation and the status of counter-examples
- the search for universals
- language variations and change

(Continued)

(Continued)

- language acquisition and learnability
- the relationship of linguistics to adjacent disciplines
- in-depth knowledge of one or more paradigms of description, theorising and research specific to the relevant sub-discipline as revealed in assessed work appropriate to the desired learning outcomes.

Management and Business Studies

Management research seeks to understand and explain the activity of managing, its outcomes and the contexts in which it occurs. As an academic field of enquiry it is heterogeneous, utilising frameworks and research methods derived from adjacent disciplines, predominantly in the social sciences. Postgraduate researchers operating within this area should show that they are capable of the appreciation and critical assessment of:

- alternative views of academic issues and management problems
- organising information and constructing a coherent argument
- ordering data and views through the writing, numerical and basic research techniques typical of a good final year undergraduate project or dissertation
- using library and online information sources
- organising an initial project outline
- individual project management.

Environmental Planning

Students entering the Planning, Environmental and Housing research fields should have an opportunity to acquaint themselves with a broader range of research issues and approaches than are offered by their own investigation. An appreciation of the various traditions in the social sciences should be supplemented by an introduction to the underlying theoretical perspectives in Planning, Environmental and Housing Studies and their relationship to research and policy analysis. Relevant core areas of training are likely to be drawn from:

- planning history, theory, techniques, law and practice
- local and regional planning theory and practice
- spatial planning
- regional analysis

(Continued)

- policy and development
- impacts of national, regional and local governance and policy guidelines
- urban analysis, policy and regeneration
- analysis of national, regional and local housing systems
- housing management, development and community planning
- social exclusion; economic development and the economics of planning
- European and international aspects of planning.

Political Science and International Studies

Political Science and International Studies covers a broad range of issues. Postgraduate students working in these areas would be expected to use material from a variety of cognate disciplines. Relevant training within these broad areas should include:

- (in the area of political behaviour) specialised training in the primary methods of collecting and analysing data at mass and elite levels
- (in Public Policy and Public Administration) training in case selection, public policy analysis, theories of decision-making, organisational theory and wider theories of governance
- (in International Politics/International Studies) specialised training in: the history of interstate practices; the key theories and concepts of advanced international politics, including the application of these to real world case studies; and international political theory
- (in International Studies and History) specialised training in the philosophy of history, the main historiographical trends of the twentieth century and case study analysis and archival research.

Psychology and Cognitive Science

This discipline area covers the scientific study of all aspects of human behaviour, though some biological areas of psychology are excluded from ESRC support. By the end of their research training, students within this discipline area should have a knowledge and understanding of a range of issues underlying the discipline of psychology, including:

(Continued)

(Continued)

- philosophy of science
- origins and nature of cognitive science
- the nature and limitations of the scientific method and the main alternatives to this method
- the nature of psychological knowledge and how it is embedded within its biological, social and cultural context
- nature of theory construction in cognitive science and methods of testing theories
- development of theories in Psychology, including current and emerging issues; this may be geared towards the general area of the student's proposed research.

Social Anthropology

Social Anthropology is concerned with the comparative study of human social and cultural life and is best characterised by the key features – ethnography, holism, comparison and theory – which are present in virtually all anthropological research. Social Anthropology's central mode of research is long-term ethnographic fieldwork. Programmes in Social Anthropology are expected to recognise and explore the following areas:

- anthropological methodologies that build upon a solid epistemological basis taught through a combination of classroom discussion and hands-on practical exercises
- anthropological practice which rests upon a critical and reflexive approach to knowledge, recognising that the construction and conduct of a programme of research are themselves social and cultural activities
- seminar participation which trains students to follow through the process by which long-term fieldwork contributes to social scientific knowledge
- the development of general and transferable skills such as critical and flexible judgement, interpersonal and collaborative skills, language acquisition, familiarity with survey methods, interviewing skills and social documentation
- the development of discipline-specific skills in social understanding, awareness of context, cultural translation and mediation, and the ability to represent diverse epistemologies within a single frame.

Social Policy and Health Studies

Social Policy and Health Studies draw on a wide range of professional and disciplinary backgrounds. Students are expected to use material from a variety of disciplines and to be able to work in a multiplicity of formal and informal research settings, with

(Continued)

differing relationships to the policy process, often alongside people with different orientations to research. Each subject area has its specific own sub-areas with their own needs and intellectual traditions. Indicative coverage within these areas includes:

- explanatory frameworks that have played a major part in the study of the subject
- an understanding of the relationship between major social trends and social and health policy and practice
- an understanding of the importance of institutions and institutional mechanisms, including organisational and professional groups, to the delivery of health and welfare
- an appreciation of the relationship between economic, social and health policies
- knowledge of the cause, development and differential experience of social and health problems (such as poverty, family breakdown or illness) among different social groups
- the consequences and impacts of policies, practices and technological advances on individuals, groups and communities and the ways in which users understand, experience or shape policy and practice.

Social Work

Social Work research takes a variety of forms and engages with a broad range of individuals, groups and communities. The diversity and complexity of Social Work as a form of practice requires variation in specific training provision. Students undertaking research training in Social Work will be expected to demonstrate:

- awareness of, and sensitivity to, the ethical and governance aspects of their research
- reflexivity about their own and others' roles in the research process
- knowledge of the social and political contexts and uses of research
- knowledge of and sensitivity to conducting research in emancipatory ways.

Social-Legal Studies and Criminology

Socio-Legal Studies and Criminology are areas in which generic social science skills are predominantly employed. These subject areas are multidisciplinary in that they draw on basic theories and methods developed in the social science disciplines.

(Continued)

(Continued)

Socio-Legal Studies may make more use of traditional legal research skills, but this is not necessarily so. Students in either area might reasonably be expected to develop skills, knowledge and understanding in the following areas:

- competing perspectives on what crime is, crime statistics, patterns and trends
- critical reading of the contribution of research to understandings of crime and justice
- an appreciation of ways in which criminological research and theory might inform social policy
- the social history of the discipline of Criminology and/or Socio-Legal Studies
- the relevance of modern social theory for an understanding of crime and punishment
- competing political science and philosophical perspectives on the role of the state in legally regulating citizens' behaviour
- an appreciation of the potentiality and limits of combining legal and other kinds of social scientific analysis and the methodological problems confronting such enquiry
- a knowledge of and ability to evaluate existing literature and research in a Socio-Legal field.

Sociology

Sociology as a subject potentially encompasses the examination and analysis of all aspects of social life and social relations, its distinctiveness arising from its focus on the social and in the approaches to understanding the social that it deploys. Sociology seeks to examine and analyse how societies, cultures, institutions and practices came into being, how they are currently organised and constituted, and how they are changing. Students undertaking research training in this area will be expected to acquire advanced knowledge of approaches to, and analysis of:

- the epistemological and ontological questions that underpin sociological research
- the range of sociological theories that have shaped, and continue to shape, Sociology as a discipline and the practical and methodological implications of such theories for research
- the interrelation between individuals and societies and between history, biography and social change
- social diversity, social division and social inequality.

(Continued)

Statistics, Methods and Computing

This area is concerned with methodological research and may include the development and refinement of new research methods; the evaluation and refinement of existing research methods; the application of research methods to empirical data, where the research is driven primarily by methodological not substantive concerns; the interrelation and/or triangulation of different methods; and the epistemological and logical foundations of research methods. Required levels of expertise and skills will vary according to the specific training route undertaken.

Generally for *Research Methods* students, coverage will include:

- building on students competence established under their generic research methods training to develop a high level of expertise in a range of research methods by learning the theory, practice, uses and limitations of these methods; they will develop expertise in critically appraising and comparing alternative methods and in assessing which methods are appropriate in different circumstances.

Generally for *Social Statistics* students, coverage will include:

- building on students competence established under their generic research methods training to develop a high level of expertise in a range of statistical methods of research design, data collection and analysis, relevant to the social sciences, by learning the theory, practice, uses and limitations of these methods; they will learn which methods are appropriate in different circumstances and develop a critical appreciation of the use of statistical methods in the social sciences.

There are additional guidelines within the broadly defined field of sociology which apply to the cognate areas of Cultural and Media Studies, and of Women and Gender Studies.

Source: ESRC *Postgraduate Training Guidelines* (4th edn, 2005) (http://www.esrc.ac.uk).

If you are currently or are considering becoming a research-based student, it might be useful to consider at what stage during your training/programme you will develop these skills, and how they might link into the skill areas identified in

Table 2.1 above. Usually, these are dealt with in formal research methods modules (as part of Masters programmes or other postgraduate-level provision). However, for some postgraduates – working in collaboration with a supervisory team or tutors – more informal development activities are employed to 'train up' researchers. Nevertheless, the skill areas defined by ESRC provide useful guidance for any postgraduate engaged in a research-based programme of study. This should help to provide an additional useful reference point of expected skill and knowledge required of competent postgraduates, researchers and future academics operating within your environment.

Reference list, useful reading and websites

Brause, R.S. (2000) *Writing your doctoral dissertation: invisible rules for success*. RoutledgeFalmer, London.

Brown, T. (2003) *Providing for the postgraduate market*. Troon: The National Postgraduate Committee of the UK.

Delamont, S., Atkinson, P. and Parry, O. (2000) *The doctoral experience*. Falmer Press, London.

ESRC (2004) Postgraduate funding information. (http://www.esrc.ac.uk/esrccontent/postgradfunding) (Accessed: 7/11/04).

ESRC (2005) *Postgraduate training guidelines 2005*. Swindon: Economic and Social Research Council (available at: http://www.esrc.ac.uk).

Harland, T. and Plangger, G. (2004) The postgraduate chameleon, *Active Learning in Higher Education*, 5(1): 73–86.

Metcalf, J., Thompson, Q. and Green, H. (2002) *Improving standards in postgraduate research degree programmes: a report to the Higher Education Funding Councils of England, Scotland and Wales*. Bristol: Higher Education Funding Council for England.

Prospects.ac.uk. Funding postgraduate education. (http://www.prospects.ac.uk) (Accessed: 5/8/03).

Prospects.ac.uk. Public funding bodies. (http://www.prospects.ac.uk) (Accessed: 5/8/03).

Sastry, T. (2004) *Postgraduate education in the UK*. Higher Education Policy Institute (available online: http://www.hepi.ac.uk).

3 Where to study and apply for funding

Chapter overview

This chapter covers the important issues you need to consider when choosing where to study at postgraduate level. It details the logistics and application procedures and processes, and specifically includes:

- Selecting a place to study based upon

  - personal circumstances
  - recommendations by others
  - familiarity with an institution
  - presence of research/teaching expertise
  - funding body recognition

- Other ways to assess institutional performance

  - league tables
  - research income
  - numbers of postgraduates
  - staff to student ratios
  - the Research Assessment Exercise

- The application process.
- Financing your programme of study.
- Questions to ask yourself when considering postgraduate study.

Selecting a place to study

Selecting an institution or programme of study can depend upon a range of factors, including personal circumstances, recommendation by others, familiarity with an institution, presence of research or teaching expertise, and Funding Council/Research Council recognition. Each of these influential areas are discussed below.

PERSONAL CIRCUMSTANCES

A growing number of postgraduate students are mature learners with family or other commitments that restrict geographic mobility in terms of where to study. It may prove difficult, or even impossible, for such students to select a postgraduate programme of study or institution based on its reputation in the field, or the presence of particular research excellence. In Sarah's case, below, family commitments were her main reason for restricting applications to a selection of local universities.

> *To gain the breadth of experience (being in a new place, studying with new people), it might have been useful to study elsewhere at postgraduate level. However, my geographical mobility is restricted because I have a family, with two young children. I could not move to another area without causing chaos in mine and my family's lives.*
>
> Sarah, PhD student, University of Westside.

For learners with other, more specialised, learning needs the options available may additionally be restricted to institutions resourced to support such needs. In Angela's case below, she was confident that the level of support she received from her institution to help her special educational need would continue during her postgraduate programme.

> *Whilst it would have been interesting to study for my undergraduate degree and postgraduate degree in different institutions, I couldn't realistically do that. The support I receive here for my specific learning needs is very good. It might take an awful long time in a new institution getting to grips with the level of support that is available – this would have had a detrimental effect on my studies.*
>
> Angela, PhD student, University of Southside.

RECOMMENDATION BY OTHERS

Studying at postgraduate level is probably going to be an intense experience, and recommendations from those who know you (those who are already studying at postgraduate level, supervisors, tutors, etc.) may help in your selection of an appropriate institution and/or programme. Your colleagues and peers will know your interests and their own experiences and knowledge of institutions and programmes of study may prove useful. Sometimes, as in the case of Anna below, their advice might be a little unexpected.

> *My friendly undergraduate tutor asked me if I was thinking of doing postgraduate stuff. He asked me if I'd thought about where I wanted to go. He asked me if I'd looked at the MAs at the institution I was currently with. He said that in all honesty, given the direction I wanted to take my research work, there were more specialised institutions offering MAs of relevance to what I wanted to do. I was surprised at his honesty really – I supposed he might have suggested that I stay where I am to add to the student numbers in his own Department! Well, he didn't do that! He suggested that I think about York, Manchester, Essex and Sussex as they all offered excellent programmes focusing on what I was interested in.*
>
> Anna, PhD student, University of Northside.

FAMILIARITY WITH AN INSTITUTION

Supporting research work conducted during the development of this text indicates that a number of postgraduates select institutions based upon their familiarity with it (Wilkinson, 2004). Having studied with an institution as an undergraduate, it might seem reasonable to continue studying at the same institution as a postgraduate. Advantages of this approach include the fact that prospective postgraduates will have a knowledge and understanding of the culture and operating procedures and processes in the institution – as well as knowing where the library is, where the best place is to park, and where the quietest bars are! As Nick indicates, below, a good learning experience and the development of working relationships with fellow students are particularly useful for future postgraduate study.

I was doing a Geography undergraduate degree at Oxford and was considering undertaking postgraduate study. I thought about it and knew that I had enjoyed the methodological parts of the Geography degree, so I went for it. I did briefly look at other institutions, but the people I knew in Oxford said Oxford's was one of the best Departments for what I wanted to do in the country. I really liked Oxford: I knew which college to apply for here because I was familiar with the colleges, I knew I had friends here.

Nick, ESRC 1 + 3 student, University of Oxford.

Familiarity with an institution might also include familiarity with an institutional 'type'. For others, familiarity might include applying to an institution that has similar characteristics to the institution where they studied their first degree.

Another reason I chose Manchester was that it was a broadly similar university to Leeds – one of the big civics, in a large city with a good, broad track record. I didn't think that I would necessarily get all of these things in York or even Essex.

Kelly, ESRC 1 + 3 student, University of Manchester.

PRESENCE OF RESEARCH/TEACHING EXPERTISE

Published material (journal articles, position papers, research reports, etc.) in your chosen field of study will often provide an indicator as to the leading scholars in the area – evidenced through the amount of material they have published. Such outputs measures are usually good indicators of academic (and their associated institution) expertise. The Research Assessment Exercise and university league tables also provide a wealth of information relating to the performance, staffing and research strengths of institutions, and for many prospective postgraduates these are crucial information sources when deciding upon where to study. These are discussed further later in this chapter.

There is a huge amount of information available for postgraduates to sift through when trying to select somewhere to study for their MA or PhD. The Research Assessment Exercise (the last one was in 2001) is a useful source to help you identify which are the top-rated departments and institutions in your particular area. Five-star institutions [denoted by the '5*'] are the best as they have been judged by their peers as consistently producing research work of an international standard. Applying to conduct postgraduate research with these institutions is quite competitive but at least you know you are in an internationally excellent environment.

Anna, ESRC 1 + 3 student, University of Manchester.

FUNDING BODY RECOGNITION

A number of organisations that fund postgraduate study have preferred institutions or programmes of study. Funding preferences can be as a result of historical links between the university and the funding body and/or as a result of programmes or institutions achieving certain quality levels or standards. 'Recognised' institutions/centres or programmes of study will be clearly indicated in application documentation issued by respective funding organisations. For example, the ESRC has a list of approved institutions and programme within its 1 + 3 PhD programme. Over 600 Masters programmes are recognised as reaching an appropriate standard for the taught element of the programme (the '1' part of the 1 + 3); many of the institutions hosting these Masters programmes are also recognised as preferred places to undertake the remaining part of the PhD programme (the '+3' element of the 1 + 3). More details relating to ESRC-recognised courses and institutions can be obtained through the postgraduate area of their website – full references are provided at the end of this chapter.

Other ways to assess institutional performance

LEAGUE TABLES

In recent years there has been considerable growth in the number of publications produced which assess university performance by reference to a range of calculations and formulas. Most of these league tables provide broad institutional indicators of performance that are of relevance to potential undergraduate and postgraduate learners, although the majority are produced as guides for those considering under-graduate study. Nevertheless, the analysis of general institutional performance, includ-ing levels of resourcing (spending, computer facilities, etc.) and student numbers, provides informative guidance to university applicants whatever their intended level of study.

Two very accessible guides are *The Guardian University Guide* and *The Times Good University Guide*, which draw upon a range of data sources in order to rank subject/discipline areas and institutions. Both of these guides also provide lively commentaries on each of the major UK universities.

The Guardian guide relates to 47 subject areas across 172 higher education institutions in the UK. It assesses and ranks subjects according to seven areas, which, following various calculations, are given a score out of 6 to 10. The seven areas are:

1. an assessment of *teaching quality* derived through an examination of Teaching Quality Assessments (TQAs) conducted by the Quality Assurance Agency for Higher Education;
2. the *spend per student* on such areas as library facilities and computing;
3. the *student to staff ratio* as an indicator of how well an institution or subject area is staffed;
4. *student destinations* as an indicator of how successful the subject area at an institution is at enabling its students to gain graduate employment;
5. the *value added* provided by a subject area within an institution where students with relatively low entry grades move on to achieve a good degree;
6. the *entry qualifications* required of a subject area at an institution; and
7. the *inclusiveness* of a subject area within an institution which enables it to successfully attract students from under-represented groups. (*The Guardian university guide*, 2005: 63–65)

The Times guide also ranks institutions according to 62 subject areas and calculates a total score out of 100. Its assessment is based upon calculations relating to four key variables:

1. *teaching assessment* based upon relevant TQA scores awarded by the Quality Assurance Agency for HE;
2. the *Research Assessment Exercise (RAE)* score or grading awarded to an institution's subject area;
3. the average *A level* score required of applicants to a subject area within an institution; and

4. the *destinations* of students following completion of their programme of study, i.e. the number that secure graduate jobs. (*The Times good university guide*, 2005: 44–45)

It is clear that both of the above guides have a number of similarities. They both provide overall institutional rankings (based upon a combination of all subject areas). They both assess performance according to a range of criteria (although only *The Times* guide includes an analysis of research activity). And they both provide additional reference points to further information and guidance. Given these similarities, you might expect the results of their analysis to be similar – but this is not necessarily the case. An arbitrary sample of three subject areas provide the following results:

Subject area	Guide	Top-ranked institution
Nursing	*The Guardian*	University of Wales, Bangor
	The Times	University of Manchester
Law	*The Guardian*	University of Oxford
	The Times	University of Cambridge
Social Policy	*The Guardian*	University of Manchester
	The Times	London School of Economics

Upon reflection, given the difference in construction and calculation, it is perhaps not surprising that the two guides provide different results – their reliance on (in places) subtly different data sets results in ultimately different rankings. Nevertheless, the way they explore and examine performance adds value for anyone seeking to select an institution at which to study. A good deal of the analysis conducted for both guides relates to data collected and collated by the Higher Education Statistics Agency (HESA). We'll take a look at some of this source data now.

HESA DATA

The Higher Education Statistics Agency works with UK universities to coordinate a wide range of institutional data relating to students, finance and HE resources. A great deal of this information is synthesised and presented in annually-released data sets. Of particular interest to those concerned with selecting a place to study at postgraduate level are the data tables relating to research income. The latest data available relate to income figures for the academic year ending 2003 (the reason for this being that it takes approximately one year to collect, verify and combine data from all relevant UK institutions). These data sets relate to research income earned by an institution across a range of approximately 40 subject areas. From these data we can establish which institution and subject area receives the most research income. It is reasonable to conclude that a subject area with the most research income is an area where a good deal of research work is conducted – an ideal environment within which postgraduates could and should operate.

An analysis of HESA research income data, by subject area, has been carried out and is provided in Appendix 3 (Top 10 institutions by research income, 2003). These analyses of HESA data rank the top 10 institutions in each area by their acquired research income and the proportion of the total UK research income they received within that subject area. By way of example, Figures 3.1–3.3 refer to research income within the subject areas of Mathematics, Social Sciences and

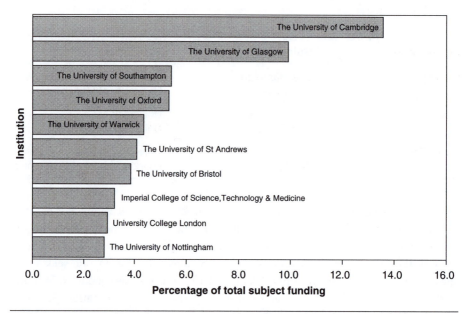

Subject: (24) Mathematics	Income £(000s)	% of total
The University of Cambridge	4604	13.6
The University of Glasgow	3361	9.9
The University of Southampton	1841	5.4
The University of Oxford	1810	5.3
The University of Warwick	1477	4.4
The University of St Andrews	1389	4.1
The University of Bristol	1307	3.9
Imperial College of Science, Technology & Medicine	1093	3.2
University College London	998	2.9
The University of Nottingham	956	2.8

FIGURE 3.1 **Institutional research income data for Mathematics, 2003**

Source: Higher Education Statistics Agency (http://www.hesa.ac.uk)

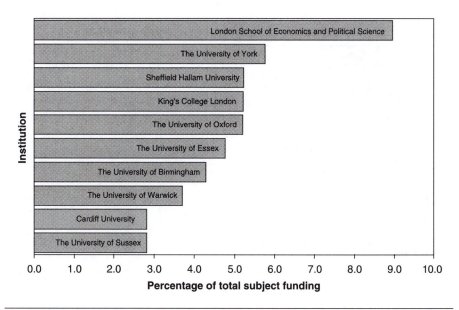

Subject: (29) Social Sciences	Income £(000s)	% of total
London School of Economics and Political Science	10745	9.0
The University of York	6919	5.8
Sheffield Hallam University	6273	5.2
King's College London	6265	5.2
The University of Oxford	6244	5.2
The University of Essex	5719	4.8
The University of Birmingham	5147	4.3
The University of Warwick	4450	3.7
Cardiff University	3382	2.8
The University of Sussex	3382	2.8

FIGURE 3.2   **Institutional research income data for Social Sciences, 2003**

Source: Higher Education Statistics Agency (http://www.hesa.ac.uk)

Education. In Mathematics, the University of Cambridge secured research income totalling £4,604,000, or 13.6% of the total research income for Maths. The University of Nottingham (in tenth place) received slightly less than £1 million, or 2.8% of the total research funding for Maths. Funding for Social Science research appears more evenly spread – the London School of Economics secured approximately 9% of the total funding, or £10,745,000, and most others within the top 10 research income-earning institutions received between 3% and 6%. Perhaps not surprisingly, in the area of Education, the Institute of Education received the most research income, securing over 22% of the total funding, or £11,610,000, compared to 2% received by Manchester Metropolitan University (just over £1 million).

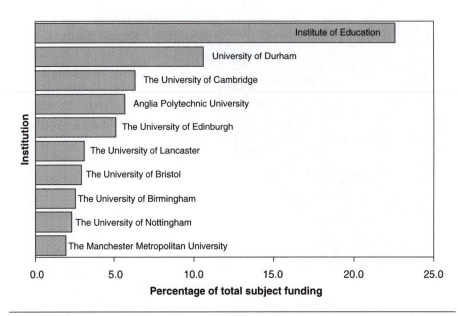

Subject: (34) Education	Income £(000s)	% of total
Institute of Education	11610	22.6
University of Durham	5468	10.6
The University of Cambridge	3260	6.3
Anglia Polytechnic University	2920	5.7
The University of Edinburgh	2624	5.1
The University of Lancaster	1606	3.1
The University of Bristol	1507	2.9
The University of Birmingham	1322	2.6
The University of Nottingham	1211	2.4
The Manchester Metropolitan University	1017	2.0

FIGURE 3.3 **Institutional research income data for Education, 2003**

Source: Higher Education Statistics Agency (http://www.hesa.ac.uk)

When considering where to apply for postgraduate study, it might be helpful to examine these and other data collected by HESA, a good deal of which is available through annually-produced HESA publications and through their website (the reference list at the end of this chapter provides full details).

NUMBER OF POSTGRADUATES

The number of postgraduate students at an institution provides a useful indicator of their success. Sizeable postgraduate numbers are usually the result of well-developed and popular postgraduate courses and programmes, an attractive work environment and the presence of skilled and competent staff (academic as well as support staff). They also often correlate with an institution's ability to attract substantial pots of research funding, upon which a great deal of postgraduate work is linked or based.

A number of commentators on higher education policy and function indicate that an appropriate mix of expertise is required to be present in university schools and departments in order to achieve 'critical mass' (Adams et al., 2000: 21–25), translated as the optimum number and type of individuals required to produce academic work of a high standard. A crucial element within that mix are the number of postgraduate students within the host school, department or institution as a whole.

There are a variety of sources through which to obtain information relating to a school, department or institution's postgraduate numbers. Institutional websites often provide this information, as do departmental or school publicity material. However, to facilitate comparability across and between institutions, HESA collects a wide range of student-based information from UK universities. As with the research income data, all HESA student information is collected at the institutional and subject levels. At the institutional level, a number of institutions have large postgraduate populations, expressed as a proportion of their total student body. One may reasonably conclude that a sizeable postgraduate population in an institution provides an indicator of a healthy postgraduate community, one where postgraduates work alongside each other, sharing ideas, collaborating and supporting each other. Drawing upon data available through HESA (relating to the academic year ending 2003), Figure 3.4 shows the institutions with the highest proportions of postgraduate students compared to other levels of study. More detailed information relating to these data are provided through the HESA website relating to student statistical information.

Exploring these data from HESA indicates that a large number of institutions have a postgraduate student population totalling over 30% of the entire institution's student population. More specialised HE institutes have higher proportions of postgraduates. For some, such as the Institute of Cancer Research, the London Business School and the Royal College of Art, all of their students are engaged in postgraduate programmes of study.

STAFF–STUDENT RATIOS

It may also be useful to think about how many academic staff you may be in contact with in your school or department. It is important to share ideas with your peers (other postgraduates), but also to do this with academic colleagues. Does the ratio of staff to students enable this to happen? You can often establish approximate numbers of academic staff in a school or department through the staffing sections of departmental or

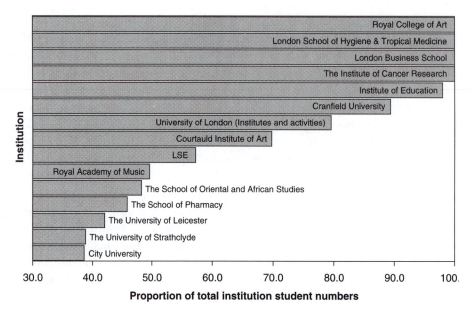

FIGURE 3.4   **Top 15 institutions ranked by proportion of postgraduate students, 2003**

Source: Higher Education Statistics Agency (http://www.hesa.ac.uk)

school internet home pages. Useful additional data relating to staffing at institutions are also provided through HESA and the Research Assessment Exercise data (see below).

THE RESEARCH ASSESSMENT EXERCISE

The Research Assessment Exercise (RAE) is carried out periodically for the Higher Education Funding Councils (the organisations which provide the substantive funds – including research funds – to universities to enable them to operate). The most recent RAE was undertaken in 2001, and the results of the exercise helped determine the allocation of over £1 billion of research funding.

Under the RAE, research activity of institutions is assessed and given a value or grade, ranging from '1' – research achieving low levels of national excellence, to 5* (five star) – research/outputs achieving international excellence in more than half of the named or submitted activities, and national excellence in the remainder. The full list of ratings, and their definitions, are provided in Table 3.1.

Based upon the gradings in Table 3.1, selective research funding was awarded – proportionally much more to the 5* institutions than those achieving lower grades. In making assessments, the exercise took into account a variety of factors, including

TABLE 3.1   RAE RATING SCALE – 2001 EXERCISE

Rating	Description
5* (five star)	Quality that equates to attainable levels of international excellence in more than half of the research activity submitted and attainable levels of national excellence in the remainder.
5	Quality that equates to attainable levels of international excellence in up to half of the research activity submitted and to attainable levels of national excellence in virtually all of the remainder.
4	Quality that equates to attainable levels of national excellence in virtually all of the research activity submitted, showing some evidence of international excellence.
3a	Quality that equates to attainable levels of national excellence in over two-thirds of the research activity submitted, possibly showing evidence of international excellence.
3b	Quality that equates to attainable levels of national excellence in more than half of the research activity submitted.
2	Quality that equates to attainable levels of national excellence in up to half of the research activity submitted.
1	Quality that equates to attainable levels of national excellence in none, or virtually none, of the research activity submitted.

Source: HEFCE (2001)

the number of articles and other material published by academics, other research outputs such as patents and conference papers, the number of academic staff engaged in research-based activities, and the level and extent of interdisciplinary-based research.

Given that the higher grades attract more funding and are often highly publicised within and outside the HE environment, many institutions make determined efforts to achieve these grades, including appointing leading scholars and those engaged in valuable research in the field or discipline area, and investing substantial amounts of university funds to areas where measurable gains in outputs (research papers, etc.) can effectively be made. As a result, a number of commentators believe that the RAE produces an environment which places undue emphasis on publications and related outputs and has resulted in a number of unintended consequences (Elton, 2000).

The results of the latest RAE (announced in 2001) are available online through the RAE website. It is relatively easy to query the various data sets to determine which institutions, given the results of the exercise, are leading the field in terms of the research work they do. For example, the sample results below (Table 3.2) show all the institutions achieving a 5 or 5* (work of national and international

TABLE 3.2   HIGHER EDUCATION INSTITUTIONS RECEIVING A 5 OR 5* RATING
IN THE 2001 RESEARCH ASSESSMENT EXERCISE

Business and Management Studies	RAE 2001 Grade
Aston University	5
University of Bath	5
University of Cambridge	5
City University	5
Imperial College of Science, Technology & Medicine	5
Lancaster University	5*
University of Leeds	5
London Business School	5*
London School of Economics and Political Science	5
University of Manchester	5
University of Manchester Institute of Science & Technology	5
University of Nottingham	5
University of Oxford	5
University of Reading	5
University of Warwick	5*
Cardiff University	5

Art and Design	RAE 2001 Grade
Bournemouth University	5
University of Brighton	5
City University	5
Goldsmiths College	5
The London Institute	5
Open University	5
University of Reading	5
Royal College of Art	5
Sheffield Hallam University	5
University College London	5
University of Wales College, Newport	5
University of Ulster	5

Civil Engineering	RAE 2001 Grade
University of Birmingham	5
University of Bristol	5*
Imperial College of Science, Technology & Medicine	5*
University of Leeds	5
University of Manchester	5
University of Manchester Institute of Science & Technology	5
University of Newcastle	5
University of Nottingham	5
University of Sheffield	5
University of Southampton	5*
University College London	5

(CONTINUED)

Civil Engineering	RAE 2001 Grade
University of Dundee	5
University of Edinburgh	5
University of Wales, Swansea	5*
Cardiff University	5*
The Queen's University of Belfast	5

Sociology	RAE 2001 Grade
University of Bristol	5
Brunel University	5
University of Cambridge	5
University of Essex	5*
University of Exeter	5
Goldsmiths College	5*
Lancaster University	5*
London School of Economics and Political Science	5
Loughborough University	5*
University of Manchester	5*
University of Oxford	5
University of Surrey	5*
University of Warwick	5
University of York	5
University of Aberdeen	5
University of Edinburgh	5
Cardiff University	5
The Queen's University of Belfast	5

Education	RAE 2001 Grade
University of Bath	5
University of Birmingham	5
University of Bristol	5*
University of Cambridge	5
University of Durham	5
Institute of Education	5
University of Exeter	5
Homerton College, Cambridge	5
King's College London	5
Lancaster University	5
University of Oxford	5
University of Sheffield	5
University of Sussex	5
Cardiff University	5*

Source: The Research Assessment Exercise website (http://www.rae.ac.uk)

quality) in the areas of Business and Management Studies, Art and Design, Civil Engineering, Sociology, and Education. To confuse matters, the next RAE (due in 2008) will adopt a slightly different grading structure from that used in the 2001 exercise. In 2008, subject areas within institutions will be assigned quality profiles consisting of grades, progressively ranging from no research activity submitted or recorded (unclassified) to work of international quality and excellence (4*). More detailed information about the results of the current RAE and format of future RAEs can be found on their website (http://www.rae.ac.uk).

THE APPLICATION PROCESS

All programmes of study at postgraduate level have pre-determined requirements of all applicants wishing to pursue postgraduate study (these often include requirements of a first degree or relevant industrial/other experience). These entry requirements will be detailed in university publicity material, such as prospectuses, or they will be explained in guidance accompanying the application form. Unlike applicants for undergraduate programmes of study (which are managed and processed by the Universities Central Admissions Service (UCAS), all applicants for postgraduate programmes are locally managed and processed. This means that there is no one system for applications – some programmes may require an application form and interview, some may require the preparation of a project or research proposal, others may require a CV outlining academic skills and related experience.

Given this, it is important that you make yourself aware of the specific application requirements of your school or department well before the deadline, which is usually between spring and summer of the year you join the programme, in order that you can prepare your application accordingly.

The Association of Graduate Careers Advisory Services (AGCAS) produce a range of guidance materials and publications, including useful advice relating to applying for postgraduate study (AGCAS, 2004). They suggest that background reading and research work relating to potential postgraduate programmes of study should begin up to two years in advance of your application, particularly if you need to build up a profile of relevant work experience or other training to help make your application look more attractive. The AGCAS recommends that you:

* Ensure that all your applications for programmes of study are sent to institutions at least six months before the beginning of the course. Many programmes call in a number of applicants for interview a few months before the programme starts so you need to be prepared for this.

* Keep in regular touch with the schools or departments at the institutions you have applied to. Towards the end of the previous academic year, institutions are much clearer about the funding and student numbers they can expect to attract in the coming year. As such, they can make clearer offers to applicants and/or confirm places (AGCAS, 2004: 9).

A less standard approach to applying for postgraduate study is provided by Michelle below. Her informal and innovative background research work proved to be very successful.

By May of the year I was supposed to start my PhD, I still hadn't applied and I was starting to think I'd just drop out and get a job. But whilst I was researching for an essay I came across a book by an academic who was writing about something I was very much interested in to do with criminal behaviour. I thought, wow this is brilliant and it fired me up to do a PhD. I looked up the author's email address through Google – it was a New York address – and I emailed him with my idea for a PhD and he replied saying he had moved to Cambridge and did I want to come to Cambridge to be his PhD student. He interviewed me here in June and I got an offer in July and that's how I ended up here!

Michelle, ESRC 1 + 3 student, University of Cambridge.

Financing your programme of study

There are a variety of funding sources available for postgraduate study, but funding at this level is not as straightforward (and easy to secure) as undergraduate funding. Postgraduate-level provision, because of its advanced and specialised nature tends to be much more expensive than undergraduate provision. As a result, those organisations or bodies willing to fund it are few, and their criteria for selection can be stringent.

SECURING FUNDING: SOME OPTIONS AVAILABLE FOR POSTGRADUATE STUDENTS

Scholarships. A number of universities/government departments provide a limited number of postgraduate scholarships for particular subject/discipline areas. Typical criteria taken into consideration when awarding scholarships are current and proven academic ability and future potential. Examples of the various university scholarships available can be accessed through institutional websites and the education-related newspapers, such as the *Times Higher Education Supplement* (usually published every Friday), and *Education Guardian* (usually published every Tuesday). For the academic year 2005–06, the University of Manchester School of Language, Linguistics and Cultures (see below) intends to offer a range of funded postgraduate places, with a level of funding which equals that provided for studentships/funding secured through the Arts and Humanities Research Board.

University of Manchester – School of Languages, Linguistics and Cultures Postgraduate Funding Programmes, 2005–06

The postgraduate community in the new School of Languages, Linguistics and Cultures is one of the UK's largest and most diverse, enjoying state-of-the-art facilities and excellent support within a high-quality research environment. To celebrate the School's establishment, we are enhancing our support for students registering for a research degree (MPhil or PhD) or an MA in 2005–06. We plan to offer:

12 Graduate Teaching Fellowships (full- and half-time AHRB-equivalent for PhD applicants with teaching experience) in Arabic, French, German, Italian, Linguistics and English Language, Mandarin, Chinese, Persian, Polish, Portuguese, Russian, Spanish, Turkish Translation Studies.

PhD Studentships (AHRB-equivalent UK/EU)
MA Studentships (AHRB-equivalent UK/EU)
Research Assistantships in Translations Studies
Full-fee Bursaries (full- and part-time for UK/EU and overseas MA and PhD students).

Source: Education Guardian, 4 January 2005, p. 37.

Sponsorship.   Some organisations provide funding (sponsorship) to students to undertake postgraduate programmes of study that are relevant to their work. With most sponsorship schemes there is acknowledgement that both parties benefit from the exercise: students receive focused training relevant to their work and the sponsoring organisations receive more skilled and knowledgeable employees capable of adding value in the workplace. The University of Leeds (as outlined below) has provided this type of support for staff undertaking a range of academic programmes of study hosted by the institution.

Sponsoring Postgraduate Study

As part of its commitment to the continuing professional development of staff, the University of Leeds provides part sponsorship of students on a range of programmes of study within the university. The MA/MSc through work-based learning is one of the postgraduate programmes recognised by the institution as providing a range of skills of relevance and use in the university workplace. Staff from the university study the programme part-time over two years and receive sponsorship centrally from the Universities Staff and Departmental Development Unit, and locally from their own school or department.

Loans. The Department for Education and Skills works with a number of high street banks to offer career development loans (CDL) to support vocational learning or education, including postgraduate study. A CDL is a deferred payment loan of between £300 and £8,000 repaid over an agreed period at a fixed rate of interest.

Charities and educational trusts. A number of registered charities provide limited financial support for postgraduate study. Awards made do not usually cover the costs of course fees and associated living expenses, although notable exceptions are the scholarships available through the Wingate Foundation and the Wellcome Trust (detailed below).

The Harold Hyam Wingate Foundation

This UK charity provides a number of annual scholarships that are awarded to individuals who show academic potential or proven excellence, and who require financial support to undertake original work in a number of defined subject areas. Project work funded by the Foundation includes activities that are broadly defined as scientific, artistic, and socially or environmentally focused. Awards are designed to assist with the costs of project work, which may include PhD study, and may last up to three years. The size of award can vary but is usually in the range of £6,500 to £10,000 in any one year. Upon completion of their funded work, students are required to produce a final report for the charity which provides an overview of the achievements made as a result of the scholarship.

Source: The Harold Hyam Wingate Foundation (http://www.wingate.org.uk).

The Wellcome Trust

The Wellcome Trust funds a number of doctoral studentships in the broad areas of science and medicine. Funded studentships are designed to enable young researchers to undertake PhD level study for up to three years. Applicants are required to hold an upper-second class honours degree in a relevant subject area and preference is given to those indicating a potential to develop as researchers in their given PhD fields. Applications are made directly to the Wellcome Trust; the deadline for submitting an application is early May in the year of enrolment.

Source: The Wellcome Trust (http://www.wellcome.ac.uk).

Whilst a number of research funding organisations do not directly fund post-graduate study, some of their initiatives do provide options for this to happen. For example, The Leverhulme Trust (see below) make regular research project grant awards to university schools and departments that also include an element to cover the resourcing of PhD students.

The Leverhulme Trust – Research Project Grant Awards

These awards are principally for the salary costs of a researcher or researchers to work on a specific and discrete research project proposed by the applicant. The aim of such awards is to enable established scholars at eligible institutions to obtain support for research project work. Eligible costs include:

- The salary of research assistants.
- The fees and maintenance cost of PhD studentship(s) at the base rate for Research Councils or for the Arts and Humanities Research Board.
- Associated costs for teaching and other support costs.

Source: The Leverhulme Trust (http://www.leverhulme.org.uk/grants_awards/grants/research_project_grants/).

Teaching/research assistanceships.   A growing number of university schools or departments now offer paid employment to those seeking to continue study during the early stages of their academic careers. A recent example is the Research Assistantship (below) offered by the Department of Computer Science at Queen Mary, University of London. Such teaching or research assistanceships usually include options which allow assistants to register for related higher degrees such as MAs or PhDs.

Queen Mary, University of London – Department of Computer Science

---

Research Assistant in Human Interaction

Applications are invited for a research assistant to work under the supervision of Dr Nicholas Bryan-Kinns, on an EPSRC-funded project to investigate Engaging Collaborations. Candidates must have a Masters in Computer Science or equivalent. In particular, the candidate should have experience of developing novel interactive systems for performing music and experience of quantitative and qualitative data collection and analysis techniques. Candidates will be considered who have a subset of these skills and are keen to develop the other required skills. In addition, candidates may have the opportunity to study for a PhD in conjunction with this post.

Source: Department of Computer Science, Queen Mary, University of London (http://www.dcs.qmul.ac.uk, March 2004).

The major sources of funding for advanced level, and certainly PhD, study are the UK Research Councils (including the Arts and Humanities Research Council). When considering such postgraduate options, it might be useful to observe the remit and awarding nature of each of the Research Councils.

Arts and Humanities Research Council (AHRC) (previously known as the Arts and Humanities Research Board)
http://www.ahrb.ac.uk
AHRB, Whitefriars, Lewins Mead, Bristol BS1 2AE
Telephone: 0117 987 6500

The Arts and Humanities Research Council (AHRC) make awards to those engaged in arts- and humanities-related postgraduate study. Its broad remit is coordinated through the work of its eight subject panels covering: Classics, Ancient History and Archaeology; Visual Arts and Media: practice, history and theory; English Language and Literature; Medieval and Modern History; Modern Languages and Linguistics; Librarianship, Information and Museum Studies; Music and Performing Arts; Philosophy, Law and Religious Studies.

The AHRC has three major funding programmes: the Research Preparation Masters Scheme, the Professional Preparation Masters Scheme and the Doctoral Awards Scheme. All funding on these programmes is allocated though an annual open national competition. Applications for programmes are usually high and applicants are usually expected to be studying for a PG Dip. (Postgraduate Diploma), Masters or PhD at a recognised higher education institution in the UK. Closing dates for most programmes is early May. Extensive details, guidance information and application forms for each programme area are available through the AHRC website.

Biotechnology and Biological Sciences Research Council (BBSRC)
http://www.bbsrc.ac.uk
BBSRC, Polaris House, North Star Avenue, Swindon, SN2 1UH
Telephone: 01793 413200

Biotechnology and Biological Sciences Research Council funded awards are allocated for those engaged in academic work within the biosciences area. Specifically, the Research Council funds activities within seven major areas: Agri-food; Animal Sciences; Biochemistry and Cell Biology; Biomolecular Sciences; Engineering and Biological Systems; Genes and Developmental Biology; Plant and Microbial Sciences.

The BBSRC allocates its funded studentships to universities and other BBSRC-recognised organisations, which then advertise for candidates. Unlike other awarding organisations, BBSRC do not award studentships directly to students. Rather, the application is made through the funded university. Two substantive funding routes are available: doctoral studentships and Masters studentships. Applicants for both programmes are expected to hold a first degree (2.1 grade). Doctoral studentships consist of over 300 research studentships awarded to institutions on a quota basis: approximately 200 strategic studentships focus upon priority objectives identified by the BBSRC, and approximately 100 are Co-operative Awards in Science and Engineering (CASE) studentships. Masters studentships (approximately 100) are provided for a range of programmes of study recognised by the Research Council as being related to the major biosciences areas identified above (details of recognised programmes are available through the BBSRC website). Application closing dates for programmes of study will be influenced by the requirements of the host university (as no direct applications for funding are made to the BBSRC).

Engineering and Physical Sciences Research Council (EPSRC)
http://www.epsrc.ac.uk
EPSRC, Polaris House, North Star Avenue, Swindon SN2 1ET
Telephone: 01793 444000

The Engineering and Physical Sciences Research Council (EPSRC) funds students within the Physical Sciences, Technology and Engineering subject areas. Postgraduate awards are made for doctoral and Masters programmes of study, the funding for these is provided directly to institutions through Doctoral Training Accounts (DTAs) and Collaborative Training Accounts (CTAs). DTAs are targeted at traditional research-based investigations, and CTAs are targeted at supporting training which has relevance and more direct application to industry. Funding allocations under each award scheme are made directly to university departments, and studentships, based upon this and other institutional funding, are awarded and managed by the host institution. Due to the direct allocation of funding by the EPSRC to institutions, application closing dates for doctoral and Masters programmes will be dictated by their host university departments. As with most postgraduate level programmes, applicants will generally be expected to hold a first degree (at grade 2.1 or above), although some institutions may have additional or other requirements.

The Economic and Social Research Council (ESRC)
http://www.esrc.ac.uk
ESRC, Polaris House, North Star Avenue, Swindon SN2 1UJ
Telephone: 01793 413000

The Economic and Social Research Council (ESRC) funds postgraduate study in the broadly defined areas of Economics and Social Sciences. It has recently focused its funding upon linked Masters/PhD awards (commonly known as 1 + 3 programmes), CASE awards and a smaller number of linked awards with other Research Councils (including the Natural Environmental Research Council (NERC) and the Medical Research Council (MRC)). A proportion of ESRC funding is awarded to university departments through a quota mechanism, and applications to programmes through this route are through the university directly. At present, a substantial element of ESRC funding is awarded through open national competition – applications to programmes through this route are made through ESRC. Approximately 700 postgraduate awards are made through the various ESRC initiatives per year, for 1+3 programmes of study awards are only available to recognised programmes and/or institutions. The list of recognised programmes and institutions is available through the ESRC website. Applicants for ESRC postgraduate funding are expected to hold a first degree (at grade 2.1 or above), and the deadline for applications directly to ESRC are usually required by early May.

Medical Research Council (MRC)

http://www.mrc.ac.uk
MRC, Medical Research Council, 20 Park Crescent, London W1B 1AL
Telephone: 020 7636 5422

The Medical Research Council (MRC) funds postgraduate study in biomedical subject areas. Three studentship schemes are funded: Capacity-Building Research Studentships, Industrial Collaborative Studentships and Masters Studentships. All MRC studentships are coordinated through university-administered Doctoral Training Accounts (a mechanism used by other Research Councils). Applications are not made through MRC directly but with the recognised institution. Capacity-Building Research Studentships are focused upon MRC-identified research areas and are allocated annually through a national competition. Industrial Collaborative Studentships are awards which are linked to an industrial partner which has some interest and input (financial) into the studentship. It is usually a requirement of such studentships that the student spends some time with the collaborating industrial partner. Masters Studentships are awarded for one-year taught programmes of study that academically build upon the discipline areas supported by MRC. In addition, a number of MRes programmes are funded which enable advanced research to be undertaken, perhaps as a foundation for further PhD study.

The MRC currently funds approximately 1,200 studentships, and awards over 300 on an annual basis. Applicants for MRC-funded studentships are required to hold a first degree (at grade 2.1 or above). The closing date for applications is dictated by the individual institution but usually falls towards the end of the academic year prior to enrolment.

Natural Environment Research Council (NERC)

http://www.nerc.ac.uk
NERC, Polaris House, North Star Avenue, Swindon, SN2 1EU
Telephone: 01793 411500

The Natural Environment Research Council (NERC) makes postgraduate funding awards in the discipline areas of Life, Environmental and Geological Sciences. Three forms of studentship are available: Research Studentships, CASE awards, and Advanced Course Studentships. As with many other Research Councils, NERC awards are made directly to universities and other recognised centres. Applications for studentships are therefore made to institutions and not NERC. Research Studentships are usually made for up to three years and cover PhD programmes of study, and some of these are jointly funded studentships with other bodies (such as the ESRC). CASE studentships are offered as either research-based or industry-focused awards. Research-based CASE awards involve some input from an industrial partner (usually supervision and some financial input), and industry-focused CASE awards are more directed by the industrial partner. Advanced Course Studentships are awarded to students undertaking Masters programmes of study recognised by NERC. These awards are designed to prepare students for employment or subsequent doctoral study.

NERC currently funds approximately 1,000 studentships each year. Applicants are usually required to hold a first degree (at grade 2.1 or above), and the closing date for applications usually falls towards the end of the academic year prior to enrolment.

Particle Physics and Astronomy Research Council (PPARC)
http://www.pparc.ac.uk
PPARC, Polaris House, North Star Avenue, Swindon, Wiltshire, SN2 1SZ
Telephone: 01793 442000

The Particle Physics and Astronomy Research Council (PPARC) funds postgraduate study within the areas of Particle Physics and Astronomy. There are two substantive postgraduate funding routes available through the Research Council: Standard Research Studentships and CASE Studentships. As with many other Research Councils, funded studentships available through PPARC are allocated to, and managed by, universities and other recognised institutes. Standard Research Studentships are awarded for three years of PhD study; they are awarded to enable students to develop research skills in areas of relevance to the Research Council. CASE Studentships (a funding approach used by other Research Councils) are awarded to enable students to develop research training skills and to work with collaborating industrial partners.

There are currently approximately 600 studentships funded through PPARC, with an annual allocation of around 300. Applicants for studentship programmes of study are expected to hold a first degree (grade 2.1 or above). Submission deadlines for applications are dictated by the managing university or institute.

The variety of places to study at advanced postgraduate level are numerous, as are the sources of funding for such programmes. Many institutions and funding sources have specific, and sometimes rigid, criteria for those wishing to study or be funded by them. The information in this chapter should help you to establish which are important for your intended area of study. A part of the application process required by many institutions and postgraduate funders is the development and submission of a research or project proposal from the prospective postgraduate (this part of the postgraduate process is detailed in the next chapter). However, before moving on to that, it may be useful to review the following key questions, which are of relevance to anyone seriously considering postgraduate study.

Questions to ask yourself when considering postgraduate study:

* What are the entry requirements and will I meet them?

* When do I need to apply?

* How much are the fees and likely living costs?

* Is funding available, how do I apply, and what are my chances?

* If I don't get funding, how will I pay for it?

* What do I plan to do afterwards?

* Where have previous students found employment?

Reference list, useful reading and websites

Adams, J., Cook, N., Law, G., Marshall, S., Mount, D., Smith, D.N. and Wilkinson, D. (2000) *The role of selectivity and the characteristics of excellence – report to the Higher Education Funding Council for England; a consultancy study within the Fundamental Review of Research Policy and Funding*. Bristol: HEFCE.

Association of Graduate Careers Advisory Services (AGCAS) (2004) *Postgraduate study and research*. Sheffield: AGCAS.

Bourner, T., Bowden, R. and Laing, S. (2000) Professional doctorates: the development of researching professionals, in T. Bourner, T. Katz and D. Watson (eds), *New directions in professional higher education*. Buckingham: Open University Press/Society for Research into Higher Education.

Darwen, J., Bell, E. and Goodlad, S. (2002) National survey of postgraduate funding and priorities. Troon: The National Postgraduate Committee of the UK.

Elton, L. (2000) The UK Research Assessment Exercise: unintended consequences, *Higher Education Quarterly*, 54(3): 274–283.

ESRC (2004) Postgraduate funding information. (http://www.esrc.ac.uk/esrccontent/postgradfunding) (Accessed: 7/11/04).

Graves, N. and Varma, V. (1997) Working for a doctorate: a guide for the humanities and social sciences Routledge. London.

Guardian (2005) *The Guardian university guide*. London: The *Guardian*.

HEFCE (2001) *A guide to the 2001 Research Assessment Exercise*. Bristol: (available online: http://www.hero.ac.uk/rae/pubs/other/raeguide.pdf).

HESA (2004) *Resources of Higher Education Institutions 2002/03*. Cheltenham: Higher Education Statistics Agency.

HESA (2004) *Higher Education statistics for the UK 2002/03*. Cheltenham: Higher Education Statistics Agency.

HESA (2004) *Students in Higher Education Institutions 2002/03*. Cheltenham: Higher Education Statistics Agency.

Metcalf, J., Thompson, Q. and Green, H. (2002) *Improving standards in postgraduate research degree programmes*. Bristol: HEFCE.

Prospects (2004) Prospects Postgraduate Funding Guide 2004/05. Prospects. (http://www.prospects.ac.uk).

Prospects.ac.uk. Alternative sources of funding. (http://www.prospects.ac.uk) (Accessed: 5/8/03).

Prospects.ac.uk. Funding postgraduate education. (http://www.prospects.ac.uk) (Accessed: 5/8/03).

Prospectsac.uk. Public funding bodies. (http://www.prospects.ac.uk) (Accessed: 5/8/03).

The Higher Education Statistics Agency – http://www.hesa.ac.uk

Times, The (2005) *The Times good university guide*. London: *The Times*.

Wilkinson, D. (2004) *Views and perceptions of postgraduate study (current 1 + 3 students at UK universities): a thematic report for ESRC*. Leeds: Leeds University Business School.

4 Developing proposals

Chapter overview

This chapter provides guidance about developing your postgraduate project and research work through the construction and presentation of a proposal. Specifically, the chapter details:

- The format and remit of research proposals.
- The importance of planning and structuring your proposed work.
- Drawing upon the guidance and support of others to facilitate the production of a professional proposal.
- Tips for success and sample proposals.
- Using the literature.
- The framework of your proposal.

The research proposal

WHAT IS A RESEARCH PROPOSAL?

The research or project proposal is a crucial element of the postgraduate application process for many postgraduate programmes of study. As Krathwohl outlines, they are:

> ...an opportunity for you to present your idea and propose actions for consideration in a shared decision-making situation. You, with all the integrity at your command, are helping those responsible for approving your proposal to see how you view the situation, how the idea fills a need, how it builds on what has been done before, how it will proceed, how you will avoid pitfalls, why pitfalls you have not avoided are not a serious threat, what the study's consequences are likely to be, and what significance they are likely to have. It is not a sales job but a carefully prepared, enthusiastic,

interestingly written, skilled presentation. Your presentation displays your ability to assemble the foregoing materials into an internally consistent chain of reasoning. (Krathwohl, 1998: 65)

The purpose or purposes of a research proposal can vary considerably, as they can depend upon a range of factors. These include the focus of the intended research, the subject or broad discipline area in which it is based, and the conventions or traditions typically observed by researchers and academics operating within the field or subject area. Generally, however, research proposals can factor some, or all, of the following purposes of research:

* research which seeks to draw together knowledge;

* research which explores or investigates a specific phenomenon or situation;

* research which seeks to provide solutions or answers to issues or problems; and

* research which seeks to generate new knowledge or create new ways of interpreting situations, issues or phenomena (Scanlon, 2000; Robson, 2002; Collis and Hussey, 2003).

It will be important, when contemplating publication of your work, to have considered some or all of these purposes (see Chapter 11 on publishing opportunities for a full discussion of the elements of the publishing process).

Research proposals provide detail on the scope and focus of your intended project work. They traditionally include an indication of the main aim or aims of the work, some background or contextual information, the methodology you intend to employ, and the substantive outputs of the work. Each of these important areas is considered in the brief proposal below.

Observing communities of practice: emerging themes and issues – FIRST DRAFT

Aims

The aim of this project is to examine the development and activities of communities of practice within a large UK-based organisation. In our examination we wish to address the following questions:

(Continued)

(Continued)

1. How are communities of practice formed?
2. What are the constituent parts of such a community?
3. How is knowledge transferred between members of the group?
4. What makes an effective community of practice?
5. How are such learning groups utilised by their employing organisation?
6. How much control over learning do communities of practice have?
7. Do such learning communities impact upon organisational performance?
8. What inhibits the development of communities of practice?
9. How important are communities of practice to the learning organisation?

Background

Review work conducted to support this research programme acknowledges that learning in an organisational or work-based setting is difficult to define. It 'encompasses a variety of overlapping and competing paradigms, each based on different theoretical premises and understandings and manifested in different practices' (Cullen et al., 2002: 30). However, there are a number of models or domains of work-based learning which facilitate professional advancement or development. These include programmes typically described as 'on-the-job' and 'off-the-job' training (Simons, 1995). Some domains identify that learning is the new form of labour and that many organisations embrace models and approaches to work-based learning because it is seen as an important component of the learning organisation (Senge, 1993).

The domains suggest that learning activity can take place at both formal and less formal levels, from within the work environment and outside it. Recent research work has identified that people learn through a variety of methods and sources – from people within their own organisation, from customers and suppliers and from wider professional networks (Eraut et al., 1998). In more recent work, Michael Eraut discusses the importance of non-formal learning to enable professional development. Here non-formal learning includes implicit learning, reactive on-the-spot learning and deliberative learning. The problematic nature of assessing and developing these learning types for professionals is discussed, as is the role of social knowledge gained through interaction with a variety of settings within and outside the work setting (Eraut, 2000).

Other work argues that the distinction between formal and informal learning suggests that learning taking place within educational institutions (formal) is superior to that which occurs in the workplace (informal) (Fuller and Unwin, 1998). Fuller and Unwin's piece commends the notion of apprenticeship, which draws many of its learning activities from the workplace. Additionally, whilst many models of development

(Continued)

and learning encourage the movement of responsibility for learning to the learners, it continues to be controlled by their employing organisations. Some identify that, as a resource, strategically managed learning can lead to, or improve, competitiveness (Leavy, 1998).

Whilst collaborative learning is encouraged, there is little research evidence which indicates the effectiveness of team and group learning. Cullen et al. (2002) identify that action research is needed which explores a number of related questions: How and when is learning happening in different kinds of teams? What factors inhibit or enhance team success? What organisational characteristics and processes affect the tasks, motivation, successes and failures of teams (in terms of learning)? How are teams linked to their organisational context? How can teams be supported/enabled to deal with complex issues where tasks and problems are not well delineated. Useful and informative work here has been conducted by Professor Joe Raelin. In his recent work examining management development and work-based learning, he details three learning types, including 'communities of practice'. Communities of practice have been defined as teams of people committed to a common purpose or enterprise who develop a shared history as well as particular values, beliefs, ways of talking and ways of doing things. There are a number of essential elements for communities of practice: mutual engagement (people engaged in actions whose meaning are negotiated and agreed), joint enterprise (people working together and accountable to each other) and shared repertoire (people with common routines and methods which symbolise their shared practice) (Raelin, 2000: 76).

Cullen et al. (2002) state the potential in developing the metaphor of 'communities of practice' as comparisons of how professional learning occurs in different communities of practice. It is the aim of this project to explore the formation and activities of one such community of learners in a large UK-based organisation in the utilities sector.

Methodology

Semi-structured interviews will be conducted with a community of learners recently enrolled on a work-based Postgraduate Diploma in Management with the University of Fairvale. This community consists of 21 learners split into sub-groups or communities specifically established with the aim of facilitating individual and organisational learning. Interviews will be informed by data collected as part of the study programme's evaluation exercise. These data include documents written by the learners themselves, outlining successful learning activities in terms of the learner, the group and the organisation. Drawing upon the combined expertise of the research team,

(Continued)

(Continued)

interview schedules will be developed which probe themes or issues emerging from the evaluation documents as well as including questions relating directly to those stated above under the aims of this research. Interview data will be analysed using appropriate qualitative data analysis software and emerging themes will be communicated to colleagues as appropriate. We anticipate that our findings will feed into other projects within the programme as well as providing information for future research.

Outputs
1. A report submitted upon completion of the research which provides an analysis of the data in relation to the nine questions identified under the project's aims and suggests areas for future study.
2. Articles (×2) discussing the content and findings of the research published in appropriate journals.
3. Conference papers (×2) highlighting emerging themes and issues raised during the research.

Draft proposals, such as the one above, are useful starting points because they formalise the research idea and provide a means by which to communicate its main ideas to others. From these notes a more detailed statement or plan can be developed, including a breakdown of aims/objectives, reference to the research/supervisory team (if relevant), and a clear timeline of activities and events.

MORE THAN A PLAN

A thorough and effective research proposal includes an outline of activities to be undertaken by the researcher. The literature, and convention, indicate that the detail of such plans varies according to the proposed research or project work. Punch defines two extremes of 'pre-structured' and 'unfolding' research (Punch, 1998). The theme or topic of your work will lend itself to a certain degree of planning or structure before you embark on the research or project work. Consider the example above – 'Observing communities of practice'. The researchers were able to provide indicative detail in relation to the fieldwork they intended to conduct and how they would begin to analyse the data collected. However, they were not able to provide substantive detail relating to how they would code, classify or interpret that data. Classifications and approaches to interpretation would emerge as the project unfolded or developed. This limited approach to planning is common within essentially qualitative research endeavours. Generally, it is the opposite for experimental or more statistical (i.e. quantitative) research. More thorough and detailed research plans tend to be developed, as research questions are tightly focused, they rely on clear conceptual frameworks and often the data to be collected can be pre-coded to facilitate analysis. It is clear, then, that the more structured a proposal or plan is, the easier it might be to organise, coordinate and project manage.

As you begin your postgraduate research you will be required to develop a proposal which maps your research intentions, focus and direction. For some, this is a solitary exercise, carefully crafting and drafting their ideas into coherent and meaningful plans. However, it need not be such a lonely endeavour; there are a host of ideas and tips you can benefit from and a number of people you can speak to. For ESRC 1 + 3 funding, you are guided to develop your proposal in collaboration with your actual or potential supervisor. This can add a much-needed critical eye to your research intentions (ESRC, 2005: para. 5.40). Other information offered by ESRC includes guidance on the content of research proposals to be considered for 1 + 3 awards, including required information on the scope and depth of your intended study:

> …you should include sufficient information for the examiners to assess your suitabil-
> ity for an award. Please, therefore indicate the theoretical background to your area
> of interest, why you consider it important and how you see it fits with your previous
> experience and possible future research work. If you have preliminary hypotheses,
> please indicate them as well as any indication of your likely methodological
> approach. (ESRC, 2005: para. 5.42)

The above guidance issued by ESRC, although specific to the requirements of the 1 + 3 scheme, has a generic relevance for many students considering the content of a research proposal.

Selecting a research theme or topic to develop into a proposal (in collaboration with your actual or potential supervisor) may be influenced by a range of factors. For many postgraduate researchers, their research theme is often a continuation of some part of their undergraduate degree. Research or reading conducted to satisfy the requirement of a course or programme essay can sometimes spark the research imagination and provide the foundations upon which to build more substantive work.

The relationship and rapport developed with course and programme tutors can also be drawn upon when deciding a postgraduate research theme. For many academics, it is flattering to be asked advice on potential research ideas and foci, and engaging with tutors in this way may enable a smoother transfer into the academic community for the budding research student.

> *Part of the reason I applied for ESRC-funding from here was because I knew my supervisor as I'd already developed a relationship with him through my previous studies. So it made sense to do it with him rather than trying to find somebody I didn't really know. He's a specialist in my area, I know him, so I could develop my application with him in person. For others, trying to find someone whom they can work with (whom they don't know) must be quite difficult. You need to know how people work and operate to make sure that you effectively get your message across about your intended research.*
>
> Peter, ESRC 1 + 3 student, University of Leeds.

For Peter, the rapport and relationship he had already developed with his supervisor (as part of his undergraduate degree) was quite important to him and proved to be extremely useful in helping him to shape his research intentions and refine his research proposal. Given the substantial time and effort it will inevitably take to complete your postgraduate research, it is crucial that you choose a topic that will not only maintain your interest during the many months (if not years) ahead, but also one that will hold some significance for your intended career path. A well planned and organised Personal Development Plan (or PDP) will highlight how and where this research sits into your overall career plan (see Chapter 10 on career planning for more information on PDPs). Additionally, in terms of selecting a topic or area worthy of investigation, by becoming aware of the literature in a given area or field, research topics or themes may emerge and present themselves to you. Consulting recent or more distant theses or dissertations may illuminate areas where little has been conducted, or they may suggest areas worthy of further work and investigation.

By utilising the resources available to you, such as critical colleagues or friends, former or current tutors, and the research literature, your application can be strengthened and your chances of funding success more likely. Although this process can be quite long and often tortuous, the resulting outline can be impressive, robust and comprehensive, and capable of dealing with/or factoring any reasonable research hiccups that may present themselves during the implementation and write-up of your project work. Consider the PhD proposal carefully crafted by Kelly, below, as preparation for her research-based activities.

Justice in Community? Locating the bases for a new politics of community

Objectives and justification of research

The principal objective of the PhD is the examination and exploration of a constructive theoretical approach to the politics of community, which argues for a theoretical division of labour between a normative theory of community justice and a rooted communal epistemology with reference to political goods, both material and non-material. Secondly, the PhD aims to provide a grounded analysis of the content and form of the communities implied by such a theoretical model, leading to some conclusions on the potentialities of a politics based on community for enactment in the UK, and further afield. Clearly, such conclusions will be preliminary claims, whose broader function will be to reinitiate an innovative debate on the place of democratic community in contemporary political theory and practice.

In defence of the appropriateness of this research at this time, a case can be made on at least three levels. Firstly, and with reference to political theory as academic discipline, it is clear that the politics of community, despite a recent upsurge in the popular political vocabulary, has not moved significantly beyond the firmly drawn battle lines of the individual/communitarian debate, with clear consequences for the normative analysis of themes such as rights and justice. It is, I believe, greatly important that continued innovation in the sphere of practice is matched by sustained theoretical analysis if political theory is to retain its claims to relevance in the twenty-first century, and hope in this PhD to offer a contribution to this endeavour. Secondly, a claim can be made arising from the political context faced, in which many territorial communities are experiencing an acute alienation from substantive power, both internal and external. On this view, I hope to prove that a new politics legitimating the domains of autonomy for specific comrnunities, must surely offer practical benefits for concrete communities and their members, and prove in turn beneficial for society as a multiply constituted whole. Finally, and referring back to the 'popular political vocabulary' of community I earlier referred to, I find it imperative to assess the usefulness of any top-down narrative ostensibly prioritising community yet maintaining a form of objectivist knowledge in practice regarding the distribution of political goods and the construction of value.

In addition, and as all research benefits from complementary work in the area, it will be of interest to see how the PhD contributes to the wider research promoted and motivated by the thematic priorities of the ESRC. In particular, I perceive linkages

(Continued)

(Continued)

with the issue of 'identity and social stability' in my analysis of the place of community within a model of social rationality; with the issue of 'participation and accountability' in my elaboration of community democracy; and with the broader theoretical question of whether 'diversity necessarily means divisiveness', a question to which I believe my work will offer support for a negative response through its analysis of the nature and composition of just democratic communities, both in theory and practice.

Questions, themes and methods

Below are five key questions to which answers will be sought and presented by the PhD, though of course it is also possible that further sub-questions will arise throughout the research period. At this stage, these questions cover the broad scope of the research and admit significant potential for drawing normative and contextual conclusions on the theme.

- What grounds are there for upholding community rights and democracy as necessary components of justice, and how would 'rights' and 'justice' be understood in such an argument?
- What notions of democracy and community are implicit in a normative theory thus premised?
- To what realms is collective action most legitimately applicable, and how might an understanding of collective goods be relevant to this, and to the constructive processes of democratic communities?
- Where in political practice does a democratic theory based on a constructive communal epistemology lead us? And according to what logic would such a model operate?
- What factors (internal and external) contribute to the 'just' functioning of democratic communities and to their potential to realise their own 'good' collective outcomes? When and where can we hope for the emergence of this type of community, and what (if anything) can be done to facilitate its construction?

Evidently, in working to answer these questions, an in-depth familiarity with key work on several themes will be a pre-requisite. I intend, in dialogue with my supervisors, to critically review the key literature on the following debates in order to engage with them constructively in answering the above questions: the choice theory of rights; utility and group rights; social autonomy and group liberties; group justice; collective

(Continued)

forms of epistemology; social capital; social rationality; collective action and collective goods; localisation.

The PhD will follow a path of constructive normative analysis in the first section, and of contextualisable epistemological theory in the second, with the aim of fostering a supportive arena for practical democratic innovation. This second section will also encompass an explicit scrutiny of the realities – both actual and potential – for concrete political communities, and the responses to these enacted by 'successful' (according to the terms of the thesis) communities currently in existence or in emergence. A comparative empirical analysis of the functioning and guiding norms of such groups will be undertaken, with a probable focus on the UK and Latin America, as a region which not only maintains important differences from the UK in the accepted measures of 'social capital', but has in addition witnessed many exciting recent instances of community formation and action.

The five key questions to be approached in the research suggest at this stage an initial working chapter structure for the PhD, with the addition of an introduction situating the research project, and a conclusion. The first four questions will be answered principally through a process of normative analysis, and last with the additional resource of my empirical findings. The balance thus hangs towards the theoretical, as formulating a paradigm for evaluating the legitimacy of social relations. Nevertheless, I believe that a short period of empirical research will not only aid me in this project, but also ensure that any claims to be made are qualified and recontextualisable. For any theory of rooted epistemology should refer to its roots and ensure that its claims are representative of real social relations, and not abstract ideals.

My plan at this stage is to spend four to six weeks engaged in interviews and ethnography with community groups in the UK (to be identified in Year 1 of the research) and in addition six to eight weeks engaged in the same process in Argentina or Mexico (communities also as yet to be identified). Clearly, the contexts of these periods of research are hugely different, and as such, and in keeping with my key questions, it will be with the voices of the groups themselves expressed in relation to their collective goods and the means elected for their enactment, and a comparison thereof, which will form the analytical framework applied to my findings. That is to say, it will be a period of qualitative empirical research, which recognises the subjective nature of its findings. Indeed, the findings cannot be otherwise, relating as they do to the grounded

(Continued)

(Continued)

construction of group values and objectives. In this way, their role is that of a support for the moral position I seek to afford community epistemology, and in no way seeks to prescribe definitive outcomes; but rather to contribute to the task of legitimating and fostering the kind of community democracy around which the PhD revolves.

Timetable

Year 1:

September 2003–February 2004: Literature review of key themes elaborated above. Development of working models of key theoretical concepts of the model, i.e. community, democracy, and justice.

Year 1:

March–September 2004: Work on social capital, analysis of secondary literature of community groups in the UK, North America and Central and South America. Identification of key groups for qualitative empirical research. Detailed planning of empirical research phase (a).

Year 2:

October–December 2004: Fieldwork in the UK, and analysis of findings.

Year 2:

January–March 2005: Detailed planning of empirical research phase (b), in light of analysis of experience of prior fieldwork.

Year 2:

April–June 2005: Fieldwork in Mexico or Argentina, and analysis of findings.

Year 2:

July–September 2005: Writing up of findings of fieldwork.

Year 3:

October 2005–February 2006: Writing up, and answering of questions 1–5.

Year 3:

March–July 2006: Conclusions.

This timetable forms the framework within which I propose to undertake the research outlined in this proposal. It is, however, subject to revisions, which will be made at regular intervals, and the timetable updated accordingly so as to ensure sufficient time is allowed at each stage.

Source: Kelly, ESRC 1 + 3 student, University of Manchester.

Kelly's outline proposal provides a crisply written statement of research intent. This document formed the substantive part of her application for the first stage of her 1 + 3 programme of study. This successful application enabled Kelly to further explore its content during her research training as part of her Masters course at the University of Manchester. All realistic researchers acknowledge that our ideas, understandings and approaches change as our research/experiences progress, and it is an important part of 1 + 3 programmes that, following completion of the taught element, funded students are given the opportunities to further develop or refine their research proposals in advance of the remaining 3 years of their studies.

A good research proposal or plan will include a timeline indicating activities or tasks to be undertaken during the lifetime of the research or project. Kelly's indicative 1 + 3 proposal, above, provides broad indicators of when the substantive parts of her research work will take place. In their proposal to explore the application and impact of e-learning in the classroom, Davies and Birmingham produced a detailed breakdown of activities to assist the coordination of the project. This, in a proposal, serves a number of purposes: it provides a chronology of events in a project, details when activities will happen (and who will be responsible for them), and allows an evaluator or reviewer to quickly gain a feel for the logistics of the exercise.

It is perhaps surprising to see such a precise level of detail in a research plan as the one provided by Davies and Birmingham, but formalising the plan in this way enables both researchers to quickly assess where the 'busy' times in the project are. For example, (Peter) Birmingham has a heavy workload planned throughout spring and summer 2006. It is therefore important that all of his other teaching and administrative activities are carefully managed around these hectic periods if the research is not to suffer a delay.

My first draft PhD proposal was difficult to write. I didn't know where to start. What should I put in it, what should I leave out? I quickly realised that there was a 'house style' for submitting proposals to our department. Reviewers have a set list of criteria and headings they are looking for in a proposed research work. If they aren't in there somewhere, then the thing falls at the first fence! It's a good idea to take a look at successful proposals in your area – some researchers and academics are more than happy to gloat about successful research bids. If you can suffer this, you can pick up some useful tips to incorporate into your work.

John, PhD student, University of Northside.

PROJECT TIMELINE

Term	Month	Event
Summer 2004	April 2004	Confirmation of arrangements for observation visits Preparation of equipment and online survey Project steering group meeting
	May	Data collection, transcription and preliminary analysis (1) Online survey administered
	June	Data collection, transcription and preliminary analysis
	July	Data collection, transcription and preliminary analysis Teacher twilight session
	August	Data transcription and preliminary analysis
Autumn 2004	September	Data collection, transcription and preliminary analysis

	October	Data collection, transcription and preliminary analysis
		Online survey administered
		In-depth analysis: day-long project team data session with
		   Birmingham, Davies, Dutton, Greiffenhagen, Luff, Watson
		Follow-up day-long data session with Birmingham and
		   Greiffenhagen

	November	Data collection, transcription and preliminary analysis Project steering group meeting
	December	Data collection, transcription and preliminary analysis
Spring 2005	January 2005	Data collection, transcription and preliminary analysis Online survey administered
	February	Data collection, transcription and preliminary analysis Project steering group meeting
	March	Data collection, transcription and preliminary analysis
Summer 2005	April	Data collection, transcription and preliminary analysis Project steering group meeting
	May	Data collection, transcription and preliminary analysis Online survey administered
	June	Data collection, transcription and preliminary analysis

	July	Data collection, transcription and preliminary analysis
		In-depth analysis: day-long project team data session with
		   Birmingham, Davies, Dutton, Greiffenhagen, Luff, Watson
		Follow-up day-long data session with Birmingham and
		   Greiffenhagen
		Teacher twilight session

	August	Data collection transcription and preliminary analysis

(CONTINUED)

Term	Month	Event
Autumn 2005	September	Data collection, transcription and preliminary analysis
	October	Data collection, transcription and preliminary analysis Online survey administered
	November	Data collection, transcription and preliminary analysis Project steering group meeting
	December	Data collection, transcription and preliminary analysis
Spring 2006	January 2006	Final preparation of data for in-depth analysis (Birmingham, Davies, Dutton)
	February	In-depth analysis (Birmingham for whole month), including two-day-long project team data session with Birmingham, Davies, Dutton and Greiffenhagen Project steering group meeting
	March	In-depth analysis (Birmingham for whole month), including two-day-long project team data session with Birmingham, Davies, Dutton, Greiffenhagen, Luff, Watson and follow-up two-day-long data session with Birmingham and Greiffenhagen
Summer 2006	April	Writing up (2) In-depth analysis (Birmingham for whole month), including two-day-long project team data session with Birmingham, Davies, Dutton, Greiffenhagen, Luff, Watson and follow-up two-day-long data session with Birmingham and Greiffenhagen Project steering group meeting
	May	In-depth analysis (Birmingham for whole month), including two-day-long project team data session with Birmingham, Davies, Dutton, Greiffenhagen, Luff, Watson and follow-up two-day-long data session with Birmingham and Greiffenhagen Writing up Preparation of data sets for archiving and dissemination
	June	Writing up Preparation of data sets for archiving and dissemination
	July	Writing up Preparation of data sets for archiving and dissemination Teacher twilight session Preparation of BERA paper

(Continued)

(CONTINUED)

Term	Month	Event
	August	Writing up Preparation of data sets for archiving and dissemination Preparation of BERA paper
Autumn 2006	September	Writing up Preparation of data sets for archiving and dissemination Project steering group meeting Preparation of BERA paper and BERA presentation (3)

(1) Includes arranging school visits, video-based observation, semi-structured interviews with teachers, pupil focus group interviews (three days per week), digitisation, cataloguing and basic transcription of videodata, transcription of interview data, collation of online survey responses, bulletin board postings and documentary materials, weekly project meetings between Birmingham and Davies, monthly project meetings between Birmingham, Davies and Dutton.

(2) Includes writing of ESRC final report (Birmingham, Davies and Dutton), academic publications, conference papers and multi-authored project book (Birmingham, Davies, Dutton, Greiffenhagen, Luff, Watson).

(3) The cost of attending the BERA Annual Conference, as well as the costs of other likely conference attendance, e.g. Becta Annual Research Conferences, will be met internally through Department of Educational Studies staff research support funds.

Source: Peter Birmingham, Department of Educational Studies, University of Oxford.

When developing proposals, the balance between a sufficiently detailed submission and a watertight blueprint with no room for deviation is a difficult balance to achieve (as John outlines above). It should be clear that an effective research or dissertation proposal does not necessarily provide minute detail relating to every possible and conceivable eventuality. Rather, it should provide sufficient information to make it clear to a reasonably knowledgeable reader that you have the necessary background, skill and resources to carry out and report on the work. It is often useful at the proposal development stage to consider the format and structure of the final piece of written work (the dissertation or thesis). This can help additionally focus your mind upon exactly what it is you are attempting to find out or discover, and how this can be effectively expressed and presented within the parameters of a written dissertation or thesis. Liz Oliver, a postgraduate student at the University of Leeds, has produced the following chapter outline in her initial proposal for PhD study, it provides an informative summary of the key areas of investigation and how they will relate to each other in the final written work.

Thesis chapter outline

Introduction
- Research Objectives
- Research Strategy
- Chapter Overview

Methodology
- Developing socio-legal research methodology at EU and national level
- The ethics of socio-legal research aimed at influencing policy
- Practical issues in the field

Fixed-term contracts and equality in science careers: introducing the issues
- Women and science in the EU and the UK: the glass ceiling and the gender pay gap
- Developing a career structure for contract research staff in the European Research Area and within UK science
- The evolving role of fixed-term contracts within science labour markets in the EU and the UK
- Introducing the legal issues

    – The evolution of EU law and policy
    – The role of UK law and policy
    – Using case studies to highlight legal issues

Emerging themes suggest a focus of the following areas
These chapters will involve socio-legal analysis across a key theme exploring the experiences of men and women in science

Fixed-term contracts and mobility
- The relationship between mobility and fixed-term contracts
- How scientists use/experience mobility on fixed-term contracts
- How fellowships and funding schemes that promote mobility use fixed-term contracts
- Social security and welfare rights in this context
- Scientists using mobility strategically
- Scientists 'moving to stand still' getting caught in a 'post-doc' and mobility trap that does not lead to further career progression
- Family life and short-term mobility

(Continued)

(Continued)

Fixed-term contracts and concepts of excellence
- Formal and informal concepts of excellence
- How concepts of excellence influence career progression
- Access to experiences and networks that will benefit career progression on fixed-term contracts
- How working conditions influence access to excellence indictors
- The role of funding provision
- Do equal opportunities policies help?

Fixed-term contracts and work–life balance
- What strategies scientists are employing to balance work and family life
- How policies to promote work–life balance help or not
- How men and women approach work–life balance
- The relationship between career progression and work–life balance
- The role of the working time directive

Fixed-term contracts: pay and working conditions
- The pay and conditions of temporary and permanent staff
- The relationship between pay and ability to manage work and home life
- Social security provision and pensions
- The role of the directive on fixed-term work

Fixed-term contracts and job security
- Job security and risk
- Policies to develop continuity and security
- The impact of job security on parenting

Conclusion

Source: Liz Oliver, ESRC 1 + 3 student, University of Leeds.

A fundamental purpose of your project or research proposal is to convince the reader or reviewer that the issue, topic or question to be examined is worthy of examination.

Consider the following draft research proposal. This outline paper provides a clear indication of intended outcomes for the research work. It identifies the supervisory team, is relatively short and provides a useful starting point for the researcher and supervisor team to begin the more formal process of developing and coordinating the research work.

Draft Project Proposal (January 1994): Cost–benefit analysis of quality assurance mechanisms in adult and continuing education

Introduction

In recent years, the issue of quality in adult, continuing and higher education has risen to the top of the political and academic agenda. As a consequence, quality assurance mechanisms have been developed in order to monitor the quality of educational provision and the institutional management structures and processes which support and validate that provision. These mechanisms now exist at a number of different levels: institutional, consortium, regional and national. A number of different models have developed with a variety of names depending on context, application, purpose and philosophy: audit, validation, accreditation, appraisal, peer group review, quality circles and so on. Some of these are new; some have been in place for a considerable length of time but may be undergoing modification. All are endeavouring to define quality and formulate ways of monitoring and improving it. The cost of these procedures often seems excessive, especially when they are new, although we are not yet clear precisely what the costs are and how to measure them. Just as importantly, we are not clear what the benefits of the various quality assurance mechanisms are, and how to measure them. This project will seek to address these questions by examining the various models of quality assurance which have been developed by Authorised Validating Agencies (AVAs) within the national framework for the recognition of Access Courses. From this an attempt will be made to develop a generalisable model and to test this in the context of university continuing education provision.

Background: quality assurance for Access Courses

In 1989, the then DES invited CNAA and CVCP to set up a national framework for the recognition of Access. Since then what has emerged is a three-tier devolved system of local agencies authorised by a central body to validate courses:

(Continued)

(Continued)

Access Courses Recognition Group (ACRG)
(A national committee of representatives of universities,
polytechnics, further education, LEAs, CVCP, CNAA, CDP)

Authorised Validating Agencies (AVAs)
(local groups usually made up of HE and FE institutions –
total number of AVAs – 40)

Access Course Providers
(usually FE colleges – total number of courses approved
July 1993 – approx. 750)

The central body, ACRG, has a system of quality assurance for the AVAs consisting of initial approval and the granting of a licence, with subsequent periodic review. AVAs have systems of quality assurance for Access Courses consisting of initial approval, annual monitoring and periodic review. Courses approved through these arrangements are awarded a national kitemark of recognition intended to provide national currency and credibility.

ACRG adopted the principle of 'lightness of touch' and devolved responsibility so that the organisational structures and procedures of AVAs are very diverse. They range from the procedures of Open Colleges which operate within the National Open College Network (NOCN) and which accredit a range of other provision besides Access programmes, at a number of different levels and provide a number of other services, to those which themselves take a 'light of touch' approach and confine their activities to the validation of Access Courses.

In parallel to the development of this range of models, interesting questions have arisen about the relative costs and benefits of the different practices, particularly as there is also great diversity in the operating budgets of AVAs. Such questions have acquired greater significance as the budgets have come under increasing pressure arising from recent Education Reform Acts. These questions are, however, extremely complex. Whilst the costs of the operations are relatively easy to identify and can be (although rarely are) fully measured in monetary values, the benefits are more problematic. Whilst some benefits may be clear, others may not be obvious; they may appear at different levels and over differing time scales; they may be direct or indirect; they may be intended or unintended; they may vary between individuals and groups; there may not be a consensus about benefits obtained from a particular

(Continued)

set of procedures. It should also be noted that whilst it may be possible to attach a monetary value to some of the outcomes of the quality assurance mechanisms, there may be others which cannot be measured in comparable terms.

Background: developments in university adult and continuing education

The new Higher Education Funding Council for England (HEFCE) has undertaken a review of the funding of continuing education provision and has indicated that radical changes will be implemented in the future. Although the precise details have not been announced, it is clear that for the 'old' universities a major programme of accreditation of adult and continuing education provision will need to be put in place. The nature of the provision and the demands of client groups make this a difficult problem. It may be that a number of different mechanisms are required for different students and the various levels and types of course. It will also be essential to min- imise the costs and maximise the benefits of whatever procedures are developed. This project will be timely to inform of these developments.

Aims and objectives

The aim of the project is to conduct a cost–benefit analysis of a number of different quality assurance mechanisms within the national framework for the recognition of Access Courses, in order to develop a more generalisable methodology which might be useful in other contexts.

Objectives

1. To identify, and where possible quantify, the costs associated with a number of different arrangements for quality assurance within the national framework for the recognition of Access Courses.
2. To identify, and where possible quantify, the benefits associated with the different arrangements.
3. To develop an understanding of the relationship between costs and benefits in the different arrangements.
4. To develop a model of the way in which costs and benefits might interact in quality assurance mechanisms.
5. To test the model in the context of university adult and continuing provision.

(Continued)

(Continued)

Methods

The project will employ a range of qualitative and quantitative approaches and will endeavour to work collaboratively with practitioners in the field. Case studies will be undertaken in five AVAs to develop a model, and two university departments of adult and continuing education will be involved in the testing of the model. The work will be undertaken in four stages over the period January 1994 to June 1996.

Stage 1: January to June 1994
* Literature review and interviews with practitioners at all levels in the case study AVAs to develop a qualitative analysis of the costs and benefits of the operation of the quality assurance arrangements. *Development of a qualitative model of the relationship between costs and benefits and the way in which they interact.

Stage 2: July 1994 to June 1995
* Identification of the costs and benefits which can be quantified and those which cannot. *Development of a methodology for quantifying the various factors. *Development of a quantitative model.

Stage 3: July to December 1995
* Testing of the model in the case study AVAs and others not involved in stage 1. *Modification of the model as appropriate and evaluation of its strengths and weaknesses.

Stage 4: January 1996 to March 1996
* Testing of the model in two university departments. *Modification as appropriate and evaluation of strengths and weaknesses.

Stage 5: April to June 1996
* Writing up of final report.

Outcomes
1. A qualitative and quantitative cost–benefit analysis of a range of quality assurance arrangements operating within the national framework for the recognition of Access programmes and in university adult and continuing education departments.
2. A proposed model for evaluating quality assurance mechanisms in qualitative and quantitative terms.

(Continued)

3. Progress reports at the end of each stage of the project and at a final report on completion.
4. Dissemination of the findings and methods through ongoing collaboration and through events at appropriate stages during the project.

Project management

The project will be based at the Continuing Education Research Unit at City University and supervised by Pat Davies (Director of Research Unit), Stella Parker (Head of Department) and Peter Roberts (Visiting Professor, Department of Systems Science).

An Advisory Group will be established, consisting of representatives from HEQC, AVAs, UCACE, University CE departments, project supervisors, and others as appropriate (e.g. funding agents).

It is proposed that a full-time researcher will be employed for three years to carry out the work. The researcher will register for a PhD at City University. The project will be funded in the first year by City University but external funding will be sought for the second and third years.

Considering the readers

WHO WILL READ YOUR PROPOSAL?

The example proposals already provided in this chapter give you an indication of a range of writing styles and approaches in research/project proposals. All the examples listed have been written with specific (although quite similar) readers or audiences in mind. It is important to consider, at drafting stage, who will read your proposal and to carefully consider the particular style of writing they will be expecting to read.

As stated earlier in this chapter, proposals for research, dissertation or project work can vary in their detail, scope, size and degree of formality. Krathwohl's summary at the beginning of this chapter indicates that it is an aim of the research proposal to convey the thoughts and intentions of researchers and academics in relation to the subject to be studied. Those thoughts, intentions, rationales and descriptions should therefore be written in a way that is familiar or expected by its intended reader. Often universities, charities, funding councils and research councils (to name but a few) have a preferred 'house style' in terms of proposals submitted to them. They are often used as initial mechanisms through which to filter proposals so if house style requirements are not observed, the proposal can fall at the first fence. Dr Blue explains why below.

It's absolutely infuriating sometimes! You can see a very good proposal in terms of an adequate consideration of the research literature, the limitations of the questions posed, good rationale for research tools to be used, but the damn thing has poor referencing, no page numbers and not even the three hard copies required are supplied with it. If they are that incompetent with the mechanics of the proposal, and what we require, it's extremely difficult to have faith in their proposed work.

Dr Blue, proposal reviewer, anonymous funding body.

Having said this, some sponsors and research funders often value an innovative proposal that does not follow the traditional format. However, this is a high-risk strategy and only those who are extremely confident about their proposed work should attempt it. Proposals which do not follow the traditional format almost always receive close and detailed scrutiny from those assessing the piece.

What makes a good proposal? Suggestions from JISC*

The Right Ideas

- Winning proposals always demonstrate that the writer has read the call for proposals thoroughly and carefully.
- A successful bid will describe a good idea for addressing one or more of the key issues identified in the call. The 'circular' will always spell these issues out in detail, so read the call for proposals thoroughly and carefully.

(Continued)

- The ideas must be applicable to a wide section of the higher and further education community, or provide results that will be of great interest to many other institutions.
- Project proposals will be evaluated against a set of criteria that are described in the 'circular'. Read the call for proposals thoroughly and carefully and check whether your proposal meets these criteria. It can help to have an independent colleague carry out a check for you. Examples of evaluation criteria in recent calls include:

  - Evidence of understanding of the problem
  - Appropriateness of the methodology and evaluation techniques selected
  - Experience of the proposers
  - Feasibility and detail of the work plan/timetable
  - Value for money
  - Likely effectiveness of the dissemination plan

- Your proposal will be marked by a panel of independent experts. They are unlikely to have much knowledge of you, your team or your institution and will usually have many such proposals to mark. Your proposal must not only stand out as a good idea, it must also be clear, concise and provide all of the information requested in the call. A well-written, brief summary of the project that sets out the aims and objectives in an easily understood form will be very helpful.
- A clear presentation of the information in your proposal is therefore the key to success.

*The Joint Information System Committee (JISC) works with further and higher education by providing strategic guidance, advice and opportunities to use ICT to support teaching, learning, research and administration. (http://www.jisc.ac.uk/) (Accessed: 15/6/04).

There are a number of reasons why proposals for postgraduate study are rejected. Most sponsors produce clear guidelines relating to the format and content of submissions put before them. The most common reasons for rejection can be classified around subjects, methods and personnel.

Subjects

- The research question isn't complex enough to merit investigation or analysis.

- Proposed hypotheses cannot reasonably be tested given the data collected.

- The theme is too complex to be dealt with using the methods proposed.

- The research has limited appeal (perhaps local) and is not related to regional, national or international policy initiatives.

- The research theme is not clear and is poorly stated.

- The research (or very similar research) is already being carried out elsewhere.

Methods

- The proposed research methods or tools are inappropriate given the scope and subject matter of the work.

- The description of the methodology is unclear and lacking in clarity, making it difficult for reviewers to evaluate it effectively.

- The overall design of the project work is disjointed and difficult to follow.

- Data analysis aspects have not been considered fully.

- The timing of the work has been underestimated.

- Risk factors have not been adequately considered.

- The proposed approach is boring and unimaginative.

- The amount of data to be collected is insufficient.

Personnel

- The researcher does not have the necessary skill to carry out the work effectively.

- Based upon the proposal, the researcher or research team are unaware of developments in the field (usually due to their lack of consideration of the wider research literature).

- The researcher does not have an established 'track record' in this field.

- The research team do not have sufficient skill in the area to be investigated.

- The workload in the project, for the researcher, is too great.

A consideration of these reasons for rejection, prior to the submission of your proposal, may save you time (in not putting forward proposed work that might reasonably be rejected), but it may also enable you to head-off such potential criticisms and develop stronger arguments for your work.

A number of organisations who fund postgraduate study now require applicants to provide details of relevant work/research experience to support their application. This requires considerable focused thought on the part of the applicant. Consider the following supporting statement made by Claire in the application to the ESRC's 1 + 3 programme.

I have spent nine months living in Bishkek, Kyrgyzstan as a student at the Kyrgyz Russian Slavonic University (August 2000 – June 2001); during my time there I gained considerable first-hand experience of Kyrgyz society and some of the key problems facing it. Furthermore, I had the opportunity to familiarise myself with the academic, NGO and international communities in Bishkek, acquiring insights into how such problems are perceived and what solutions are being proposed.

During the course of my degree I have completed a range of Russian and Eastern European Area Studies courses each year, thus facilitating the development of a sound overview of the region on both a political and societal level. My experience of living in Russia (Krasnoyarsk and Voronezh) and Kyrgyzstan has further informed my studies of the Former Soviet Union on an anecdotal level. I feel my knowledge and skills would be further enhanced and consolidated by the proposed course of study, thus putting me firmly in a position to pursue a career within the research community, either in the academic field or a related area such as NGOs working in the region.

In addition to advancing my skills within a specific academic capacity, the course will enable me to strengthen related and

(Continued)

(Continued)

complementary capabilities, including the facilitation of learning and cross-cultural awareness. My teaching and mentoring experience to date has included EFL teaching and cultural orientation programmes for international students. Completing the proposed MA and PhD will strengthen my position to make full use of these skills in the context of an academic career in conjunction with my existing skills. The course will also permit me to fully utilise my existing language capabilities and allow me to further develop them in parallel with the acquisition of advanced research skills such as data collection techniques and methodology.

I have independently maintained an active interest in CIS affairs through attendance at CREES departmental seminars and round table discussions and will shortly be attending a conference, which includes seminars on security issues. This year I have actively contributed to seminars on defence and security in the Former Soviet Union, including a presentation on security issues in Central Asia pre- and post-9/11. Continued academic study will provide opportunities to enhance my overall awareness of Area Studies issues, on both a theoretical and area-specific level, and to increase my participation in the field, assisted by the acquisition of more refined written and oral presentation skills.

Claire, ESRC 1 + 3 student, University of Birmingham.

As a result of the considerable growth in research funding applications, many funding organisations now require reviewers to structure their comments around a set of themes contained in an evaluative grid. These reviewer grids are then used to evaluate or assess the worthiness of a proposal or bid for funding. The example below groups the assessment around four key areas of: quality of submission, timeliness of submission, researcher track record, and value for money. A sifting mechanism is often used by funding organisations utilising such assessment frameworks, whereby proposals scoring below a threshold minimum are not put forward for funding.

Framework for evaluating proposals

(Please circle the appropriate response)

Quality criteria

- Does the proposal consider appropriate literature and utilise the best research methodology for the subject under investigation?   Yes   No
- Is the proposed work free of any substantive weaknesses in approach?   Yes   No

Timeliness

- Is this proposal related to current policy initiatives?   Yes   No
- Is the work unique (i.e. you are not aware of similar work being carried out elsewhere)?   Yes   No
- Is the proposed work innovative?   Yes   No

Track record

- Are you aware of the work of the proposer?   Yes   No
- In your opinion, does the proposer have the experience/knowledge/skill to conduct the work?   Yes   No

Value for money

- Is the project adequately costed?   Yes   No
- Does the project represent value for money?   Yes   No

Note to reviewers:
If 'Yes' is recorded 7 or more times, proposals are put forward for funding. If 'Yes' is recorded fewer than 7 times and you believe the proposal merits funding, please state your reasons on a separate sheet and return to the Funding Manager.

Many of the frameworks for evaluating proposals are similar to those used by reviewers of papers considered for academic journals. Some funding organisations, as do journal publishers, make public their evaluative criteria, so it might be useful to investigate, prior to submitting your work, the criteria used by the organisation from which you are seeking funding or resourcing. It might also be extremely useful to consider the following before finally submitting any proposal. Ask yourself:

* Have I established appropriate aims and objectives?

* Have I provided a well-thought out research design?

* Have I given a full and detailed description of the proposed methods?

* If I am using data collection, have I considered already existing resources?

* Have I demonstrated a clear and systematic approach to the analysis of data collection?

* Have I thought about ethics?

* Have I anticipated potential difficulties and addressed them?

* Have I provided a bibliography?

* Have I identified potential users and thought about how to engage them?

* Have I provided a clear dissemination strategy?

The Economic and Social Research Council receive a huge number of proposals for research funding. Some are in response to specific invitations or calls within particular research areas or themes, others are more speculative expressions of interest in research-based activity, and a large number are from potential postgraduate researchers seeking to join the prestigious number of ESRC-funded students. Paul Rouse, within the Postgraduate Training Directorate at ESRC, provides useful suggestions for those seeking ESRC research funding (primarily postgraduate study applicants, although other funding-seekers may well benefit from his advice).

* Allow plenty of time to develop, draft, re-draft and submit your proposal.

* Read the rules and regulations and guidance notes on preparing and submitting funding proposals.

* Familiarise yourself with the funding source. Do they fund the particular research work you intend to conduct?

* Discuss your application with peers, tutors and potential supervisors.

* Justify your costings.

* Consider the content and presentation. Is it written in a suitably professional style?

* How will dissemination be achieved (a report, presentation, journal article, books etc)?

* Check the detail for typos etc. Have you included everything you should have?

The literature

It is important to incorporate relevant research literature into any proposal or research plan you may develop. This adds authority to what you write and provides reference 'markers' or 'positions' for those reviewing your work. Consider, in the extract below, the way Davies and Birmingham utilise the research literature to help sharpen their research focus. They draw upon a range of sources to help clarify their research aims, they use the literature to provide a clear rationale for their intended investigations, and they demonstrate, through the variety of material cited, that considerable relevant reading has taken place in the development of their proposal.

E-learning in the classroom: the educational affordances of broadband

Introduction

Broadband provides high-speed, reliable and permanent connection to the internet. By connecting classrooms and local networks to the internet more effectively, it is hoped that broadband will also help to integrate ICTs generally into classroom teaching and learning. The government's heavy investment in e-learning is intended to result in improved standards across the curriculum. Broadband connectivity, as a major instance of state investment, must demonstrate its worth in particular in this respect.

Following ImpaCT2's major contribution to research in this field, further research must now attempt to describe and theorise with some precision the ways in which teachers and students achieve educational benefit from their uses of new technologies within classrooms. Claims made on behalf of broadband internet (YHGfL, 2002;

(Continued)

(Continued)

Becta, 2003) refer to gains in relation to learner autonomy, motivation, classroom management, access to information, content delivery and enhanced opportunity for communication. These all have some foundation in earlier forms of ICT-supported practice and have been demonstrated to some extent in previous research, especially: NCET (1994), Cox (1997), Denning (1997), Grabe and Grabe (2001), Harris and Kington (2002), Loveless (2003), and Scrimshaw (2003).

Very little detailed substance exists in support of such claims in relation to broadband specifically. What there is consists largely of short-term (by comparison to the proposed project) classroom-level inspections of Regional Broadband Consortia, conducted internally (e.g. YHGfL, 2002), by Ofsted (e.g. 2001, 2002), or small case studies relayed at occasional conferences, such as Contagious Creativity organised by NESTA Futurelab in 2002, which take broadband as their focus. The present application therefore proposes to make a significant and original contribution to research into educational uses of technology by providing in-depth, data-driven understandings about the educational benefits afforded by broadband connectivity in classrooms, and into the teaching and learning practices that surround its use.

Research questions

The notion of affordances provides a key aspect of the theoretical orientation for this research. We recognise that 'there is nothing inherent in the Internet that guarantees learning. But in a specific context involving learning activities, such as research, collaboration, self-expression, and reflection, the Internet offers multiple affordances' (Ryder & Wilson, 1996). Such a perspective focuses our attention primarily on what the intended beneficiaries of broadband here, teachers and pupils, are actually gaining from the technology in the course of subject teaching and learning in classrooms, in terms of both direct practical and educational benefit.

The setting of classrooms is central to the proposed research, which will take close account of how broadband is incorporated into the 'multidimensionality' (Doyle, 1986) of classroom teaching, with its 'one adult figure responsible for the learning of a substantial number of young people ... for substantial periods of time' (McIntyre, 2002, p. 127). Research into classroom teaching and learning indicates an ongoing tension between teachers' need to reduce the complexity of classrooms to manageable levels, and pupils' need to take ownership of their learning in varied ways, a tension which broadband technology is likely to highlight. The research will focus on how the work of using broadband is negotiated and carried out between teachers and pupils,

(Continued)

and on the values accorded to different affordances of broadband by the various actors in specific settings. Therefore, this research will address the three following closely-related questions:

1. What are the affordances of broadband internet in specific, situated encounters between teachers, pupils and broadband resources?
2. How do teachers and pupils collaborate in achieving the affordances of broadband internet in the classroom and what are the distinctive characteristics of their respective contributions to that work?
3. What do these complex interactions suggest about effective processes and practices for using the internet in teaching and learning?

We see the emphasis on specific, situated encounters as crucial in establishing the relevance and validity of our answers to these questions: 'Whatever policy recommendations are made in terms of the world as it ought to be, our point is that they must be based on careful analysis of the world as it is' (Hemmings et al., 2000, p. 113). In line with Woolgar's observation that 'attention at the macro level gives rather little clue as to how these technologies are actually used and experienced in every day practice' (2003), the orientation of our proposed research reflects the growing emphasis in recent years since the 'shift to the social' (Baecker et al., 1995) in human computer interaction (HCI) on the observable ways we act and interact when using technologies in specific social settings.

By closely examining 'the practices and procedures, the *in situ* reasoning and knowledge, relied upon by participants in accomplishing their practical actions and activities' (Luff et al., 2000, p. xiii), Workplace Studies provide an array of observations and findings concerning locally organised human competencies and practices operating in work settings which feature the use of technology. Whilst important studies have focused on such complex organisational environments as command and control centres, news rooms, architectural practices, medical consultation rooms and financial institutions, formal educational settings such as classrooms have received little analytic attention and remain as a result a neglected workplace deserving of close study.

In order to focus on classrooms in this way, it is necessary to recognise that the use of educational technology in lessons depends for its success upon factors such as pupils' other work in the classroom away from the computer, discussions and

(Continued)

(Continued)

gestural interactions between pupils and between pupils and their teacher, the ways teachers initially 'set up' computer-based activities, the nature of the interventions teachers make during the activities, and the ways before and after such activities that pupils are enabled to relate them to other, non-computer-based educational experiences (Wegerif and Scrimshaw, 1997; Mercer and Fisher, 1998; Wood, 1998; Littleton and Light, 1999; Crook, 1994 and 2000; Cazden, 2001; McConnick and Scrimshaw, 2001).

Such approaches to the study of classroom-based work formed the basis for our own previous research into the kar2ouche Shakespeare storyboarding software (Birmingham, 2001; Birmingham and Davies, 2001a; Birmingham and Davies, 2001b; Birmingham and Greiffenhagen, 2002a; Birmingham and Greiffenhagen, 2002b; Birmingham, Davies and Greiffenhagen, 2002; Davies and Birmingham, 2002; Wilkinson and Birmingham, 2003). In this present proposal, we aim to extend this approach to a wide range of classrooms in which uses of broadband internet are currently being developed and refined.

Source: Davies, C. and Birmingham, P. E-learning in the classroom: the educational affordances of broadband. Research proposal submitted to ESRC.

There are a number of excellent texts which focus upon drawing from published material to aid, enhance, steer and inform research activities. Essentially, accessing and reviewing literature in your research field enables you to 'get up to speed' in your area of interest. You will become aware of the leading writers and issues, and the developments in subject areas that may affect your work.

Birmingham (2000) provides a practical approach to assessing and evaluating literature for project and research work. He suggests that when critically analysing published material, we should consider:

* *Does the material go into sufficient depth?* Is it clear what the piece is about and why any research upon which it is based was conducted? Is a clear context for the article provided? Are any data missing from the piece or is any information unclear?

* *Are there any inconsistencies?* If the piece is based upon substantial analyses of data, are figures provided and consistent (e.g. are references to initial and achieved samples consistent)? Are attrition (non-response and drop-out) rates clearly explained and rationales provided?

- *Where did the author obtain his/her information?* Do you recognise the sources of the authors information (e.g. other journals, textbooks, research papers) or are they obscure references? Did the author collect information from more than one source or could the information and data collected be biased in any way?

- *Are the authors claims reasonable?* Are claims made based upon an analysis of information or data collected by the author? Is there sufficient evidence provided for claims made? (adapted from Birmingham, 2000: 35–36)

We might also add to the above list: how does this literature add to my work or help shape, develop or steer it? Effectively, what value is this published work to my intended research or project work endeavours?

When you are developing a research proposal to conduct an in-depth study or investigation it will not be necessary (or even desirable from the reviewer's point of view) to conduct a full-scale literature review of the research area. Such a professional undertaking would naturally take many weeks, months or even years of hard work to complete. It is appropriate at the proposal writing stage to conduct such a review as to enable you, as a competent researcher, to identify important and influential pieces as might reasonably affect your work. We might refer to this as a pre-scan of the literature (Wilkinson, 2000: 19). An analysis of the various types of literature source that you can draw upon when reviewing your work are provided in Chapter 11 on publishing opportunities.

Elements of project or research proposal

Jonathan Grix, an academic at the University of Birmingham, provides some focused advice for those seeking research proposal success. He suggests that research proposals should include:

- a crisp and clear summary of the problem to be tackled,
- an indication of how the proposed project fits in with the wider, relevant literature,
- a discussion of the theoretical approach adopted,
- a number of clearly set-out research questions or hypotheses,
- a discussion of the methods to be employed to answer, refute or validate research questions or hypotheses,
- an awareness of relevant data sources and data analysis; and
- a timetable for the completion of the thesis. (Grix, 2001: 11)

As mentioned earlier in this chapter, research and project proposals can take various forms. However, a useful, if somewhat basic, structure might be to frame a proposal that will allow you to competently consider the following:

* framing your questions;

* exploring the literature;

* developing a strategy;

* collecting data;

* analysing data; and

* drawing conclusions (Wilkinson, 2000: 15–16).

Considering these fundamental areas of the research process will provide you with the building blocks to move on to develop a fully-worked research proposal. More specifically, most proposals are structured around the following format or headings and sections:

Title   The title of your work.

Introduction   Providing the context for your proposed work, with reference to the key literature sources and perhaps a refinement or clarification of the remit of your intended work.

Aims/Objectives   The substantive elements of your work – what you hope to achieve. Often, the aims/objectives section of a proposal is provided as a list of research questions, related to your title, which you wish to explore.

Methodology   The approach to research that you intend to take, and the tools you intend to use within your research framework.

Analysis   An appreciation of the data you will collect, and indications as to how these data will be analysed. Here you might discuss particular computer packages or statistical techniques you will use with the data.

Timetable   The chronology of events/activities within your project work.

Dissemination   How and where you intend to share the results of your work with others (e.g. through interim reports, workshops, conferences, journal articles, monographs).

Budget   How much the work will cost (usually not necessary for standard PhD funding, but crucial for research grant funding and post-doctoral work).

Staffing or CV   Those who will work on the project (usually only the applicant for postgraduate funding), with contact details and relevant previous experience, such as research assistance work, undergraduate dissertation experience, conference papers, seminar presentations, etc.

References   The names and contact details (usually two) of those who can comment upon your academic ability and potential.

Reference list, useful reading and websites

Beginners guide to the research proposal. (http://www.ucalgary.ca/md/CAH/research/res_prop.htm) (Accessed 15/1/05).

Birmingham, P. (2000) Reviewing the literature, in D. Wilkinson (ed.), *The researcher's toolkit: the complete guide to practitioner research*. London: RoutledgeFalmer. pp. 25–40.

Blaikie, N. (2000) *Designing social research*. Cambridge: Polity Press.

Clough, P. and Nutbrown, C. (2002) *A student's guide to methodology*. London: Sage.

Collis, J. and Hussey, R. (2003) *Business research*. Basingstoke: Palgrave.

ESRC (2005) *ESRC postgraduate studentships in the social sciences available in 2005: guidance notes for applicants*. Bristol: Economic and Social Research Council.

Grix, J. (2001) *Demystifying postgraduate research: from MA to PhD*. Birmingham: Birmingham University Press.

Krathwohl, D.R. (1998) *Methods of educational and social science research: an integrated approach*. New York: Longman.

National Postgraduate Committee. (http://www.npc.org.uk).

Phillips, E.M. and Pugh, D.S. (2003) *How to get a PhD: a handbook for students and their supervisors*. Third edn. Buckingham: Open University Press.

Prospects. (http://www.prospects.ac.uk).

Punch, K. (1998) *Introduction to social research: quantitative and qualitative approaches*. London: Sage.

Punch, K. (2000) *Developing effective research proposals*. London: Sage.

Robson, C. (2002) *Real world research*. London: Blackwells.

Scanlon, M. (2000) Issues in research, in D. Wilkinson (ed.), *The researcher's toolkit: the complete guide to practitioner research*. London: RoutledgeFalmer. pp. 1–13.

Thackray, D. Proposal writers guide. (http://www.research.umich.edu/proposals/pwg/pwgcomplete.html).

University of Newcastle, Careers Service – guide to research funding. (http://www.careers.ncl.ac.uk/students/pages/rfesfund).

Wilkinson, D. (ed.) (2000) *The researcher's toolkit: the complete guide to practitioner research*. London: RoutledgeFalmer.

Wisker, G. (2001) *The postgraduate research handbook: succeed with your MA, MPhil, EdD and PhD*. London: Palgrave.

Wisker, G., Robinson, G., Trafford, V., Creighton, E. and Warnes, M. (2003) Recognising and overcoming dissonance in postgraduate student research, *Studies in Higher Education*, 28(1): 91–105.

5 Finding your feet – the culture of academia

Chapter overview

This chapter covers the workings and operation of higher education institutions in the UK, including:

- The operation and function of HE institutions.
- Different types of university (pre- and post-1992 institutions).
- The importance of research and the Research Assessment Exercise (RAE).
- Pay structure and differences by institutional type.
- Typical structure of a university.
- The academic year.
- Academic roles and typical functions.

HE institutions in the UK

Charlotte's views (below) on postgraduate study and the university environment indicates that the culture and work environment inside universities differ from those found in other work environments. This chapter describes the different types of HE institution in which postgraduates may find themselves. It outlines the HE contract and its express and implied terms and, to assist your movement within and through the university, it provides an account of the variety of academic ranks, structures, role and responsibilities. The aim in all this is to help demystify academia.

> *There are very different cultures inside and outside academia. I forget how different it is and then I come back and think 'oh yeah I remember'. It's difficult and it depends on why you come into academia. I've come back and I'm doing what I do because I want it to be relevant. It's a means to an end. I want to know about this. I want to work in policy. It's something I'm interested in. You arrive in academia and you realise there are different rules, different everything, and you present your work in a different way. The pace is different: I was working in a consultancy and I worked until twelve every night with deadlines every other week, but the pace in academia is deceptive. You think the idea of being a student is all relaxing. It's not. It's actually really hard. It never leaves you, it's always there whereas in a job you can walk out and think 'that's it, I've done it'. It's hard to switch because they each demand very different things of you.*
>
> Charlotte, ESRC 1 + 3 student, University College London.

Higher education institutions come in many shapes and sizes and do not exclusively include universities (although to achieve the title 'university' in the UK is closely guarded and controlled (Bekhradnia, 2003: 2)). In the United Kingdom there are 90 universities, 116 university institutions and 55 colleges of higher education (Universities UK, 2003).[1] Each of these institutions has a specific remit or mission to work variably within the areas of: teaching and training, research, collaboration with industry, and the development of links with local communities. The mission and remit of an institution will influence its operation and culture – an institution with a strong commitment to the local community may not be engaged in internationally renowned research and, conversely, a research-led university may not necessarily have strong links with the local community. Of course, these are extremely broad generalisations. Each HE institution is often a complex mix of

---

[1] There are 115 university institutions in the UK, counting separately the colleges of Wales and London. If Wales and London are counted as single institutions, the total is 90 university institutions (Universities UK, 2003).

people with competing agendas in terms of research, teaching, widening participation and collaboration with industry. Nevertheless, broad institutional types do exist that can be said to display typical characteristics. In his analysis of the university sector, Peter Scott (a university Vice-Chancellor himself) classifies seven HE institutional types:

1. Oxford and Cambridge – having their own unique approaches to higher education;

2. the University of London – with its many associated colleges and institutes (such as Queen Mary and Birkbeck);

3. the large 'civic' universities (such as Leeds and Birmingham), broadly established during the Victorian age;

4. 'redbrick' universities – more recent institutions founded during the first half of the twentieth century (such as City University);

5. the campus universities – built on Greenfield sites during the 1960s (such as York and Warwick);

6. the technological universities – those that were formerly colleges of advanced technology (such as Loughborough); and

7. the 'new' or 'post-1992' universities – those that were formerly known as polytechnics (such as Huddersfield, Sheffield Hallam and Liverpool John Moores). (Scott, 2001: 195)

Other organisations and policy-writers define universities in a variety of ways according to the subject of analysis. In terms of research and related output, Evidence UK Ltd, a supplier of bibliometric research data, classify institutions in a way which allows comparison between like or similar institutions:

1. Pre-1960 institutions, which include the collegiate universities, the big civic institutions and the largest London colleges;

2. 1960–1990 institutions, which include those university creations associated with the Robbins expansion, of which some were in existence prior to 1960 under other guises; a small number of older institutions with similar research profiles are also included;

3. Post-1990 institutions, which include the polytechnics, which gained independent university status and received a significant increase in core research funding after the 1992 Research Assessment Exercise; and

4. Specialist colleges with research activity only in one or few subject areas. (Evidence, 2002: Section 1.4.5)

As with many things in life, the group you belong to helps define your power and strength, and many argue that universities are no different (Eccles, 2002; Jobbins, 2002; Goddard, 2004). These differences and groupings may become clear during your selection of institution and supervisor (see Chapter 3: Where to study and apply for funding, and Chapter 8: Working with your supervisor), but for the purposes of more simplified analysis we will apply an almost universally accepted (and understood) approach to classification of HE institutions in the UK – pre-1992 and post-1992 institutions.

PRE-1992 INSTITUTIONS

Before 1992 university provision in the UK was offered by a select number of institutions. These 'older' universities were established by Royal Charter or statute, or an Act of Parliament. Many 'older' universities have been institutions of higher education for hundreds of years, conducting research and teaching undergraduate and postgraduate students. These include the Universities of Oxford and Cambridge, which date from the twelfth and thirteenth centuries, and the Universities of Glasgow and Aberdeen, which have been in existence since the fifteenth century. However, some institutions have more recently enjoyed the status of being an 'older' university. This is as a result of, in part, the expansion of higher education in the UK initiated by the Robbins Report, published in 1963. Institutions classified as more recent 'older' universities include City University and the University of Warwick. The full list of institutions belonging to the pre-1992 group is provided in Table 5.1. Typically, these institutions receive more research funding than their post-1992 institution counterparts as they have been in existence (usually) longer and have therefore had the opportunity to develop and nurture research expertise.

POST-1992 INSTITUTIONS

The Further and Higher Education Act of 1992 granted university status to former polytechnics. Post-1992 universities are often referred as 'new' universities, although many of them were in existence long before 1992, operating as alternative and more flexible providers of higher education than their traditional (older institution) counterparts. Unlike traditional institutions of higher education, these providers embraced the needs of the time, offering part-time and sub-degree work, as well as full-time programmes of study. One of the fundamental aims of these institutions is to make higher education more relevant and accessible to a broader student base. As such, they were developed primarily as teaching institutions. Since being granted university status in 1992, these institutions have considerably developed

TABLE 5.1   PRE-1992 INSTITUTIONS

Aston University	University of Exeter
Brunel University	University of Glasgow
City University	University of Hull
Cranfield University	University of Kent
Heriot-Watt University	University of Leeds
Imperial College of Science,	University of Leicester
Technology & Medicine	University of Liverpool
Keele University	University of London[2]
Lancaster University	University of Manchester
Loughborough University	University of Newcastle upon Tyne
Open University	University of Nottingham
Queens University Belfast	University of Oxford
UMIST	University of Reading
University College London	University of Salford
University of Aberdeen	University of Sheffield
University of Bath	University of Southampton
University of Birmingham	University of St Andrews
University of Bradford	University of Stirling
University of Bristol	University of Strathclyde
University of Cambridge	University of Surrey
University of Dundee	University of Sussex
University of Durham	University of Ulster
University of East Anglia	University of Wales[1]
University of Edinburgh	University of Warwick
University of Essex	University of York

[1]Includes associated institutions: Cardiff, Lampeter, Aberystwyth, Bangor, Swansea.
[2]Includes associated colleges and institutions: King's College, Birkbeck, Goldsmiths, Queen Mary, Royal Holloway.

their research capacity. A major change for universities in this category has been the development of the ability to award their own degrees. Previously, pre-1992, degree awarding powers for polytechnics were controlled by the Council for National Academic Awards. A full list of institutions belonging to the post-1992 group is provided in Table 5.2.

DIFFERENCES BETWEEN THE TWO UNIVERSITY TYPES

Anecdotal evidence collected throughout the development of this text suggests that pre-1992 institutions tend to be viewed and represented as hierarchical – with clear and historical lines of responsibility and remit. As a result, images of inflexibility and rigid adherence to tradition may be seen to emerge in such institutions. Post-1992

TABLE 5.2   POST-1992 INSTITUTIONS

Anglia Polytechnic University	University of Central England,
Bournemouth University	Birmingham
Buckinghamshire Chilterns University College	University of Central Lancashire
	University of Derby
Coventry University	University of East London
De Montfort University	University of Glamorgan
Glasgow Caledonian University	University of Gloucestershire
Kingston University	University of Greenwich
Leeds Metropolitan University	University of Hertfordshire
Liverpool John Moores University	University of Huddersfield
London Metropolitan University	University of Lincoln
Middlesex University	University of Luton
Napier University	University of Northumbria, Newcastle
Nottingham Trent University	University of Paisley
Oxford Brookes University	University of Plymouth
Robert Gordon University	University of Portsmouth
Sheffield Hallam University	University of Sunderland
South Bank University	University of Teesside
Staffordshire University	University of West of England,
Thames Valley University	Bristol
University of Abertay, Dundee	University of Westminster
University of Brighton	University of Wolverhampton

institutions tend to be more loosely organised, perhaps around a broad and flexible faculty base. They are (perhaps as a result of their comparative youth), evolving organisations that are responsive to market (student) needs. A great number of post-1992 institutions continue to have, as their focus, the provision of programmes of academic study, rather than being involved with substantive research-based activities.

A great deal has been written to explore the workings, operation and function of these two broad types of HE institution. It is clear, through an examination of research funding tables (as provided in Chapter 3: Where to study and apply for funding) that the key research movers and shakers (in terms of total funding received) are within the pre-1992 group of institutions. However, there are pockets of research excellence, in terms of volume of research output and funding attracted, within the post-1992 sector. This is particularly so outside the Science and Engineering sectors.

RESEARCH ABILITY AND COMPETENCE

In the recent national assessment and evaluation of research output (the Research Assessment Exercise (RAE) of 2001), conducted by the key university funding organisations (the Higher Education Funding Councils of England, Scotland and

Wales), a number of subject areas (or units of assessment, as they are referred to in the exercise) had a high proportion of institutions within the post-1992 group producing work reaching the level of international excellence – receiving the prestigious '5*' rating in the exercise. For example, of the five institutions judged as internationally excellent within Sports-Related Subjects, three were post-1992 institutions; in Art and Design, of those receiving high RAE grades (grade 4 and above), over half were post-1992 institutions; in Sociology, a number of post-1992 institutions achieved a level of research which equated to a standard of national excellence; in Psychology, a similar proportion also achieved this level of excellence; and in Other Studies Allied to Medicine, a substantial proportion also achieved the very respectable 'nationally excellent' 4 grade.

It is true that a sizeable number of post-1992 institutions are places targeting vocational learning, meeting local and regional needs. However, others, led by ambitious and hungry academics, are beginning to snap at the heels of their 'traditional' university (pre-1992) counterparts. These institutions are eager to promote their abilities and can often produce rigorous and high-quality research that is so competitively priced and packaged as to cause concern within the traditional university competition. The fictional differences in quality and standard of research conducted by pre- and post-1992 institutions are becoming increasingly difficult to justify.

THE PAY DIVIDE

Although many differences between the two institutional types are fading or becoming, at best, blurred, one difference remains for those considering employment within one of the two. Pay scales for those engaged in research or other academic activities within the two institutional types are currently calculated through the use of different methodologies and are promoted and protected through different institutionally and sectorally recognised unions. In pre-1992 institutions, the Association of University Teachers (AUT) has long negotiated on behalf of its academic/research university staff membership. Regular rounds of negotiation have led to the development and production of pay scales to reflect the role and responsibilities of academics and researchers. Within post-1992 institutions negotiations have been more fragmentary and less unified within the sector until relatively recently. The National Association of Teachers in Further and Higher Education (NATFHE) represents a large majority of academics and researchers within post-1992 institutions, and its less intricate (in comparison to that of the AUT) pay scale agreement indicates discrepancies for staff carrying out academic and research duties. Essentially, Tables 5.3 and 5.4 show that those employed as academics or researchers in post-1992 institutions earn less than they would in a similar post in a pre-1992 institution. Understandably, many academics and researchers across the two institutional types are unhappy with this

TABLE 5.3   PRE-1992 ACADEMIC, ACADEMIC-RELATED, OTHER-RELATED AND RESEARCH SCALES (FROM 1 AUGUST 2002)

Academic	Academic-related	Spinal point	Salary on 1/8/02	Other-related	Research
***	Grade 1	4	£18,265	Grade 1	Grade IB
		5	£19,279		
		6	£20,311		
Lecturer A		7	£21,125	bar	
	Grade 2	8	£22,191	Grade 2	Grade IA
		9	£23,296		
		10	£24,121		
		11	£25,451		
		12	£26,270		
Lecturer B		13	£27,339		
	Grade 3	14	£28,498	Grade 3	Grade II
	disc. points	15	£29,621	disc. points	
	Grade 4	16	£30,660	Grade 4	
		17	£32,125		
		18	£33,679		Grade III

(CONTINUED)

disc. points	Senior lecturer			Grade 5	disc. points
	Grade 5	**20	£35,251	Grade 5	
		21	£36,712		
		22	£37,629		
		23	£38,681		
		24	£39,958		
disc. points	disc. points	25	£40,841	disc. points	
		26	£41,876		
		27	£43,067		
Grade 6 min'm	Grade 6 min'm	Highest grade: minimum	£40,841	Grade 6 min'm	Grade IV min'm
	Professorial min'm			Grade 6	Grade IV

* Age 27 point

** Point 19 was deleted with effect from 1.4.91

*** Point 7 from the lecturer A scale deleted.

Source: Association of University Teachers website (http://www.aut.org.uk) (Accessed: 3/5/04)

TABLE 5.4   POST-1992 LECTURERS' COMMON INTEREST GROUP HIGHER
EDUCATION PAY SCALES (FROM 1 AUGUST 2002)

Grade	1 February 2002 £ pa	1 August 2002 £ pa
Lecturer		
6*		
7	19,575	(22,191)
8	20,453	(22,191)
9	21,350	22,191
10	22,236	22,948
11	23,130	23,870
12	24,017	25,033
13	24,906	25,708
14	25,793	26,618
15	26,686	27,669
Senior Lecturer		
−1	24,906	25,708
0	25,793	26,618
1	26,686	27,669
2	27,577	28,498
3	28,459	29,621
4	29,348	30,376
5	30,249	31,217
6	31,129	32,125
7	32,021	33,046
8	32,910	34,191
Principal Lecturer		
0	31,129	32,125
1	32,021	33,046
2	32,910	34,191
3	33,795	34,940
4	34,690	35,800
5	35,574	36,712
6	36,462	37,629
7	37,360	38,681
8	38,252	39,476
9	39,141	40,394

(CONTINUED)

Grade	1 February 2002 £ pa	1 August 2002 £ pa
Researcher A		
1	11,562	11,962
2	12,451	12,997
3	13,344	13,771
4	14,236	14,692
5	15,120	15,734
6	16,008	16,520
Researcher B		
1	16,905	17,624
2	17,785	18,409
3	18,681	19,279
4	19,575	20,311
5	20,453	21,125
6	21,350	22,191
7	22,236	22,948
8	23,130	23,870
9	24,017	25,033
10	24,906	25,708
11	25,793	26,618
Part-time Hourly Rates		
I/II/III	28.48	29.48
IV	24.28	25.13
V	17.77	18.39

Source: National Association of Teachers in Further and Higher Education website (http://www.natfhe.org.uk) (Accessed: 3/5/04)

apparent unfairness in approach to payment. Negotiations have recently been initiated with all HE institutions to develop and agree a common and universal pay scale, although the implementation of this may be some way off.

HE COLLEGES/OTHER INSTITUTIONS

In addition to the pre- and post-1992 institutions, higher education provision is also offered in the UK by a growing number of higher education colleges. These institutions are, like universities, self-governed and independent. A number award their own degrees (having been granted the right to do so through statute or Act of Parliament), whilst many award degrees which are validated by collaborating (usually nearby) universities. As with universities, colleges can vary considerably in size and scope of operation, although their student intake numbers tend to be much smaller than their university counterparts. Many HE colleges provide programmes spanning a range of general discipline areas of use and relevance to the local and regional population. However, some focus on particular niche areas, such as the Cumbria College of Art and Design, the Dartington College of Arts, and the Royal Agricultural College.

Working in a HE environment (as all postgraduates do, even if only on a part-time basis) is quite different from participating in undergraduate study. It will become important, as you progress through your studies and academic career, to have a knowledge and understanding of the main offices, operations, structure and various personnel functions within higher education. The following section describes the typical structure of a UK university in order that your 'place' as a postgraduate operating within an academic environment may become clearer and you may be in a better position to plan where you want to be and determine your route to getting there.

Structure of a university in the UK

Whilst there are differences between pre- and post-1992 institutions, their governance and academic management is broadly similar. This section provides an overview of the typical structures, roles and responsibilities within UK universities. The description and presentation of structure and roles are simplified in order to provide a functional indicator of a typical university (see Figure 5.1 below). For those interested in a more detailed examination of the operation of universities, there are a range of publications discussing the area (Cuthbert, 1996; Deem and Brehony, 2000; Burton and Steane, 2004; Delamont and Atkinson, 2004).

The ceremonial head of a university is its **Chancellor**, who serves as the most senior public face of the institution, offering support and wise counsel to the university's functional management. He or she is elected through nomination of the Council. Typical duties may include the conferment of degrees at graduation events, supporting fundraising efforts, and chairing meetings of importance to the university's public image.

The university **Council** (or **Court** in Scotland) is responsible for finance and the general control of institutional resources. It has a 'lay' (non-academic) majority of members who have no other direct involvement in the university's activities. The academic leadership of the university is provided through the office and function of

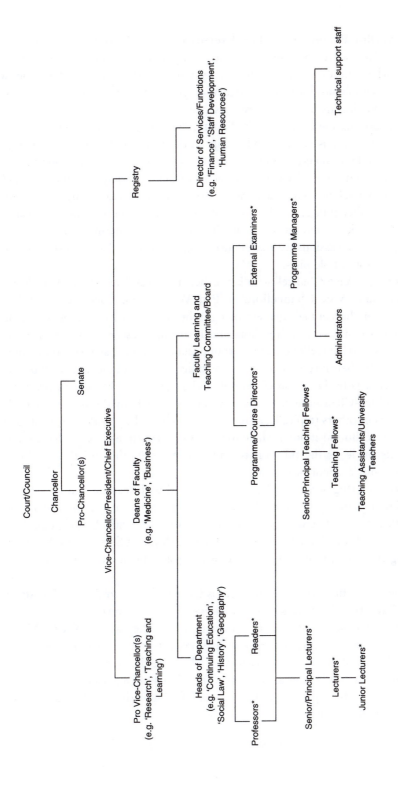

Court/Council
Chancellor
Pro-Chancellor(s)
Vice-Chancellor/President/Chief Executive
Senate

Pro Vice-Chancellor(s)
(e.g. 'Research', 'Teaching and Learning')

Deans of Faculty
(e.g. 'Medicine', 'Business')

Registry

Director of Services/Functions
(e.g. 'Finance', 'Staff Development', 'Human Resources')

Heads of Department
(e.g. 'Continuing Education', 'Social Law', 'History', 'Geography')

Faculty Learning and
Teaching Committee/Board

Programme/Course Directors*

External Examiners*

Senior/Principal Teaching Fellows*

Programme Managers*

Administrators

Technical support staff

Professors*
Readers*

Senior/Principal Lecturers*

Lecturers*

Junior Lecturers*

Teaching Fellows*

Teaching Assistants/University Teachers

* Those with whom postgraduates are likely to work/liaise.

FIGURE 5.1 **Typical structure of a UK university**

Vice-Chancellor/President or **Chief Executive**. He or she is ultimately responsible for the day-to-day operation of the university and its academic development, reporting, where necessary, to the university Council. By way of comparison, a university's Vice-Chancellor is similar to a Managing Director of a business and the university Council is its Board of Directors.

Also supporting the Council is the **Senate**, the university's sovereign academic authority. As such, it has no lay membership. In most universities Senates are large organisations and thus do not meet in their entirety very often. A good proportion of the work of most university Senates is conducted through a variety of committees and other related bodies. One such organisation is the Academic Development Committee, which, among other things, decides upon the direction and development of academic-related activities within the university. It is within this committee that deliberations take place and decisions are made concerning the development of new academic units or the closure of old ones.

Assisting the Vice-Chancellor in his or her many institutional roles or duties are the **Assistant Vice-Chancellors** or **Pro Vice-Chancellors**. Typically, Pro Vice-Chancellors have a management or figurehead role, focusing upon a specific area of the university, such as Teaching and Learning, Research, Student Affairs. Usually, Pro Vice-Chancellors help determine and operationalise institutional policy in relation to their given areas of responsibility, and the implementation of this policy is often devolved to faculties, schools and departments. In some institutions, posts of Pro Vice-Chancellor are permanent positions held by the appointed academic, whereas in others (typically, although not exclusively, pre-1992 institutions) Pro Vice-Chancellor positions are held for a set period of time before either a reappointment is made or the position is undertaken by another suitably qualified academic (usually a senior professor).

The role of **Registrar** is primarily concerned with leading and coordinating the administrative function of the university, ensuring the provision of a wide range of efficient and effective support services to academic staff. As such, functions such as Personnel (or Human Resources), Finance, Student Services, IT Services/Computing are usually ultimately directed or controlled by the Registrar and his or her Office.

The academic function of a university is most visibly controlled by **Heads** or **Deans of Faculty**. These are senior academics within the university who control the direction and output of the faculties with which they are involved. Within faculties/schools are academic units such as divisions, departments or institutes. These are also led by, usually, quite senior academics. These are the tangible and more visible (to students) areas of the academic structure. Heads of Department/Faculty are commonly seen to be experts in a field of study falling within the broad remit of the department they lead.

The **Faculty Learning and Teaching Committee/Board** help determine and operationalise the curriculum development areas for the Faculty. It is here where new programmes within a department, school or faculty are discussed and approved/rejected. The processes, procedures and decisions of Exam Boards are also the responsibility of the Faculty Learning and Teaching Committee/Board. It is here where student work, such as PhD theses, are finally (upon examiner advice) approved.

The **departments** or **schools** are seen as the academic powerhouses of a university, as it is here where all the academic activity is based. Most, or all, teaching provision in a university is hosted by department or school, research students and assistants are attached to Schools or Departments, and research output is (broadly) assessed by subject areas fitting into a school or departmental structure. Because academic activity is based around one of these two organisational units, this is where all academic staff are primarily based. In generally accepted order of seniority, this is where professors, readers, senior/principal lecturers, lecturers and junior lecturers carry out their academic roles and functions. Also, housed by school or department are teaching fellows, teaching assistants and university teachers. As their titles suggest, the primary role of these staff is to teach, or assist with teaching that is led by other 'academic' staff.

ORGANISATION: THE CHAIN OF COMMAND

The structure and organisational management of higher education institutions varies according to its fundamental classification, as outlined earlier. However, even within these areas there is considerable variation. Therefore, this text does not set out to provide the definitive structural arrangement for each institutional type; rather it provides information relating to broad structural commonalities that are often present. Indicated on Figure 5.1 with an '*' are those members of staff who are most likely to work with postgraduate learners. This may be for a variety of reasons. For example, a sub-division of Faculty Learning and Teaching Committees are Faculty or Departmental Exam Boards (often chaired by the Head/Director of postgraduate study, or a similarly senior academic member of staff). During these meetings (often held once or twice per year), primary decisions are made concerning the final grades awarded to learners who have completed programmes of study that fall within their remit.

The position of Head/Director of postgraduate study will usually be held at a School or Faculty level. It is the responsibility of the Head of postgraduate study to ensure appropriate procedures and mechanisms are in place to induct postgraduates into the university and advanced-level programmes of study. They are involved with the appointment and distribution of tutors and supervisors to postgraduate students. Heads of postgraduate study are also centrally involved with the examination of student work, often approaching and appointing external examiners, overseeing the *viva* process and often chairing Exam Boards. Most university systems and procedures require that postgraduate Directors of study also, initially, deal with problems/issues involving learners within their school, faculty or department. Directors of postgraduate study are responsible for postgraduate provision within their School/Faculty. They are responsible (and answerable) to colleagues and postgraduate students within their School or Faculty, and they are also held accountable for postgraduate issues by the university's hierarchy (academic as well as administrative). You should make yourself aware of your own Director or Head of postgraduate study, as you may require his or her assistance in the appointment of supervisors or, along with the help of your supervisor, the appointment of an external examiner.

External examiners (or 'Externals' as they are often called) are important elements of postgraduate programmes of study. They provide objective comment upon the programme as a whole and make decisions concerning the grading of student work. Most postgraduate programmes utilise the skills and knowledge of an external examiner through elements of the examination process. They may be asked to help select examination or assessment topics or questions, and they may also be asked to provide an input in oral examinations (or *viva voces* or *vivas* as they are also known). Utilising externals in *vivas* is standard practice for PhD examinations, but it is a tool that is also used to examine (usually a small selection) of Masters level students. At Masters level, *vivas* are generally reserved for exceptional students, and situations where learners are within the borderline of degree classification.

Those of you engaged in teaching and tutoring work as postgraduates will also work with module or programme leaders. These are usually senior lecturers with considerable experience of teaching at this level. Module and Programme Leaders are responsible to the appropriate Head or Director of study for the academic content of the modules or programmes that they manage. This responsibility usually requires them to monitor and assess your teaching and to satisfy other learning and teaching quality assurance requirements. Lively analyses and evaluations of this and other areas of the HE environment are provided in a number of academic texts (details of these are provided at the end of this chapter and in the annotated bibliography at the end of the book).

THE HE CONTRACT

Why work in higher education? Murlis and Hartle (1996) indicate that when we enter a contract to work in a university, we effectively agree to two types of contract: the economic and the psychological. The economic contract is the more tangible of our contracts. It contains all of the standard details in relation to salary, performance rewards, teaching year (and perhaps teaching load), research expectations, administrative duties, and benefits of working for the university. The psychological contract is less clear because it is invisible. This is the contract that typically draws postgraduates into continuing to work in the university setting beyond completion of their studies.

> *The autonomy is great! Before I came to academia I worked in a bank, that was awful and really dreary – everything you did was thought about and decided by someone else, it seemed. It's completely different here. I come in when I want, I work when I want – it's my decision. The work I do is mine. If I make a mistake it's my mistake. If the work is good, then I get the reward for that through recognition in the department and university.*
>
> Sharon, PhD student, University of Westfield.

Sharon's psychological contract included the potential for recognition of the work she is doing and has done within the university. The psychological contract is concerned with the academic challenges you will face and the perceived elevated status attached to working in such an environment. It is concerned with the power to determine (to a greater or lesser extent) your own academic development, and to draw upon a range of structured training and development opportunities to support and enhance that development. It is concerned with an environment which facilitates (either locally, nationally or internationally through seminars or conferences) networking with like-minded individuals. However, not everyone seeks to join this 'academic club', as Colin tells us below.

> *I don't see myself as training to become an academic – that is just one big myth perpetuated by the funders and universities. It helps maintain a healthy stock of cheap, very cheap, teaching staff. I didn't come into this [studying for a PhD] to become an academic. I did it because I was interested in the subject. I don't know what I will do when I have finished the PhD but it won't involve becoming a lecturer.*
>
> Colin, PhD student, University of Northside.

Academic ranks and structures

As discussed previously, academic ranks and structures can, and do, vary within and across institutions and data collected throughout the development of this text has sought to synthesise information from a range of institutions to provide a useful analysis of broad roles and responsibilities. Within the carefully structured hierarchies of universities, are the following key positions.

RESEARCHER

Assisting with or sometimes providing leadership for university research projects are research assistants, research associates, research officers and research fellows. Researchers are usually associated with one or more research-based projects in the host department, school or faculty. They are often charged with managing or coordinating part of a project, under the supervision of a more senior academic, and are usually expected to provide assistance with teaching, particularly teaching relating to specific research tools or instruments used in the projects they work on.

In a number of institutions the hierarchy of research posts is demonstrated through the use of the word 'junior' or 'senior' within the title. The range of terms used by institutions to refer to those solely engaged in research activity often leads to confusion, particularly when comparisons are made between institutions. A position of research fellow at one institution may involve very different duties (and secure a different rate of pay) than a similarly titled position at another institution. Generally, the differences appear to be more noticeable between pre- and post-1992 institutions. Typical responsibilities are difficult to describe for this diverse group. However, they will often include:

- providing administrative support for various research activities;

- drafting research instruments, such as questionnaires or interview schedules;

- collecting research information;

- analysing data and reporting on the research; and

- supporting the development of journal articles.

I studied for a Social Science Masters degree at Manchester and it was here that I caught the 'research bug'. ... I learnt a great deal from some of the leading academics there and I decided to pursue a career in this area. I applied for a research assistant post with a national charitable organisation, and got the job! I spent almost two years there, but I got bored with the monotony of just designing and administering questionnaires. Because this organisation was so large (and dedicated to conducting large-scale, mainly survey-based research projects), I was restricted to working within a very narrowly defined area of their operations. I wasn't happy with this and felt that my abilities and potential as a researcher were not being utilised or developed. I trawled through the education jobs sections of all the national newspapers and applied for quite a few jobs. The experience gained from the interviews for these was extremely valuable – it might seem obvious but reading around the subject related to the post you are being interviewed for really does work wonders. I did this for the post at Oxford. I stated in my application form how I met all the criteria for the job and drew attention to this at interview. I was successfully appointed to a two-year contract to work on a specific project. I've really enjoyed this as I've been able to draw upon a range of my researching skills – from designing questionnaires and interview schedules, through to analysing the data and presenting our findings at conferences.

Peter PhD student, University of Oxford.

TEACHING ASSISTANT

Teaching assistants have traditionally been employed by universities to lessen the teaching load of academic members of staff (usually more senior lecturing staff).

Teaching assistants typically support courses and programmes of study by leading seminars, tutorials and discussions groups; they usually have little or no prior experience of teaching at HE level. Teaching assistants are heavily used in science-based subjects to manage and coordinate lab work of undergraduate and postgraduate students. Teaching assistant work can also involve marking submitted work on behalf of more senior teaching colleagues. Many teaching assistants in HE are postgraduate students who wish to secure teaching experience as well as additional income.

Typically, job descriptions for teaching assistants might include:

* preparing laboratory space for students to use;

* marking student work;

* supporting and leading seminar sessions;

* providing tutorial support to students;

* assisting with research work of more senior colleagues;

* developing course notes and handouts; and

* providing summaries of relevant texts for students.

ASSOCIATE LECTURER

Associate lecturers are members of teaching staff affiliated to a university department, school or faculty. Associate lecturers are often paid on an hourly basis and are not usually full-time members of university staff. Instead, they are traditionally 'bought in' to modules, courses or programmes as required. They usually have some experience of teaching at HE level and are often used to provide focused teaching support in particular, sometimes niche, areas.

Typically, job descriptions for associate lecturers might include:

* leading teaching/lecture sessions;

* supporting and leading seminar groups;

* marking student work;

* moderating (second marking) student work; and

* developing course notes and handouts.

UNIVERSITY TEACHER

This is a relatively new position, but is becoming increasingly utilised to broaden an institution's teaching capacity. University teachers are usually junior academic members of staff with generalist expertise to teach across a range of subjects within a department, school or faculty. University teachers are often full-time members of staff and are usually salaried, rather than paid on an hourly basis. This post traditionally consists of teaching (often at undergraduate level), administration and programme development.

Typically, job descriptions for university teachers might include:

* marking student work;

* moderating (second marking) student work;

* supporting and leading seminar sessions;

* leading teaching sessions; and

* providing tutorial support to students.

LECTURER

Traditionally, a university lecturer is department or faculty-based and works as part of a team. The role of a lecturer would, in part, be dictated by the remit or mission of the host department or institution. However, in general, the role of lecturer would consist of a mix of three major functions: teaching, research and administration. Teaching would usually involve supporting undergraduate and postgraduate programmes managed by the host department. Research activities would usually include support for work which is within the scope of expertise of the lecturer. For example, a lecturer in Industrial Relations might reasonably expect to support research projects related to this, working with trade unions and/or exploring human resource issues in organisations, etc. Often lecturer grades (particularly in relation to pay) are expressed as either 'A' or 'B'. A lecturer within the 'A' banding would usually be a more junior member of staff, perhaps with little experience of teaching, whereas a lecturer within the 'B' banding would be expected to have more experience of teaching and/or research.

Typically, job descriptions for lecturers might include:

* developing course materials;

* programme/course development;

* moderating (second marking) student work;

* attendance at conferences/seminars;

* attending university committees;

* conducting research;

* supporting and leading seminar sessions;

* leading teaching sessions; and

* providing tutorial support to students.

SENIOR LECTURER

As with the lecturer, a senior lecturer's role would, in part, be dictated by the remit or mission of the host department, school or faculty. Traditionally, a senior lecturer's role would consist of teaching, research and administration. Often senior lecturers, with a strong or developing research track record, secure a lighter teaching or administrative load. Conversely, if teaching is a particular strength, a senior lecturer may secure a lighter research or administrative load. For a number of senior lecturers, the title and role provides management responsibility within the host department, school or faculty. This can take a variety of forms, but may include coordination and management of particular courses or programmes within the institution.

Typically, job descriptions for senior lecturers might include:

* contributing to the host department, school or faculty's portfolio of teaching;

* marking student work;

* moderating (second marking) student work;

* developing national and international research collaborations;

* attracting research funding;

* attendance at conferences/seminars;

* attending university committees; and

* making substantial contributions to curriculum/programme development.

PRINCIPAL LECTURER

Typically, job descriptions for principal lecturer positions include many of those listed for a senior lecturer. In a number of institutions, principal lecturers have a slightly lighter teaching load than senior lecturers and they tend to provide more leadership for programmes of study than senior lecturers.

PROFESSOR

Traditionally, academics at the professorial level have lighter teaching duties or responsibilities than their junior colleagues. Often, teaching is limited to flagship programmes or courses offered within their host department, school or faculty. The substantive part of a professor's post is usually taken up by providing a leadership role on research projects and identified curriculum areas. The management of working groups, units or institutes in many universities is a role taken by professors.

Typically, job descriptions for professorial positions include:

* engaging in substantial research activity;

* attracting research students and significant research funding;

* developing national and international research links to promote the host department, school or faculty;

* supervising MPhil and PhD students;

* contributing to teaching programmes offered by the department, school or faculty;

* chairing appropriate department, school or faculty committees/exam boards; and

* contributing to the strategic planning and development of the host department, school or faculty.

READER

A reader is a senior academic charged with providing excellence through research and/or teaching. Readers often provide academic leadership in focused areas, for example, Adult Education, Strategic Marketing, Business Excellence. Many university readers have progressed through more junior teaching posts to reach this level. A critical part of a readership is the ability to secure and attract research funding. In a similar way to professors, readers are sometimes 'poached' from institutions because of the funding and prestige they attract. A number of universities specify criteria for conferment to readership and professorial posts, and the successful application of these criteria are reviewed by a conferment panel of fellow academics and senior institutional officers prior to any appointment. Readerships/professorships are usually conferred on individuals who are considered to have achieved an outstanding/significant record and reputation as academic leaders, teachers and/or scholars.

Typically, job descriptions for readership posts include:

* pursuing a personal, innovative research programme of international status and quality;

* securing external research funding;

* taking a leading role in a specific research team and/or group;

* supervising and managing research projects;

* supervising higher degree students;

* acting as Director of Research for research students;

* contributing to collegiate development and support of research activities;

* promoting the department's own research internationally;

* teaching undergraduate and postgraduate students, and carrying out the associated examining processes; and

* being proactive in the development of his or her own teaching in terms of content, delivery and assessment.

HEAD OF DEPARTMENT

Traditionally, department heads are experienced academics who have substantial knowledge and understanding of the academic environment in which they operate. Often, department heads have worked their way up the ranks within a university, gradually experiencing ever more involvement in teaching, research, administration and the general operation of academic work within the institution. In general terms, a key and substantive role of the head of department is to ensure that there is a clear and consistent vision of the aims of the department. These aims are met through the development and implementation of strategy which complements that of the broader university.

Typically, job descriptions for heads of department include:

- academic leadership and performance management of the department (including sub-units, centres and institutes);

- the effective management, development and appraisal of staff allocated to the department;

- developing and enhancing appropriate research and commercial activities consistent with the strategic aims of the department and broader institution;

- developing and maintaining close relationships with organisations in the industry, regulatory and industrial agencies, and other HE providers;

- ensuring the quality of the design, implementation and review of the department's academic programme; and

- ensuring the development and delivery of the curriculum and the development of appropriate teaching, learning and assessment strategies, having particular regard for the student experience.

As with many senior academic posts, the position of Head of Department is reached following a lengthy employment journey. In her research work exploring the training and experiences of university managers, Rachel Johnson collected the following information from a current Head of Department:

> I did postgraduate work ... started working as Assistant Lecturer, ... [then] started here as a Lecturer ... and I moved up to be a Senior Lecturer and ... Principal Lecturer with responsibility for a combined honours programme. ... I became, eventually, Director of Undergraduate Studies ... in charge of all the undergraduate programmes. [When the department was formed,] I was the only candidate to be Head of Department. ... I think the opportunity then came to do something I'd never done, which was to actually manage a group of staff – and I thought this was a good career move: the opportunity to do something different and [gain] a considerable increase in my salary [Head of Department, post-1992]. (2002: 36)

VICE-CHANCELLOR

The traditional and typical role of Vice-Chancellor is to provide a university's academic leadership, but he or she may also be more centrally involved with the functional operation of the institution. It has been stated that Vice-Chancellors' duties 'oscillate between high-level strategy and minor housekeeping operations. A meeting with the chief executive of a hospital trust might be followed by discussion of a relatively minor problem with a member of the academic staff' (Bargh et al., 2000: 157). Vice-Chancellors are experienced academics, and are usually appointed to such posts towards the end of their careers – with a typical age at appointment of 50+ (Bargh et al., 2000: 42).

PRO VICE-CHANCELLOR

A Pro Vice-Chancellor can be effectively termed a deputy Vice-Chancellor. Universities often have more than one Pro Vice-Chancellor (PVC) to provide leadership to key strategy operations of the university. For example, it is common for institutions to have a PVC for research and a PVC for teaching and learning. A substantial number of the smaller universities have proportionally fewer PVCs than their larger counterparts. Often, the various posts of PVC are fixed-period 'secondments' of suitably qualified staff (academics) from across the university. However, some universities (more often the newer post-1992 institutions) have permanent PVCs or deputies.

Pro Vice-Chancellors are senior academic positions in a University and candidates for posts are generally selected from an institution's senior academic (usually professorial) stock. An account of the position of Pro Vice-Chancellor is indicated in the following interview note collected by Johnson:

> It's invariably the case that Pro Vice-Chancellors are chosen amongst the four Deans in the university. And the Deans, in turn, are chosen from amongst Heads of Department. ... The Vice-Chancellor will say that his view of Pro Vice-Chancellor is that they are an elder statesperson – or, as he would say, elder statesmen – of the university who have seen a wide variety of different facets of the university and how it operates. ... Simply because we have been there, got the T-shirt, we've done our role as Head of Department and we are continuing to operate as a tutor and as a lecturer and working within a department [PVC, pre-1992]. (2002: 48)

REGISTRAR

The university registrar is often viewed as the institution's 'General Manager'. Usually registrars coordinate the day-to-day running of the university. Typically, this includes managing institutional processes of quality assurance, programme assessments and awards, admissions, and the management and coordination of student records. The university registrar works closely with a variety of senior officers and academics across the institution.

Typically, job descriptions for university registrars include:

- providing effective leadership, management and professional development of Registry staff;

- ensuring that the academic infrastructure of the university is fit for purpose and supports the achievement of institutional programme aims and student needs;

- ensuring the effective communication to all academic administrative staff and other key post-holders of the standards and objectives they are required to meet;

- maintaining awareness of the changing environment (both internal and external) relating to academic regulation and administration, and advising the institution on how to plan and respond effectively; and

- developing effective external professional networks to facilitate benchmarking and the identification and adoption of best practice.

ACADEMIC LIBRARIAN

Many university departments or faculties utilise the services of an assigned academic librarian. It is the role of the librarian to manage and share information for potential use by his or her host department or faculty. Often these librarians have responsibility for specific areas within the general university library, for example a Business librarian may be responsible for ordering business-related stock not only for the Business department or school, but also for general use by those in other parts of the university. It is usually the case that academic librarians affiliated to a particular department, school or faculty provide teaching input on information retrieval skills of use to both academics and students. Much of this teaching or facilitating role is focused upon exploiting online bibliographic databases and general use of the internet.

Typically, job descriptions for academic librarians include:

- securing and acquiring access to journals and electronic publications of use to the host departments;

- preparing teaching materials on library information retrieval;

- managing a small team of assistant librarians;

- liaising with academic publishers;

* acting as a library point of first contact for staff in the host department;

* liaising with host department staff and students to assist the development of the library service;

* attending relevant external events/conferences; and

* developing and managing information resources with an institution's virtual learning environment.

ADMINISTRATORS AND PROGRAMME MANAGERS

Within the university environment, administrators and programme managers perform a vital role. In essence, they oversee and coordinate the administrative activities and systems that enable effective teaching, research or other university activity to take place. Many university administrators work within an institution's central administration section or area (for example, in student admissions, finance, quality assurance or examinations); others may work within a department, school or faculty, supporting or organising activities of staff or students. Often, programme managers are those administrators who work more closely with students and support the work of courses or programmes within departments, schools or faculties. The work of administrators and programme managers can be diverse and varies across (and within) institutions.

Typically, job descriptions for administrators and programme managers include:

* coordinating, producing and circulating course and programme-related material;

* dealing with general enquiries relating to the submission of student work;

* servicing relevant committees and exam boards;

* communicating information to staff and students;

* coordinating recruitment activities;

* marketing programmes, events and seminars; and

* dealing with general quality assurance issues relating to programmes.

Knowing your organisation

It is clear from the above discussion of key actors and their roles and responsibilities that universities can be large and difficult organisations to work in and understand.

However, it is crucial for anyone seeking to gain the most from such an organisation and its operating environment to have at least a working knowledge of its history and development, its approach to teaching, learning and research, and an awareness of the various types of people who work there (academic and non-academic). Blaxter, Hughes and Tight (1998) suggest a number of useful exercises for the novice academic, many of which apply to postgraduate learners.

Learning tasks for new academics

Get hold of copies of, and read, the following:

- *The history of your university or college.* This will provide invaluable information relating to the development of your institution. It should provide some indications as to why an institution favours certain areas for research or teaching over others. Such documents are usually kept in the university library although your school or department may hold a copy for you to look at.
- The publicity material published by the institution (by school or faculty if you can). This information will help you to identify particular specialisms and strengths within the institution.
- *The university or college calendar.* This will provide a wealth of useful information for the postgraduate learner keen to understand the institution and make contacts with others. Most calendars are now available through the institutional intranet and they typically include information such as complete staff lists (with contact details), the management structure and administration of the institution, and information on key dates in the university year (such as committee meetings, exam boards, etc.).
- *Recent reports published by your school or department.* These provide further insights into the work that is currently taking place and the quality of that work. From this, you should also be able to gauge who, in your area, is producing the output that you are most interested in.

Arrange to meet people in your own school or department. Invite them for coffee or lunch and ask them to tell you about their recent research or project work. If it is linked to your area(s) of interest, make them aware of this so that they can consider you as a contributor in future work.

Source: Adapted from Blaxter, Hughes and Tight (1998: 48).

Collaboration

In accessing and fully utilising the cultures and work environments relevant to your postgraduate work, it will be necessary to liaise or work with a broad range of people who hold the various posts discussed in this chapter. Such liaisons or working relationships can occur in a variety of ways and at a number of levels within and outside your institution. The list below is indicative of the many approaches and opportunities that exist for postgraduates and academics to collaborate effectively with one another.

Working relationship	Benefits
Research unit	Other researchers in your unit may be working on similar projects or have encountered similar problems.
Department	In order to explore what's going on in your department and its particular areas of expertise, it may be useful to speak with colleagues and ask them about their work. Opportunities may arise for work in which you can become involved.
Across the university	Attending meetings, seminars, training events, discussion groups, etc. across your institution will allow you to develop cross-disciplinary linkages and, if necessary, publicity and support for your work.
University to university	Developing links and partnerships with other universities may enhance your work and will allow you access to other experts in the field. This can be developed through your attendance at conferences, contributions to discussion groups or special interest groups, etc.
University to sponsor	In order to secure continued funding for your work, it may be useful to develop links with key sponsors on your field. Again, this can usefully be achieved through attendance at conferences and seminars, and other sector- or industry-related events. It may be useful to establish what other activities your institution is involved in with regard to key sponsors.

An example of effective collaboration with colleagues was the production of a study guide, *The researcher's toolkit* (Wilkinson, 2000), which explores and explains approaches to research for those new to the subject. *The researcher's toolkit* brought together a number of academics and university support staff (from a variety of institutions) with the aim of sharing responsibility for the production of the text. Each collaborator compiled at least one chapter and during the production of the text meetings were held at various locations across the UK to facilitate its speedy production and delivery to an eager publisher. There were two major benefits of this endeavour: the production of a textbook (a new and exciting experience for almost all of the contributors); and the development of relationships between the collaborators which have lasted beyond the production of the text, and have since led to further fruitful collaborations.

It is clear that working or collaborating with others to pursue a common research goal has a number of benefits, and examples of successful collaborative efforts are increasingly reported in the literature (Smith and Katz, 2000; Smith, 2001). Building and developing these useful career relationships is covered in more detail in Chapter 8 (Working with your supervisor) and Chapter 9 (Working with other researchers).

THE IMPORTANCE OF SUPPORT STAFF

Liaising with university support staff and drawing upon the assistance they can provide are crucial activities for postgraduates to undertake. The term 'support staff' embraces a variety of university posts and typically includes computer technicians, porters, secretaries and personal assistants. These people are important because they are often gatekeepers to resources you may need to access. Computer technicians are the people you turn to when your printer does not work, when you have corrupted your hard-drive, or when you require the latest data analysis software for your office PC. Maintaining good working relationships with this group (and others that similarly might usefully support your academic endeavours) will pay dividends in the long run. You may not need them right now, but you probably will at some stage during your postgraduate programme of study, so build the relationship now. Rita Brause (2000) crisply summarises the value of computing and IT staff:

> If you are friendly, you may find that [computer lab] space 'reserved' for you. On the other hand, you may find that your equipment is frequently 'down' or your software has been removed from the system. By being friendly to all, you will not only feel better about yourself, but you are likely to make more rapid progress. (Brause, 2000: 75)

Reference list, useful reading and websites

Bargh, C., Bocock, J., Scott, P. and Smith, D. (2000) *University leadership: the role of the chief executive.* Buckingham: Open University Press/Society for Research into Higher Education.

Becher, T., Henkel, M. and Kogan, M. (1994) *Graduate education in Britain*. London: Jessica Kingsley Publishers.

Bekhradnia, B. (2003) *Implications of the government's proposals for university title: or what is a university?* Higher Education Policy Institute (available online: http://www.hepi.ac.uk).

Blaxter, L., Hughes, C. and Tight, M. (1998) *The academic career handbook*. Buckingham: Open University Press.

Brause, R.S. (2000) *Writing your doctoral dissertation: invisible rules for success*. London: Falmer Press.

Burton, S. and Steane, P. (eds) (2004) *Surviving your thesis*. London: Routledge.

Cuthbert, R. (1996) *Working in higher education*. Buckingham: Open University Press/ SRHE.

Deem, R. and Brehony, K.V. (2000) Doctoral students' access to research cultures – are some more unequal than others?, *Studies in Higher Education*, 25(2): 149–165.

Delamont, S. and Atkinson, P. (2004) *Successful research careers: a practical guide*. Buckingham: Open University Press/SRHE.

Eccles, C. (2002) The use of university rankings in the United Kingdom, *Higher Education in Europe*, 27(4): 423–432.

Evidence (2002) *UK higher education research yearbook* (2002 edition). Leeds: Evidence Ltd.

Goddard, A. (2004) Gang of four run away with research lead, *Times Higher Education Supplement*, 2 January.

Handy, C. (1985) *Understanding organisations*. Harmondsworth: Penguin.

Hockey, J. (1995) Change and the social science PhD: supervisors responses, *Oxford Review of Education*, 21(2): 195–206.

Hockey, J. (1996) Strategies and tactics in the supervision of UK social science PhD students, *Qualitative Studies in Education*, 9(4): 481–500.

Jobbins, D. (2002) *The Times/The Times Higher Education Supplement* – league tables in Britain: an insider's view, *Higher Education in Europe*, 27(4): 383–388.

Johnson, R. (2002) Learning to manage the university: tales of training and experience. *Higher Education Quarterly*. Vol. 56. No. 1. pp. 33–51.

Johnston, S. and Broda, J. (1996) Supporting educational researchers of the future, *Educational Review*, 48(3): 269–281.

Marshall, L. and Rowland, F. (1998) *A guide to learning independently*. Buckingham: Open University Press.

Murlis, H. and Hartle, F. (1996) Does it pay to work in universities?, in R. Cuthbert (ed.), *Working in higher education*. Buckingham: Open University Press/SRHE.

Powell, S. (1999) *Returning to study: a guide for professionals*. Buckingham: Open University Press.

Scott, P. (2001) Conclusion: triumph and retreat, in D. Warner and D. Palfreyman (eds), *The state of UK higher education*. Buckingham: Open University Press/SRHE.

Smith, D. (2001) Collaborative research: policy and the management of knowledge creation in UK universities, *Higher Education Quarterly*, 55(2): 131–157.

Smith, D. and Katz, S. (2000) *Collaborative approaches to research: report to the Higher Education Funding Council for England*. Leeds: Higher Education Policy Unit, University of Leeds.

Tight, M. (1996) *Key concepts in adult education and training*. London: Routledge.

Universities UK (2003) *Higher education in facts and figures* (Summer). London: Universities UK.

Wilkinson, D. (ed.) (2000) *The researcher's toolkit: the complete guide to practitioner research*. London: RoutledgeFalmer.

Wisker, G. (2001) *The postgraduate research handbook: succeed with your MA, MPhil, EdD and PhD*. London: Palgrave.

Reading and searching for information and seeking advice

Chapter overview

This chapter examines the information you will need to successfully navigate a post-graduate learning journey. It includes:

- Accessing the literature:

    - what and how much to read
    - tools you need to help focus your reading
    - tips for reviewing literature.

- Using online bibliographic databases to help tailor your searches.
- Citation reports and impact factors.
- Types of literature and their strengths and weaknesses.

In order to successfully conduct any project or research work, we must access various information sources and report upon the data collected from them. The most obvious and commonly accessed source of information is that provided through published (written) research and professional literature. Effectively drawing upon this resource to add value to project or research work can be time-consuming unless a methodical approach is used. Sally Rumsey (2004: 2), a librarian with substantial experience of accessing and using research literature and other forms of information, provides a useful framework with which to access information sources:

- Analyse the question or problem.

- Define the scope of the research – detailing what information is required.

- Identify the key sources of that information.

- Establish where that information is located or stored.

- Gain access to the information.

- Ensure, through relating it to your research question or problem, that the information you retrieve is (a) required, (b) reliable, and (c) current (if this is important to your work).

- Make sure that searches and results are effectively managed and stored.

- Ensure you maintain the currency of your information trawl by keeping it up to date.

Accessing literature

Accessing and reading literature forms a substantial part of postgraduate study. An integral part of any postgraduate research process is the ability to read, assess, synthesise and evaluate published work in the field. As research outputs – and particularly publications such as journal articles, books, research and government reports – become even more important indicators of research competence, it is crucial to be aware of what is being published in your field or area of study. To do that you need to read.

USING THE LIBRARY AS AN INFORMATION SOURCE –
WHAT YOU SHOULD KNOW

- Most universities employ a number of subject area librarians. Find out the names of yours and get in touch with them to tell them of your work and ask how they can help you (see how useful this was for Peter's work, below).

When I started my postgraduate programme, I didn't really know what literature was available in my field of study. I knew the library had huge stocks of educational journals, databases and texts, but I didn't know how to deal with all of these in a structured way. The subject librarian was extremely helpful with this. She asked me quite a lot of questions initially about what I was doing in my project work and

(Continued)

(Continued)

the information I had already consulted. She suggested that I speak to some colleagues in another department, who had sought similar types of information from the subject librarian (I linked up with these shortly after my library visit and secured access to the literature they had already collected). We spent some time querying a range of databases, including Zetoc and the Web of Knowledge. I was able to quickly obtain (using some of the tips and shortcuts suggested by the librarian) a great deal of key material through this exercise. I think I saved quite a few days work there!

Peter, PhD Student, University of Oxford.

* Find out the loan and other entitlements. The 'Issues desk' staff or your colleagues within your department should be able to tell you this information.

* Obtain a library card so that you can access the library.

* Make sure you have the relevant usernames and passwords if you wish to access online or electronic resources. Some of these are now standardised (so that you'll only ever need one login), but many are not, so be prepared to make a note of them.

* Find out what inter-library loan facilities are available at your institution (how many books etc. can you borrow from other libraries? Do other university libraries have reciprocal arrangements with yours? How much does it cost to request documents from other libraries if they are not available at your own).

* Note the opening times for your campus libraries. Some now open well into the night during term time, and often at weekends. Make sure you know the latest time you can take a book out of the library on an evening (some institutional libraries now provide a self-service facility).

* Check what facilities and/or services are available through your library. For example, check the databases to which the institution subscribes and any training it offers, such as literature reviewing or using bibliographic data management tools.

WHAT AND HOW MUCH TO READ

What you should read can encompass a wide and varied area if your research work impacts upon, or is associated with, a range of themes or issues. A useful starting point to assist with a more focused exploration of literature may be to seek the guidance of your research supervisor or course/programme tutor. As established experts in the exercise of reading and using the literature, these informants will be well placed to guide you to at least some of the useful and authoritative literature sources in your field. Postgraduate colleagues may also be able to steer you to suitable and relevant literature. Through your networking efforts with such colleagues, they will become aware of your areas of interest and may well suggest materials, journals and texts that they have found particularly useful.

TOOLS YOU NEED TO HELP FOCUS YOUR READING

It is clear that the amount and type of literature you can consult and draw upon for your studies/research investigations is immense. There are tools and techniques you can use to help manage this and prioritise the material you consult. Such tools can effectively be used to assist with the first-level evaluation of literature that you may be considering using for your research or project work.

Academic journal articles are by far the most popular literature sources for researchers and academics. However, such sources can vary considerably in the quality of material they contain. In addition to the peer review procedures that almost all articles undergo (a process whereby other researchers and academics review and comment upon work to establish its worthiness for publication), there are journal rankings which assign quality indicators to published material. Journal ranking in its most simple form operates through the recommendation of others – your supervisor or tutor may identify certain journals in your area as prestigious in the field. Reading articles in such journals ensures you are reading high-quality literature.

More elaborate journal rankings have been developed that explore the number of citations received for articles within a journal in any one year. The rationale behind this ranking procedure is that the more frequently articles within specific journals are cited, the more popular and widely read (and therefore respected) these journals are. This approach to ranking journals is not without its critics, but it is broadly accepted in academia as a useful way to identify top journals in a given field, and the high-quality articles within them.

Journal Citation Reports®

Journal Citation Reports (JCR)® presents quantifiable statistical data that provides a systematic, objective way to evaluate the world's leading journals and their impact and influence in the global research community.

Features
- Covers more than 7,500 of the world's most highly cited, peer-reviewed journals in approximately 200 disciplines.
- Offers access to citation statistics from 1997 onwards.
- Enables users to sort data by clearly defined fields: impact factor, immediacy index, Total Cites, Total Articles, Cited Half-Life, or Journal Title.

The JCR® is available in two editions: the Science Edition covers over 6,100 leading international science journals from the ISI database; the Social Sciences Edition covers approximately 1,800 leading international social sciences journals from the ISI database.

Intended users
Enables a variety of information professionals to access and assess key journal data:

- *Librarians* – helps users manage and maintain journal collections and budget for subscriptions.
- *Publishers* – enables publishers to monitor their competitors, identify new publishing opportunities, and make decisions regarding current publications.
- *Editors* – assists in assessing the effectiveness of editorial policies and objectives, and tracking the standing of their journals.
- *Authors* – enables authors to identify journals in which to publish, confirm the status of journals in which they have published, and identify journals relevant to their research.
- *Information analysts* – lets users track bibliometric trends, study the sociology of scholarly and technical publication, and study citation patterns within and between disciplines.

Formats and delivery options
Web – via JCR® on the Web; published annually in the summer following the year of coverage.

(Continued)

CD-ROM – via JCR® on CD-ROM; published annually in the summer following the year of coverage; networking options available.

Source: http://www.isinet.com/products/evaltools/jcr/

The Institute for Scientific Information's (ISI) Journal Citation Report® (JCR®) is the most widely used international journal ranking service. It ranks over 7,500 journals across a broad range of subject or discipline areas. For example, the 'Social Work' area ranks 29 journals from across the world that publish in this area. Within the broader and more active subject area of 'Management', there are 67 journals for which data are consistently collected, including the number of papers or articles published and the associated citations of those papers or articles. Essentially, the higher the number of citations received for articles from a journal, the higher its importance, or 'impact factor', is deemed to be. A journal's 'impact factor' is determined by dividing the number of recent articles by citations received for those articles within the year. Take a look at the following two examples:

Journal Citation Reports®

Journal title:	*Advances in Nursing Science*
Citations received for recent articles:	65
Number of recent articles:	40
Impact factor (65 divided by 40):	**1.625**
Journal title:	*American Journal of Nursing*
Citations received for recent articles:	52
Number of recent articles:	269
Impact factor (52 divided by 269):	**0.193**

Source: ISI Journal Citation Reports® (http://www.isinet.com).

The second journal of the two certainly publishes far more papers or articles than the first journal, but the citations for those papers are far less. As a result, the impact factor is also far less. The above analysis shows that more academics, researchers and commentators refer to pieces in the first journal than in the second one. As a result, the first journal, using this operation, is deemed to contain more relevant and significant material than its comparator.

In addition to selecting journals and articles to read by the total number of citations they have received, you can also use similar services for individual writers or academics in that field. ISI's HighlyCited.com Researcher's service collects citation information across 21 broad subject categories in Life Sciences, Medicine, Physical Sciences, Engineering and Social Sciences. From this information (collected over a period of 20 years) it then produces lists of leading academics (based upon citations received) in those subject areas. This may be a useful way to identify important writers in the broad subject areas defined by the service.

ISI HighlyCited.com reveals the face of research – the people behind the accomplishments in 21 broad subject categories in Life Sciences, Medicine, Physical Sciences, Engineering and Social Sciences. These individuals are the most highly cited within each category for the period 1981–1999, and comprise less than one-half of 1% of all publishing researchers – truly an extraordinary accomplishment.

ISI HighlyCited.com will grow to include in each of 21 subject categories the top 250 pre-eminent individual researchers who have demonstrated great influence in their field as measured by citations to their work – the intellectual debt acknowledged by their colleagues. The information for each researcher is as follows:

- Biographical information: education, faculty and professional posts, memberships and/or offices, current research interests, and personal websites.
- Full listing of publications: journal articles, book or book chapters, conference proceedings, websites and other internet resources.
- Bibliography enhanced by links to the full bibliographic information indexed in the ISI Web of Science. ISI HighlyCited.com: (http://www.isinet.com)

ISI's Journal Citation Reports® and their HighlyCited.com authors service enable you to search large databases of thousands of journals and millions of journal articles or papers. Depending on the access to the service your university library subscribes to, you can often secure direct electronic access to the papers and/or journals cited. There is, however, a caveat to this. Most of the services provided by ISI were originally developed for the Sciences and Engineering disciplines. This is, therefore, where materials are strongest, holding many of the journals within their lists, and the majority of the millions of articles, records and references. However, these services are continually evolving, and the Social Sciences are developing into substantive databases that are used as reference points by many academics and researchers.

As you investigate and explore the literature available in your discipline or subject area, you will become aware of the most prolific authors. It may be useful to explore other work published by them across a range of journals or related subject areas. A number of bibliographic databases enable you to search for material by author, including the British Library database, Zetoc (http://zetoc.mimas.ac.uk/) and ISI's Web of Science service (http://wos.mimas.ac.uk/).

The Zetoc service provides Z39.50-compliant access to the British Library's Electronic Table of Contents (ETOC). The database contains details of approximately 20,000 current journals and 16,000 conference proceedings published per year. With around 20 million journal and conference records, the database covers every imaginable subject in science, technology, medicine, engineering, business, law, finance and the humanities. The database covers the years from 1993 to date and is updated daily. A list of journal titles covered by the database is available. Copies of all the articles and conference papers listed on the database can be ordered online from the British Library's Document Supply Centre in Yorkshire.

Eligibility
Zetoc is made available to institutions through MIMAS (Manchester Information and Associated Services) at the University of Manchester, on behalf of the British Library. It is free of charge to JISC-sponsored UK further and higher education institutions. Zetoc: (http://zetoc.mimas.ac.uk/about.html)

A simple search within the author field of the Zetoc database for work published by Tony Bowers, an expert in the field of special educational needs, returns a large number of records. Some of these records relate to other authors with the surname and initial 'Bowers T', but examining the content (title, abstract, etc.) of these returns to determine material within the general content areas of educational studies and special educational needs reveals articles and papers he has published in relation to his work on the special educational needs Code of Practice.

When you have identified an author who writes about the subject you are interested in, it's worth a quick scan of his personal or institutional website. You can often have the inside track on a lot of material listed that is still being developed. If the academic or researcher concerned keeps their site up to date (which isn't always the case!), you can collect some focused pieces of work using this approach.

Ian, ESRC 1 + 3 student, University of Manchester.

As Ian indicates above, once leading writers have been identified, it can be very useful to explore their websites (most journal articles will have contact details, including email, for the writer concerned). A growing number of researchers and academics now detail their complete publication lists on their websites, with many providing hyperlinks to downloadable draft or complete copies of papers.

TIPS FOR REVIEWING LITERATURE

> A literature review enables a researcher to accomplish a number of more specific aims. It is likely, for example, that in the early stages of your research you may have only a vague idea of the area you would like to explore more fully. You may have only a tentative outline of your research problem. This should not give you cause for concern. A review of the literature will help you to sharply focus your tentative problem by both limiting and more clearly defining the topic you are interested in researching. Look out for recommendations made by researchers for those intent on continuing with research in a particular field. You may be provided with advance warnings of possible pitfalls, or research questions which have been thus far neglected. Reading around the subject will help you to distil the issues you wish to concentrate upon and leave you with a concise, detailed and distinct plan of action. (Birmingham, 2000: 27)

The 'literature'

> *Accessing and reading the literature in your field of enquiry helps you to flesh out your ideas. You can find out what else has been done, by whom and where. By drawing upon the work of others, you can explore your own ideas and locate them in an academic context.*
> Peter, PhD student, University of Oxford.

Without doubt, the essential sources of your reading and information relating to your chosen research/study area will be the published, usually research-based, literature, including journal articles, textbooks and monographs. However, there are many other literature sources you may wish to consult, so the sheer variety and volume of material available can make evaluating the multiple formats and their contents difficult. Nevertheless, there are a range of factors that can assist in the identification of typical strengths and weaknesses of standard literature formats.

BOOKS

Books come in many shapes and forms, and the quality of their content varies considerably. There are essentially three broad types of book: the textbook, the research book and the edited book. Textbooks are usually based upon the expertise of the author, containing some reference to research and the experiences of the writer (perhaps through teaching the subject). Research books report upon an area specifically investigated for the purposes of the text. As such they tend to be more focused and exploratory than textbooks. Edited books usually consist of a collection of pieces (written by a variety of authors) drawn together by a common theme or issue. Whilst it is the role of the editor of the volume to draw together the many different pieces within the text, quality and consistency can sometimes vary considerably within the chapters of the text.

Most books, prior to publication, undergo some form of peer review process. The larger and more established academic publishers, such as Sage, the Open University Press, Routledge, Oxford University Press and Cambridge University Press, etc., commission academics and other experts to review draft chapters and materials, and employ copy-editors and proof-readers to ensure quality and consistency. When evaluating books to assess their relevance and use for your own research or project work, consider the expertise of the author (has he or she published other material in this area?); consider the data or arguments upon which the text is based (are the arguments backed up by relevant research data); consider whether others (such as tutors, supervisors or other postgraduates) quote this work.

JOURNAL ARTICLES

Journal articles are by far the most accessed forms of literature. Journals, and the articles published within them, can also vary in their quality. The Journal Citation Report® provides one way of assessing the quality or value of journals and their content, but there are other approaches to assessing journal and article quality. Most academic journals have panels of experts (usually academics) who review and approve the material for publication. Details of these 'peer review' panels can be found on the inside cover of the journal. They are termed 'peer review' panels as they consist of fellow academics and researchers (your peers) from your own and other institutions. A useful assessment tool for postgraduates accessing any journal might be:

• Do you recognise any of the experts on the peer review panel?

• Are you aware of their work in the field?

• In your opinion, are they well-placed to comment upon the material published in the journal?

Editors of journals often have the final say regarding the publication or rejection of journal articles. Further evaluation considerations may therefore include:

• Do you recognise the editor?

• Have you read any of his or her work?

• Do you consider him or her to be an expert within the broad subject area of the journal?

• Is the editor affiliated to or associated with a respected university school or department?

If the editors are any of the above, does that suggest to you that these are good quality journals? Speak with your tutors or supervisors to obtain their views on the leading journals; ask them what criteria they use to assess quality?

CONFERENCE PAPERS

The conference paper is often a journal article in its preliminary or draft form. Conference papers often present initial ideas and the emerging formulations of 'theory' not yet fully tested by research data. As a result, they should be used with some degree of caution. That is not to say that they should be dismissed as of no value. A good number of conference papers afford you access to 'new' ideas that are closer to the research than their journal article superiors. Through accessing conference papers you may become aware of emerging difficulties or successes in your area of study. You may be directed to new avenues of investigation that your analysis of journal articles has not revealed.

MONOGRAPHS

Monographs are sometimes referred to as 'short books'. Typically, within universities, monographs are short pieces focused around a specific subject or issue. Size varies according to subject matter, although around 50 or so pages is a reasonably sized monograph. They are usually produced and published 'in house' (i.e. by the institutional employer of the author – usually a university), and for a number of novice researchers and academics the monograph is their first opportunity to experience publication of their work. In terms of assessing or reviewing the work published, a number of institutions expect supervisors or colleagues to comment on the content of the monograph prior to publication. However, as this is not a consistent practice across all institutions, care should be taken when referring to pieces produced by junior members of academic staff. A number of the assessment criteria outlined above can equally be applied to monographs.

THESES

A thesis is typically a report detailing the results of an original investigation. They are usually submitted in part-fulfilment of Masters/PhD programmes of study. Length and style of theses are dictated by the university making the award and the quality of content is assessed by a panel of academics – these are helpful quality indicators for postgraduates wishing to cite material published within them. As a result of their *detailed* examination of a topic or issue, theses provide excellent background material relating to specific areas of study. Good publications of this type provide a focused examination of the issues within a specific area. They provide a full description of what was known about the subject previously (within a literature review) and a full account of new investigations. They also analyse these results with reference to previously published materials, and they make conclusions and recommendations based upon their analyses.

NEWSPAPER/MAGAZINE ARTICLES

Newspapers and magazine articles can provide an interesting source of reference material or data for your research/project work. However, they tend to be written in a less objective way than the other forms of literature previously discussed. The review process is less rigid for this type of publication. Newspaper and magazine articles are often written for a more general readership, rather than those engaged in academic research, and can therefore appear superficial in their discussion of issues or subjects relevant to your own work. However, they are often topical (as a result of the frequency of publication – daily, weekly, monthly, etc.) and can assist with locating research within a practical/relevant context.

WEB-BASED LITERATURE

Web-based literature includes almost anything that a reasonably IT-literate individual can upload on to a website. As a result, the quality and content of material collected through the internet can vary considerably. For a great deal of the material available, there are no mechanisms to review or validate the content. Typical questions to consider when evaluating web-based material might include:

* Who hosts or coordinates the website where the material is found?

* In what capacity is the author writing – is it a personal piece, or affiliated to an organ-isation or institution?

* Is the piece written in an acceptable academic way?

* Do others reference this web-based material?

For many postgraduates, accessing and fully utilising the research literature is a daunting exercise. Kelly, a postgraduate researcher from the University of Manchester, indicates that using literature for postgraduate study involves a much more proactive and systematic approach to data collection and synthesis. She offers the following advice to fellow researchers.

> *I suppose it's small things really, like keeping up to date with academic journals, etc. What I tend to do is to go on to one of the online databases (such as Web of Science or Zetoc) and search for key wordsassociated with my subject area. Obviously, you can do this by date range – so you could look for more recent stuff, or material published quite a while ago, or in a specific year that is important to your work. Some of what you read might not be useful but at least you will become more knowledgeable of what material is out there.*
>
> Kelly, ESRC 1 + 3 student, University of Manchester.

Keeping track

Given the huge range of materials and resources you can access as part of your studies, it is essential that you keep clear and thorough notes of the information you have consulted. University or subject librarians should be able to offer assistance and suggestions on appropriate forms of record keeping for your discipline area. There are also several computer-based bibliographic tools to help you construct a database of your literature sources. The most popular packages for this are Endnote and Reference Manager. Many university libraries or IT departments support at least one of these packages, so it might be worthwhile exploring this before you purchase any software for yourself. A standard form of record keeping for literature items includes the following (a sample record, using this format, is also provided):

Name   The name(s) of the authors of the piece – surname first, then initial(s).

Title   The title of the literature – for example, the book, chapter, article, or research report.

Date   The date the literature was published, and the edition if given.

Publisher   The name of the publisher and place of publication if the literature is a book or report.

Name   The name of the book or journal that the literature piece was taken from and page numbers if a journal article or chapter is within a book.

Location   The location of the literature, so that you can consult it again if need be. Usually, this would include a catalogue number/library reference and the ISSN or ISBN (unique identifiers for all journals and books which are found on the back cover of books and inside cover of journals).

Sample literature record

Name	Ramsden, B.
Title	Academic staff: information and data
Date	1996
Publisher	Society for Research into Higher Education/The Open University Press
Name	*Working in Higher Education.* Rob Cuthbert (ed.), pp. 23–33
Location	Main campus library 'University' section. ISBN 0335197213

Reference list and useful reading

Birmingham, P. (2000) Reviewing the literature, in D. Wilkinson (ed.), *The researcher's toolkit: the complete guide to practitioner research*. London: RoutledgeFalmer. pp. 25–40.

Burns, T. and Sinfield, S. (2003) *Essential study skills: the complete guide to success at University*. London: Sage.

Clough, P. and Nutbrown, C. (2002) *A student's guide to methodology.* London: Sage.

Phillips, E.M. and Pugh, D.S. (2003) *How to get a PhD: a handbook for students and their supervisors.* Third edn. Buckingham: Open University Press.

Potter, S. (2002) *Doing postgraduate research.* London: Sage.

Prior, L. (2003) *Using documents in social research.* London: Sage.

Rumsey, S. (2004) *How to find information: a guide for researchers.* Maidenhead: Open University Press.

Wisker, G. (2001) *The postgraduate research handbook: succeed with your MA, MPhil, EdD and PhD.* London: Palgrave.

7 Managing your time, academic writing and presenting your work

Chapter overview

This chapter examines useful approaches to time management, academic writing and presentation skills. In particular it provides coverage of:

- The importance of time management.
- Identifying how time can be wasted.
- Tips for effective time management.
- The importance of good academic writing skills.
- Different types of writing for different academic audiences.
- Sample material from those engaged in postgraduate study.
- Approaches to writing.
- Styles and standards in report writing.
- Tips for those wishing to develop their academic writing.
- The importance of presentation skills and getting value from presenting your work.

Producing project timelines and an appropriate project plan are key project management skills. Indeed, many research funders recognise that those are important skills for postgraduate students to develop. This and other project and research management tools and techniques are discussed in this chapter.

Managing your time

There are numerous student texts that address the subject of time management. The advice provided in most is usually good and almost all cover the basics of how to manage your time more effectively (a number of excellent reference guides are provided at the end of this chapter and in the annotated bibliography at the end of the book). Time, and its effective management, is difficult for many of us to get to grips with. Whilst we all have time in which to complete work, many don't really value it until it has gone. The remedy is clear: although we cannot control time, we can, by thinking and acting strategically, be more in control of its efficient and effective use. Claire, a current PhD student, presents common concerns in relation to time management, and she formulates some useful solutions.

We haven't had much guidance on time management and I am really bad at it. I always think that I have loads of time – no problem. It goes in waves. You start the term and there's loads of it, then suddenly you realise that you have two essays to do in two weeks. So you have to think about juggling things around a bit, trying to do different things at once for different courses. It's very easy to get engrossed in one thing and concentrate on that – at the cost of not doing anything else. You need to be able to carefully manage what needs to be done and when. It's often useful to begin by actually recording how many hours of the day you actually work (not including the coffee breaks or fag breaks, answering emails, talking around the computer), and try to get this up to around 35–36 hours per week. It is really useful. It gives you the focus to think about what it is you are actually doing. It gives you an idea of where you are.

Claire, ESRC 1 + 3 student, University of Birmingham.

As Claire (along with many other postgraduates consulted throughout the development of this text) acknowledges, effective time management assists with the smooth management of your studies, project and/or research work. In essence, good time management is empowering for students because:

- it allows you to feel in control, especially when the pressure to produce work is at its highest;

- it allows you to allocate and spend time in your personal life without the fear that this personal time-out will have a negative impact on your postgraduate studies;

* it allows for time to revise and refine your work before it is submitted for scrutiny by your tutor or supervisor; and thus

* it helps to reduce stress levels which should, in turn, allow you to enjoy and make the most of your period of study.

The difficulty with time management is that there is only one individual who can make a difference to personal time management – and that is you. Students who cover time management skills on structured courses often ask the impossible – pens at the ready, they expect to be given some magic formula that will transform their lives. Clearly, this is an unrealistic expectation, but with structured research, a realistic approach and an honest appraisal of personal time management skills, most students should be able to dramatically improve their competency in this important but often neglected skill. The place to begin your search for improved time management is with an objective and critical self-assessment. Consider the following questions:

* Can I identify my priorities in my programme of study?

* How do I apportion time to my priorities?

* Do I have a daily target for my research/project work?

* Is it easy for me to put things off?

* Do I take up too much of other people's time?

* Do I usually meet the deadlines I set (or others set for me)?

* Are the activities I carry out necessary for my work?

* Do I work better at certain times of the day rather than at others?

* Do I concentrate on activities that are interesting rather than ones central to my work?

* Am I easily distracted from my work?

The honest answers to some of these questions might be uncomfortable to acknowledge, but they should help you to begin to think about how effectively you utilise the time available for your studies. The following guidance might be useful in helping you to identify important tasks or activities, and to manage effectively the time you commit to them and other areas of your postgraduate studies.

EFFECTIVE TIME MANAGEMENT

- Where possible, develop a daily routine – this is especially useful for dealing with routine tasks.

- Undertake important tasks, or allocate time to them, at the point in the day when you function best.

- Give yourself a time frame – an action plan is a good way both of focusing on what you have to do and of keeping a check on your deadlines.

- Prioritise! Make a 'to do' list and work through it each day. One of the most important lessons you will learn in life is that those people who know how to prioritise are the ones who get things done with minimum stress. As Kelly and Francesca indicate below, thinking about research or project work as discrete elements or 'chunks' of work can be useful. Francesca highlights other benefits of effectively managing your work – sharing your plan with others helps them to understand what you are doing and when you are doing it.

I think it's very important not to get too overwhelmed by it all. When you think about it, a PhD or any postgraduate dissertation is a huge undertaking that requires careful and effective project management. A key part of this is to break your work down into manageable packages of activity. This is what project managers do in business – they identify the important areas of work, which bits need to be done first, which can wait, which require the support of specific expertise, etc. That's what we should be doing as postgraduate students, breaking it down, planning it carefully and managing the various elements (with assistance from others as and when necessary), to eventually link it all up in the final product – the dissertation or thesis.

Kelly, ESRC 1 + 3 student, University of Manchester.

I work very differently now from when I did when I first began my postgraduate studies – I work to a tight schedule now which maps out my entire research journey. I'm now much clearer and articulate at segmenting my project work, and thinking about how to develop the skills I will need (and when I will need them) for the various parts of my research work. My supervisor is very keen on that and he likes to see the schedule, what I am doing, when, and my rationale for it. He helps me to break things down into manageable chunks and exploring where activities best fit within the overall scheme of things.

Francesca, ESRC 1 + 3 student, University of Cambridge.

- Do not delay or put-off important tasks because they seem to be difficult, or perhaps they are boring. Make an objective assessment of how important the task is and, if it is important, make it a priority.

- Plan your time – if you have research to undertake, phone calls to make or emails to send, factor them into your day. Be aware that although emails can be a great time-saver, they can also be a time-waster if they are not kept succinct and related to your research or project work.

- Keep a notebook handy to jot down ideas, websites, text references or notes to follow up. A postgraduate's workload can be heavy and diverse, so keeping track of information and events (as Ian indicates below), is critical.

I think it's crucial to have a research diary to keep a record of your progress. Note down everything (who you spoke to, who wasn't helpful, how difficult it was to get a meeting with them, how useful the information was that they gave you, etc.). Diaries are useful to help you think about planning for when essays are due in, to help you think about the process (and time taken) of conducting the interviews, collecting the data and synthesising and analysing it.

Ian, ESRC 1 + 3 student, University of Manchester.

* When studying, take a break when you are at your least effective – this will help to clear your thoughts and should make you more productive when you return to your study.

* Think things through before acting – ensure that you know what you are supposed to be doing, and think about the most effective way of working as this will save time in the longer term.

* If you know that you have a tendency to be perfectionist, then step back and think about your workload – mundane or everyday tasks should be done adequately as you need to think about a return on your time and efforts. If you take time doing things with little or no visible return, then you could be encroaching on time that could be spent on a high-return task, such as writing an article or part of your thesis.

* Where possible, share the workload – work cooperatively with colleagues and fellow students.

* Set your workload appropriately – some tasks may be short-term, others may be set over a longer period of time, so good planning is needed to allocate time frames for work.

* Make a daily list of things that you have to do and cross-off tasks when they are completed. This is a good way to keep up to date with your workload and, psychologically, it is good to see your achievements written down. You may also be surprised at just how much you achieve in a relatively short space of time. Conversely, if you keep a daily list and are not achieving your targets, this fact will soon become evident and you can take steps to rectify this before too much time has been lost.
(Adapted from guidance provided to postgraduate students, Leeds University Business School)

It is clearly important to organise and plan your studies – and to give yourself time to do other things. Some, like Adam below, structure their studies around a traditional working day, leaving the evenings and weekends for socialising and doing things other than work.

> *What I want to do is come in at nine and go home at six, and have the evening off. I have friends who will go for a coffee for two or three hours and will produce great PhDs, and I just can't do that. I'd feel really guilty because in the evening and at weekends I do other things. I don't ever do work. So I have to make sure that during the daytime that's what I'm doing.*
>
> Adam, ESRC 1 + 3 student, University of Oxford.

For others, the approach to study and its management is different. Many will recognise Michelle's approach, below, which is less structured around a typical working day. However, Michelle suggests some useful strategies for managing this style or approach to study.

> I've found that doing a Masters and a PhD is not like an ordinary 9 to 5 job. I've found I'm always thinking about my work, even when I'm out at the pub. If I've had a problem that day, I find myself thinking it through. It's constant. I find myself working on Saturdays and Sundays. Having no office space at the moment doesn't help: I work from home and I wake up, turn over and see this pile of books which I know I have to read. If I had an office space it might be easier for me to divide my work and recreational time up a bit better. For the moment, I have my diary and at the beginning of each week I write down the things I have to do. Depending on how I'm feeling I'll do them in a certain order, but I won't set myself strict deadlines in terms of completing them. I might go shopping in the morning and work late into the night or I might start my work early and mess around in the evening. If I'm feeling distracted, there's no point in making myself sit down and do something because it's a certain time of day – I know I won't be able to do it properly.
>
> Michelle, ESRC 1 + 3 student, University of Cambridge.

There are a variety of tools available online to help you identify your strengths and weaknesses in your own approach to time management (details of some of these are provided at the end of this chapter). Rita Brause (2000) offers the following lively advice based upon her own research work with postgraduate learners:

> You will need to be a real researcher. Start early. Join the appropriate professional organizations. Get and read journals. Develop researching skills.
>   Everything important should go into a file or notebook immediately.

Make sure all references are complete so none have to be looked up later.

Force yourself to write every day, tired or not. Set and meet your own deadlines.

Document everything.

Never throw anything away.

Get the library to support your efforts.

Establish your agenda, your questions as you progress, and what you want feedback on.

Get organized and reorganized again and again.

Expect unplanned diversions.

Provide some leeway in your schedule.

Make time to smell the roses! (Brause, 2000: 31)

Writing skills

In order to effectively communicate our thoughts and ideas, or the findings, results and conclusions of our research/project or other assessed work, we need to be able to write in a clear and academically acceptable way. This requirement strikes fear into many, as summarised by Stephanie, below.

I was nervous before I wrote the first essay for my Masters because I wanted to write better having progressed to postgraduate level. I try to read as much as I can to get a good idea of what a good writing style is. ... Because I'm still at the research stage of my dissertation I find the prospect of writing 20,000 words very daunting.

Stephanie, ESRC 1 + 3 student, Aberystwyth University.

However, it need not continue to be as frightening an experience as Stephanie describes. Good academic writing, like most things, takes practice and a little bit of planning. As Stephanie indicates, one of her strategies involves reading about the subject matter from a variety of sources to enable her to develop a similar academic style. Another technique successfully adopted by Miranda, below, is to develop draft pieces of writing, and continually refine them as the topics or issues under discussion in the piece become clearer through your continued reading around the subject.

I'm not naturally gifted at academic writing. I need to do draft upon draft upon draft and I need feedback and I'm still learning. I don't know why that is but I guess I'm someone who really has to think about what I want to say. So I first have to write down the concept of what I want to say, then rethink it all.

Miranda, ESRC 1 + 3 student, University of Surrey.

In an attempt to ensure everything is covered in the piece of writing, many resort to a 'scattergun' approach of considering an overly ambitious range of ideas and topics. Whilst this can result in an impressive range of material covered and sources cited, not a great deal tends to be covered in depth. Adam, below, provides honest analysis of the drawbacks of this approach to writing.

I think my skills in academic writing are very poor. I compress a huge number of ideas into a very dense paragraph stuffed full of ideas, links and tangents. I'm having to be much clearer, much more concise and explicit. Part of it is just making my sentences more focused, making them easier to read.

Adam, ESRC 1 + 3 student, University of Oxford.

The above three cases all highlight the difficulties associated with writing in an academic way. The ability to write clearly and say what you mean takes time and effort to develop. Some, as Nick points out below, view academic writing as relaying information and ideas to your peers, although it need not be a rigid, inflexible process.

I actually look at writing as a skill. I know a lot of people I work with in the university see writing as just the means to translate bits of information or research across to other people and they never actually focus on the skill of writing itself. I read loads of creative writers – people like George Orwell and Mark Twain – to see what they do. They wrote loads of good fiction but with a creative, expressive element. I've tried to do that all the way through but it's a fine line. You can meet people who mark essays who have a very strict idea about what academic writing is all about and they say, well that doesn't fit the criteria. Well I've always done it and a couple of times I've crashed and burned, but most of the time it has worked and because I've had success I'm not going to stop. I'll push the boundaries even more now and see how far I can go.

Nick, ESRC 1 + 3 student, University of Plymouth.

DIFFERENT WRITING FOR DIFFERENT AUDIENCES

Good academic writing is clear, objective (not emotive), usually written in the third person, and draws upon previously written work in an appropriate way. Conference or seminar papers are usually less formal articulations of research work and activities than journal articles. Consider the piece below, an extract of a piece written by Jeff, a 1 + 3 student from the University of Hull. This piece formed part of preparatory work for a research seminar discussing access issues for the field researcher.

Working in the field – Jeff Smith, University of Hull

This presentation is based upon research recently conducted in a local Hull secondary school, work that is the first phase of an ESRC-funded study concerned with providing a contemporary ethnographic account of school experience and its impact on teachers and pupils. It is intended that a further period of extended fieldwork will allow for a cross-cultural comparative analysis that will draw on material from the

(Continued)

Irish Republic as well as the UK context of Hull, which was chosen for the initial stage of research.

One of the primary theoretical motives in carrying out this research is to take a fresh look at what is happening in our schools today. Hopefully, in so doing, I will be trying to reassess those theories derived from the sociology of education, which have a considerable history and thus a well established literature and influence, that have sought to focus attention on the role of culture in reproducing unequal social relations. Typically grounded in a blend of phenomenological and interactionist approaches, coupled with a conflict-oriented methodology that favours ethnographic research techniques, this work characteristically identifies schools as a major investigative site for their role in the reproduction of successive generations of disaffected adolescents, who are socially and economically disadvantaged by their lack of achievement in education.

I should stress at the outset that at this present time this project is ongoing and incomplete, lacking as it does at the moment any comparative data from which to begin to map out a broad pattern of findings that will form the basis of my final thesis. However, as part of the process of reflecting on one's data and beginning to engage with it theoretically, I have almost immediately been struck by how the importance of the personal dimension in fieldwork emerges as soon as one starts to carry out research in a chosen field setting.

Indeed, in the course of undertaking a prolonged period of participant observation in an institutionally based field site, it increasingly became apparent to me that one's own personal research experience is a crucial and highly influential factor in shaping not only the kind of work that gets done, but also the way that it is recorded and written up, ultimately leading me to suspect that, consciously or otherwise, it goes a long way towards colouring the whole complexion of the final written account. Is this something we need to be concerned about, for the possible effects it is having on our findings, or do we simply choose to exercise a form of professional discretion and try to avoid mentioning the issue wherever possible. This is, of course, except among our peers, where they become our equivalent of 'war stories', 'tales of the field', that we can swap with each other in a socialising process that largely serves to increase our own sense of academic and professional solidarity.

With this question in mind, and taking into account the incomplete nature of the study, I thought that today instead it might be interesting to focus on the issue of personal experience in relation to what I have actually done, which is just over six months of ethnographic fieldwork in a local school.

(Continued)

(Continued)

In particular, I'd like to talk about the process itself, and more specifically, what the experience of fieldwork has been like for me, both personally and methodologically, and in doing this I would like to take a lead from William Foote Whyte and come clean about some of the errors and mistakes I have undoubtedly made and the possible repercussions that may well have resulted from them.

This allows me, quite conveniently, to capitalise already on the benefits of hindsight and take those of you yet to embark on the enterprise of ethnography on a fairly brisk walk through the potential minefield of pitfalls and perils that await anyone choosing to work in a research context on an extended, day-to-day basis with real live human beings. I need hardly add that it will also provide another opportunity for some professional bonding as I give an initial airing to one or two of my own personal 'war stories', by winding back the tape on my initiation into fieldwork.

By way of contrast, journal articles are usually de-personalised pieces of writing, in that they remove first-person references within the text (such as 'I carried out the fieldwork in this way…'), and provide a more distant, formalised account by framing the writing in the third person (such as 'The research team explored this issue with a range of interviewees…'). Examine the excerpt below from a draft text for a journal article. It displays some of the typical characteristics of this form of academic writing. For example, it provides a number of references to other written material, it is written in an objective, third-person style, and arguments follow a logical sequence – with each section developing from previous elements. Although minor variations may occur, usually references in journal articles follow a standard Harvard referencing style.

Encouraging enterprise in business clusters

Price, A. Robertson, M. and Wilkinson, D. (draft)

As part of a Yorkshire Forward funded project to encourage business start-up and explore notions of enterprise, Business Start-Up at Leeds Metropolitan University has undertaken an Entrepreneurial Intentions Survey of students across the four universities of Leeds, Leeds Metropolitan, Bradford and Huddersfield (Wilkinson, 2004). This survey has its roots in previous survey work conducted by Business

(Continued)

Start-Up at Leeds Metropolitan designed to explore enterprise and entrepreneurial intent amongst its student base.

Enterprise and entrepreneurship are not new to Higher Education in the UK (Price and Wilkinson, 2002). In recent years there have been a considerable number of studies and publications on the subject from a range of leading scholars. Some attempt to examine the traits and characteristics of entrepreneurs (Brandstatter, 1997; Chen et al., 1998; Llewellyn and Wilson, 2003), or explore enterprise in relation to particular groups within the population, and others even wrestle with the very notion of what an entrepreneur is – given the lack of clarity and agreement in relation to its definition (Wilkinson, 2001). To help explore the landscape of issues and concerns around enterprise education in the UK, and to facilitate the development of competent regional entrepreneurs, the Entrepreneurial Intentions Survey collected data from students within the West Yorkshire area to explore and unpack their views on enterprise and entrepreneurship. This is a timely investigation which relates to a number of regional and national policy objectives. In particular the work addresses a number of Yorkshire Forward's key strategic objectives: it addresses Objective 2 of the Regional Economic Strategy by examining the attitudes of would-be entrepreneurs, exploring the impact of school-based enterprise activities, and examining attitudes/beliefs and values of women, black and ethnic minorities. By exploring and examining attitudes to enterprise, entrepreneurship and related educational programmes, we hope to additionally inform Objective 4 of the Regional Economic Strategy – 'to radically improve the development and application of education, learning and skills, particularly high-quality vocational skills' (Yorkshire Forward, 2003a: 39). A further strength of our work is that it assists in the realisation of an important part of the Higher Education Funding Council for England's (HEFCE) strategic plan to enhance the contribution of HE to the economy and society, and by 'ensuring that funding is properly informed by regional economic development priorities' (HEFCE, 2003: 26).

Our current investigations build on similar, smaller-scale, work conducted in previous years to enhance the regional understanding of students and their entrepreneurial intentions – to better inform university strategic decision-making and applied educational approaches and practical interventions.

Survey

Building upon work conducted in 2003 which examined, among other things, barriers to business start-up (Robertson et al., 2003), this survey obtained the views of

(Continued)

(Continued)

a broad range of students enrolled on programmes of study with the four partner universities of Leeds Metropolitan, Leeds, Huddersfield and Bradford. Changes were made to the questionnaire used to collect the data, based on feedback from a broad range of sources, including academics, students, and colleagues at Yorkshire Forward. The questionnaire included both quantitative and qualitative questions, and aimed primarily to gather information about the students and the university that they attended. As with the previous year's exercise, questionnaires were administered face-to-face at various locations frequented by students across the four partner university campuses. The questionnaire was administered in Semester/Term 1 of the 2003–04 academic year and collected the views of 4,172 students.

APPROACHES TO WRITING

There are a variety of approaches or models to academic writing, and many provide useful frameworks through which to develop or focus your written work. It may also be helpful, when considering academic writing skills, to observe the key elements required of written work at postgraduate level within your school, department or institution. Such assessment criteria often include:

The development of an argument or framing of an appropriate research question. Indicative questions here might include: Is your work logically presented and written? Is the research question clearly written and unambiguous? Has the same or similar work already been done? If so, what does your work add to the body of knowledge?

Reference to the literature. Indicative questions here might include: Does the piece refer to relevant published material? Are relevant academic journals used as source material? Does the work refer to recognised experts in the field?

Criticality. Indicative questions here might include: Are arguments presented clearly, articulately, and objectively assessed? Does the piece evaluate the work of others in a critical way? Is evidence provided for competing or opposing views?

Progression. Indicative questions here might include: Is theory linked with evidence collected in an articulate way? Does the method or approach to analysis complement the tools and techniques used to collect information and data? Are conclusions made based upon the data collected or information/literature consulted?

REPORT WRITING

Whilst the traditional format of academic writing follows an essay style, an increasing amount of postgraduate work is presented in report format. Action-oriented research projects, dissertations or even PhD theses are particularly well suited to this structured approach to writing. The main elements of a report, and their sequence, are as follows:

A **title page** which usually provides the title of the report, the name of the author, and the date of publication.

A **contents page** detailing all the sections of the report and their sub-sections, with page numbers.

An **executive summary** which summarises the main points raised in the report.

An **introduction** that explains the scope of the report. A typical introduction also includes coverage of the following:

* Terms of reference – for whom the report has been written, and its purpose

* Procedures adopted – how the information presented in the report has been obtained

* Topics covered – a broad indication of the report's content

A **findings/discussion** section which develops and discusses ideas, issues and arguments raised. Descriptions and arguments should be built logically and progressively. This section of the report should be broken down into discrete sections and sub-sections to guide the reader through its content. Each section and sub-section should have a title/heading and be numbered.

A **conclusion**, indicating what the report has found based upon the literature consulted and data collected.

A **recommendations** section which highlights areas for suggested future action.

Appendices at the end of the report can incorporate detailed information relating to the report. Each appendix should be numbered and referred to in the text of the report.

A **bibliography** which lists all references to information sources used in the report.

TIPS FOR WRITING REPORTS

* Make sure your report answers the question or questions set. Does it address the brief or terms of reference?

* Is it well structured, sequenced and to the point?

* Are all the main issues you have raised covered in sufficient depth?

* Is each substantive point supported with appropriate evidence?

* Can any claims made in your report be reasonably attributed to the data you have collected or the literature/information you have consulted?

* Is there a clear distinction between the work of others and your own? Have you accurately acknowledged all your sources?

* Is the report the required length? Can some sections be made more concise? What do they add to your main arguments?

* Is your report clearly written and presented? Have you proof-read it and eliminated all ambiguities?

TIPS FOR WRITERS

There are a number of excellent textbooks that provide detailed advice and guidance on the topic of writing for academic audiences. One particularly useful text, for those interested in developing their own professional writing skills, is *Professional writing* by Sky Marsen (2003). This publication unpacks the whole writing process and includes a number of helpful tips for effective writing, which are summarised below (see Marsen, 2003: 14–15):

* *Don't wait for inspiration.* Make time to write, and stick to it. Even if what you initially write does not clearly relate to the central theme, you have at least started the process and this will eventually help you to focus upon your topic.

* *Revise as you write.* Writing and re-writing helps to clarify your thoughts about a subject and the subsequent way you write about it.

* *Become observant.* Good writing is developed from experience; the more you know about a subject (either through extensive reading and/or experience), the better and more informed your writing will become.

* *Record different types of material that you may one day use in your writing.* Keep a record of ideas and thoughts about the subject area of your writing (perhaps in a notebook, on post-it notes or scraps of paper) as they occur. This might be whilst out walking the dog, on a bus or train journey, or whilst discussing your work with friends or colleagues. The important thing is to write the thought down and refer to it when re-drafting your work.

- *Use physical details of writing consistently.* We all work best in certain places, using certain tools. This might include a particular 'writing chair' or 'desk', a particular type of pen or lined paper.

- *Get feedback.* Try to secure the assistance of a friend or colleague to read through and comment upon your draft work. We are often, as writers, too close to the material to see inconsistencies or ambiguities in what we write.

- *Learn the conventions and standards of your language.* Ensure your written work observes grammatical rules and conventions. Sometimes, as writers, we may wish to make more of an impact by breaking these rules – in order to do this we still need to know what they are and how far we can manipulate them.

Presenting your work

As postgraduates, you will present your research or project work through a variety of methods. An essay, assignment, journal article or thesis submission are all crucial methods of transmitting and sharing our work with others. In addition, you may be required to present your research work, your work-in-progress, to others who have a similar interest in your subject area at a conference or seminar. If you wish to develop a career in academia (either as a researcher or an academic), the development of sound skills in terms of presenting your work and communicating ideas, findings and theories will become crucial. For many postgraduates and academics the development of sound presentation skills takes considerable practice to achieve. Peter outlines a useful training activity at the University of Leeds to help postgraduates develop and hone these skills. It might be useful, when working with other postgraduates in your own school or department, to trial your presentations with them in a similar way.

Our lunchtime departmental seminars are really good events to help critique aspects of your work, or get the views of others on what you are doing. I've got some really useful guidance from other people's talks on the practicalities of running a research project. What to do, what not to do – that kind of thing.

Peter, ESRC 1 + 3 student, University of Leeds.

Presenting work at a seminar, conference or other live event employs many of the same structural requirements of a formally *written* presentation of your work. The content for both is crucial. In written work, you can provide more detail relating to methodology, sample size, response rate and the analysis of the data. When presenting your work to a live audience, the level of detail needs to be carefully gauged to fit the time available, the level of general expertise of the audience, and their ability to absorb information and data presented to them in order to reasonably maintain their interest. This combination of variables usually dictates that presented work should be succinct and of relevance to the group of people in front of you – a lesson learnt the hard way by David, below.

I remember the first paper I presented at a conference on Special Educational Needs. The subject of my presentation was taken straight from a paper I was preparing for an academic journal. That was a big mistake! I tried to condense far too much theory and background material into my presentation. I should have thought more carefully about concentrating on the essence of my article content [a survey of perceptions in relation to a piece of Special Educational Needs legislation] rather than making comment upon everything I'd read on the subject of Special Educational Needs.

David, PhD student, University of Southside.

Good presentations are always well prepared. It is extremely rare for someone to have delivered a well-received conference paper who has not given considerable time to its preparation (at least half a day to prepare a 20-minute presentation is not unusual). Essentially, all successful presentations rely on a detailed structure and plan, which includes an analysis and consideration of the following:

* *The remit of the presentation (or its objectives).* What is the intent of your presentation? Is it to review the literature in a given area? Is it to present interim results of your field work?

* *The audience.* Who will be your audience and what level of understanding do you believe they currently have in relation to the subject of your presentation? Are they experts in the field and already 'up to speed' on the key areas of concern? Are they

unaware of the subject area and do you therefore require 'scene setting' to explain your research work?

- *Structure.* How are you going to structure your presentation? The most common format is to have an introduction, a discussion or review of data, and a conclusion where you draw together the main themes or issues of your presented work. To ensure the audience engages effectively with the subject matter of the presentation it is often necessary to simplify the structure of your work by removing unnecessary sections which obscure your main objectives.

Gina Wisker suggests that effective presenters should consider the four Ps: plan, prepare, practise and present (Wisker, 2001: 307). *Planning* includes an appreciation of the framework presented above, precisely focusing on the elements of your work that you wish to discuss and can manageably cover in the time available to you. *Preparation* includes producing outlines and headings or 'signposts' within your presentation. This can help you to monitor and assign 'chunks' of time within your presentation, as Peter used to great effect when presenting his work for the first time.

> *I had quite a lot to get through and I was aware that I tended to speed-up my talking a bit when I became nervous. I found that by splitting the presentation up into short 5-minute bursts I was able to tackle the presentation much more easily – it wasn't a horrible 30-minute presentation anymore, it was a collection of six 5-minute presentations! The total presentation was an incremental process of linking the sections together and it helped me to keep to time.*
>
> Peter, PhD student, University of Oxford.

Practise is crucial for the delivery of a smooth and appropriately paced presentation. Only with practice and by rehearsing what you will say, will you become reasonably confident about your presentation. Practice (in front of supportive colleagues) can also usefully reveal structural weaknesses in your presentation of research or project work. It is also important, if you are considering using presentation equipment (such as PC projectors, interactive whiteboards, group activities), that you are confident in using such tools. This can only be achieved through practice. It is painful for many, but practice really can make perfect – a point clearly made by Elaine, below.

Everybody wets themselves with worry about presentations, but it's a fact of postgraduate life that you have to do them. There's no getting away from it. I hate it but I've made the decision to get some practice in and from next year I'll be doing some teaching assistant work in Psychology to gain the experience and learning the ropes. So, every week next year, I will have to engage with students and develop my presentation (through teaching) skills. You can read as much as you like about the art of presenting, but nothing beats actually doing it.

Elaine, PhD student, University of Eastside.

Reference list, useful reading and websites

Becker, L. (2004) *How to manage your postgraduate course*. London: Palgrave.

Bell, J. (1999) *Doing your research project: a guide for first-time researchers in education and social science* (2nd edn). Buckingham: Open University Press.

Blaxter, L., Hughes, C. and Tight, M. (1998) *The academic career handbook*. Buckingham: Open University Press.

Brause, R.S. (2000) *Writing your doctoral dissertation*. London: RoutledgeFalmer.

Marsen, S. (2003) *Professional writing: the complete guide for business, industry and IT*. London: Palgrave.

Marshall, S. and Green, N. (2004) *Your PhD companion*. Oxford: How to books.

Phelan, P.J. and Reynolds, P.J. (1995) *Argument and evidence: critical thinking for the social sciences*. London: Routledge.

Potter, S. (2002) *Doing postgraduate research*. London: Sage.

University of Surrey – Skills Project Pilot Pack. (http://www.surrey.ac.uk/skills/contents.html) (Accessed 30/9/04).

Van Emden, J. and Becker, L. (2004) *Presentation skills for students*. London: Palgrave.

Wisker, G. (2001) *The postgraduate research handbook: succeed with your MA, MPhil, EdD and PhD*. London: Palgrave.

8 Working with your supervisor

Chapter overview

Securing the support and guidance of your tutor or supervisor is an important part of postgraduate study. This chapter covers:

- The role of supervision.
- Selecting supervisors.
- Jointly supervised projects.
- Making contact with your supervisor.
- Supervisor responsibilities.
- Student responsibilities.
- Managing the relationship.
- Keeping in touch with your supervisor.

The role of supervision

> *A good supervisor is a critical friend. He's your mate – that is really important. You've got to get on – if you don't it's going to be a really miserable experience.*
>
> Jeff, ESRC 1 + 3 student, University of Hull.

WHAT IS SUPERVISION?

You should not be expected to undertake postgraduate research without support and guidance from your host institution. That support can take many forms but perhaps the most influential and important is that provided through your supervisor or supervisors. A supervisor's primary role is to assist your progress whilst you undertake your research journey. Most universities have clear guidance on the role and function of supervisors, often expanding the baseline requirements as set out in the Quality Assurance Agency's (QAA) Code of Practice on Postgraduate Research Programmes (Quality Assurance Agency, 1999). All research councils subscribe to this code and expect institutions in receipt of research council funding to adhere to the guidance contained within them. Specifically, for supervisors, the code states:

* Supervisors should possess recognised subject expertise.
* Supervisors should have the necessary skills and experience to monitor, support and direct research students' work.
* Research students should receive support and direction sufficient to enable them to succeed in their studies.
* The progress made by research students should be consistently monitored and regularly communicated to students. (Quality Assurance Agency, 1999: 10–11)

> *There are definitely people who shouldn't supervise. When you think about it, a lot of people are not that sociable are they? Particularly academics! I mean, you do think sometimes – how on earth did they get into this game (working with others) because many of them don't appear to be good at it or like it a great deal?*
> Colin, PhD student, University of Northside.

Colin's comment about who should, and who should not, supervise is a common one, but based upon the QAA guidance and institutional convention, it is clear that supervisors should be skilled individuals with the appropriate subject expertise and experience of conducting research themselves. Postgraduate and PhD supervisors are senior members of academic staff with substantial experience of such academic mentoring and guidance work. As such, they commonly possess skills and techniques to enable the effective personal development of postgraduate supervisees.

To be an effective supervisor, you have got to like being with people – or be good at faking it at least! And a lot of them aren't even good at that – and they are going to have to manage somebody's work for the next three years. So there are some people who are much better at it than others, some do it purely to progress their own careers. It's a feather in their cap, isn't it – to say 'I've supervised X number of PhD students'. You've just got to make sure you work with a supervisor who is, or at least looks like they are, interested in your work.

Peter, PhD student, University of Westfield.

Supervisors can have a dramatic impact on the learning and professional development of their students, and most supervisors recognise and value the importance and responsibility attached to the role. For those of you engaged in PhD-level study, you and your supervisor will collaborate over a number of years – it is therefore advisable for you to make efforts to nurture and develop this relationship in order for you to gain the most from this element of your postgraduate experience. If carefully coordinated and managed, your collaboration can last well beyond the completion of your programme of study.

Selecting supervisors

I first met my supervisor during the last two years of my undergraduate course when she was teaching the psychology module. I wrote a couple of essays for her and she clearly liked what I wrote. We hit it off straight away. We have shared interests in discourse analysis, social constructionism, visual rhetoric and visual discourse and I write very much like she does.

Nick, ESRC 1 + 3 student, Plymouth.

It's important to be able to 'get along' with your supervisor, as Nick did. After all, your supervisor's assistance and involvement with your project or research work will undoubtedly facilitate it's progression and completion. Unfortunately, however, there is no clear recipe for success in selecting a supervisor. For some, this is decided for them by their host institution, or they may have managed to nurture the relationship whilst studying for their undergraduate degree (something successfully achieved by Peter, below).

> *I think, if I am honest, a part of the reason I applied for a 1 + 3 was that I already had this relationship with my supervisor and I knew that here was somebody I could get along with and do some research with. For others, trying to find someone whom they can work with (whom they don't know) must be quite difficult.*
>
> *You need to know how people work and operate to make sure that you effectively get your message across about your intended research. This takes time – you need to read up around potential supervisors, possibly go and see them, and establish whether or not they would be willing/interested in supervising you.*
>
> Peter, ESRC 1 + 3 student, University of Leeds.

In some of these cases it is the luck of the draw – some are successful and some are not. However, for many prospective postgraduate research students there is the opportunity to influence or even select a supervisor or supervisors. ESRC 1 + 3 students are encouraged to develop their applications for the scheme with their actual or prospective supervisor: part of the application is assessed on the supervisor's contribution, comment and guidance indicates that whilst your proposed research should be your own, the ESRC strongly suggests that you talk with your prospective supervisor before outlining in your application your proposed research (ESRC, 2005a: 31).

What useful criteria might you apply to aid your selection of supervisor? A key selection criterion for supervisors might be how well known they are in the field – this is usually determined and measured by the number of research outputs (for example, journal articles, research papers, chapters in books, etc.) they have. In your reading around the subject of your intended research, have you come across any of their work? Is their work referred to (or cited) by others? If so, in what context is it cited? Occasionally, authors can secure high citation rates through the production and publication of low quality material. Such 'negative' citations can easily distort mechanisms which measure the impact (citations divided by the number of sources or articles) of journals and other outputs.

> *Don't do what I did and become blinded solely by an academic's success in the field – demonstrated by their prolific research output. Instead, try to work out if you'll actually get along with them. What types and kinds of research methodology do they use – are they similar or the same as the methods you wish to use? What's their educational and academic background – are there any similarities to your own? What 'common ground' in experiences and understandings do you share?*
> Professor Smith, University of Northfield.

Experiences and expertise in conducting research are useful considerations when exploring supervision possibilities. In-depth knowledge and experience of qualitative research and the technological tools to support and enhance it might be particularly relevant considerations for the budding ethnographic researcher. Indicators of expertise in this area might be displayed through the potential supervisor's teaching commitments and duties. For example, are they involved in teaching the particular research methods you are interested in using for your work? Do they publish material drawing upon/utilising certain methodological approaches?

Recommendation by others can be an effective way to determine suitable supervisory assistance for your postgraduate work. It is often helpful to seek advice from current or recent tutors on the matter – given what they know of you and your work, who would they recommend? Do you have peers who are currently engaged in postgraduate work – who would they recommend? Many University departments have postgraduate research tutors – who would they recommend? It might be useful here to provide the postgraduate tutors with an outline of what you intend to explore in your research, so they can effectively match up your research with relevant potential supervisors.

It might be worthwhile considering and approaching someone who is new to supervision to become involved in offering guidance and related support to your work. Whilst for some dealing with the unknown like this is a high-risk strategy, it does have its benefits. For example, an academic who is new to supervision may, understandably, wish to make a good impression (both on you and the academic hierarchy within the school or department). He or she may therefore be prepared to offer you more time and support than their more experienced counterparts. They may have innovative and more accessible approaches to supervision and perhaps, given their relative junior status, they may be more compassionate and understanding of the postgraduate's lot (after all, it might not have been so long ago that they were in your position).

Jointly supervised projects

Research or project work that is jointly supervised requires clear and professional management by you as the student. Careful and reasoned consideration should be given to the viewpoints and expertise of your co-supervisors. As part of their guidance for postgraduate research, the ESRC recognise the benefits of such supervisory arrangements. Specifically, they encourage: 'dual supervision, or supervisory panels, particularly where the student is engaged in cross-disciplinary research or research involving collaboration between an academic department and an outside organisation, where meetings of all the parties concerned may be necessary from time to time' (ESRC, 2005b: 16).

> *A lot of people I know have two supervisors and that's a great strength – you can always go to the other supervisor for a second opinion on things etc. It really helps strengthen your work and your arguments.*
>
> Kelly, ESRC 1 + 3 student, University of Manchester.

> *I've been very happy with my supervisors but part of the problem for PhD students is that you can't always choose who your supervisor is. Also, I've found it very*
>
> *(Continued)*

> *(Continued)*
>
> *beneficial to have two because you get different perspectives and so on, but I understand it's more common to have just one. I've found the mix very helpful: one of my supervisors is much older and more experienced, the other much younger. Obviously it's important to be able to get on personally as well as sharing research interests or approaches.*
>
> Alexej, ESRC 1 + 3 student, Aberystwyth University.

On a practical level, it may be difficult to arrange meetings between yourself and supervisors who have demanding teaching and/or research duties. Because university research managers anticipate that these and other problems or issues may arise, they often assign a lead supervisor role to one of your supervisory team. It is the commonly accepted duty of your lead supervisor to then liaise with others to suggest and arrange suitable and convenient times for meetings. Your lead supervisor will also coordinate and manage your progress on your programme of study. In some departments and institutions the lead supervisor has the final say when contradictory advice or guidance is received in respect to, say, your progression through the stages of your degree programme. Most co-supervisor issues can be resolved, however, through discussion and negotiation between the parties involved, but if problems or concerns remain you should approach your school or departmental postgraduate tutor or head of postgraduate studies indicating your concerns. It is fair to say, however, that in most cases the benefit of receiving two separate supervisory inputs on your work far outweigh any difficulties or issues you may encounter.

Communication is crucial when you have more than one supervisor, everyone should be aware of what you are doing, and when. Make sure that all relevant documentation, plans, interim results, reports, are copied to all supervisors. Keep them informed of your fieldwork activities and any changes or amendments to your work. Doing all of this will help you to avoid a situation as described by Maureen below.

> *The politics of working with two supervisors might be difficult for some postgraduates to get to grips with. I know of some situations where a postgraduate has shown draft*
>
> *(Continued)*

(Continued)

material to one supervisor without copying the joint-supervisor into the communication. This caused some difficulty, for some time afterwards, between the postgraduate and the supervisor concerned. The other supervisor thought he was being side-lined and therefore not consulted on the postgraduate's progress. Always keep joint supervisors equally informed about your work – it avoids confusion and keeps them both on your side.

Maureen, ESRC/CASE student, University of Leeds.

Initial contact

The initial formal meeting with your tutor or supervisor can be an intimidating experience for you. This is probably the first time you've enjoyed one-to-one support for the duration of your programme of study. Many students will have benefited from the experience of support for undergraduate dissertation work, but this will rarely have required more than one or two meetings with a dissertation or project tutor. At postgraduate level (and particularly PhD level), the guidance you receive from tutors or supervisors, and the influence they have on your work, is (and should be) considerable. This being the case, it is important to get things off to a good start. At your first meeting you should think about discussing and clarifying the following with your tutor or supervisor.

* *Meeting times*   How often, and for how long, will you meet each other? For some, agreement is reached that meetings will take place informally throughout the academic year. This doesn't suit everyone, so ensure that your supervisor is aware of the way you would like to approach this. Be prepared to negotiate and compromise – supervisors will have other calls on their time and they may not be able to meet you as frequently as you wish, or at the times of day you suggest.

* *Agenda-setting and preparing work*   Some supervisors prefer to set agendas for meetings with supervisees, whereas others believe it is the responsibility of the student to structure their format and coverage. It may be a useful demonstration of your control of your own work to set the agenda for meetings held between yourself and your supervisor. Some postgraduates fit in with the timetables of their tutors or supervisors; others (such as Gareth below), proactively seek regular, focused support.

> *You should be proactive in seeking an appointment with your*
> *supervisor. I need mine to look at my work and make some*
> *comments so that I can move on to look at other things, or carry*
> *out some more work on it if she feels it needs it.*
>
> Gareth, ESRC 1 + 3 student, University of Edinburgh.

Responsibilities

RESPONSIBILITIES OF STUDENT AND SUPERVISORS

All higher education institutions have procedural notes, Codes of Practice or other similar guidance documents designed to clarify the duties, roles and responsibilities of students and supervisors. Information can vary by discipline, department and institution, but this guidance can usefully be employed as a starting point for discussions relating to roles and responsibilities between you and your supervisor. Ian, below, drew upon this institutional guidance to clarify further the expectations he had of his supervisor.

> *I expect a supervisor who you can go and speak to about your*
> *research work. You can knock on his door and see him there and*
> *then or arrange to meet with him at a later time. Also, if you*
> *have a problem of any kind, your supervisor should be there for*
> *you to assist with this where they can. I think a lot of PhD*
> *students suffer in their relationship with their supervisor because*
> *they (the supervisor) aren't on campus a lot. I've always been*
> *aware of my supervisor's 'office hours' and that's helped me plan*
> *my time and study.*
>
> *My supervisor provides useful pointers towards reading I*
> *should be taking a look at. After all, he is a key author in the field*
> *and he can get hold of a lot of forthcoming work – stuff that*
> *hasn't even been published yet. So I can have the inside track*
>
> *(Continued)*

(Continued)

on a lot of material. His website is very useful for this. He keeps it up to date and I can see some of what's new in my area by accessing his, and other experts' websites.

Because my supervisor is seasoned at academic work and styles, etc, he can provide me with invaluable advice as to how I frame some of my arguments or present aspects of my work for an academic audience.

Ian, ESRC 1 + 3 student, University of Manchester.

SUPERVISOR RESPONSIBILITIES

As noted above, supervisor responsibilities may differ within institutions and across subject or discipline boundaries. However, there are a number of core duties or responsibilities of postgraduate supervisor. These might usefully include providing support, help and assistance with:

- induction to the university – including information on its structure, history and research strengths;

- the standard and amount of work required of postgraduate students within your discipline area;

- searching for appropriate literature;

- planning and managing the project/research work;

- preparing a thesis for submission including, university conventions and requirements;

- assisting with networking opportunities;

- accessing university training and development events;

- arranging for tailored instruction to support the student's research or project work (such as advanced statistical modelling courses for highly statistical research projects); and

- development of material suitable for publication.

(Adapted from Finn, 2005)

It is clear that a good supervisory relationship provides support and guidance for the postgraduate student, as Nick suggests below. However, as Gareth moves on to also explain, supervision includes support not only in relation to a variety of formal mechanisms, but also with the subtleties of operating within an academic environment.

When I started, my supervisor quite often checked how the research training was going and gave me reading to do which would prepare me for later on with my Masters dissertation. So he started as a guide and then turned into a kind of critical evaluator, asking me to justify the decisions I had taken in my research. After my Masters he put the brakes on me and gave me a term of reading and asked me to take stock. At the moment, because I'm on fieldwork, I don't really see him at all, but I can phone him if I have a problem. That was something we discussed and it works fine.

Nick, ESRC 1 + 3 student, University of Oxford.

Key areas where supervisors can assist include: agreeing to regular meetings, reading and commenting on work, pointing out mistakes, suggesting new literature to look at, and warning me about the implicit rules of the research and academic game. For example, whether I should email a person, give them a phone call, or ask my supervisor to make the first approach.

Gareth, ESRC 1 + 3 student, University of Edinburgh.

There are a growing number of textbooks detailing the general and specific duties of postgraduate study supervisors. In their work exploring the PhD process, Phillips and Pugh (2003) devote a chapter to supervision considerations, and they outline the main expectations of students when being supervised:

- Students expect to be supervised.
- Students expect supervisors to read their work well in advance.
- Students expect their supervisors to be available when needed.
- Students expect their supervisors to be friendly, open and supportive.
- Students expect their supervisors to be constructively critical.
- Students expect their supervisors to have a good knowledge of the research area.
- Students expect their supervisors to structure the tutorial so that it is relatively easy to exchange ideas.
- Students expect their supervisors to have sufficient interest in their research to put more information in the student's path.
- Students expect supervisors to be sufficiently involved in their success to help them to get a good job at the end of it all! (Phillips and Pugh, 2003: 110–19)

To assist institutions and students in fully exploring their roles and responsibilities, the National Postgraduate Committee has developed guidance designed to support both student and supervisor – details are available through their website (http://www.npc.org.uk). In addition, the UK Grad Programme (a collaborating partnership of organisations interested in postgraduate education and training) provides useful suggestions on getting the most out of the student-supervisor relationship (http://www.grad.ac.uk).

In Rita Brause's useful and informative text on the subject of doctoral study, she presents a list of questions for supervisors (Brause, 2000). Asking these (and others like them) of your potential and actual supervisors might facilitate a clearer definition and understanding of what both of you expect from the supervision process.

QUESTIONS FOR SUPERVISORS

- How do you usually work with your doctoral students?
- What do you think are my responsibilities?
- In what ways can I expect that you will help me?
- Will you give me assignments each week?
- Are there other students who are working with you on a similar topic, whom I might work with?
- Do you have a research group that meets periodically to talk about projects?
- Do you have preferences for one research methodology, one theory, or one topic over others? Why do you prefer these?
- Is there a way in which I might work on one of your research projects for my dissertation?

- Will we be able to meet during the summer and during semester breaks?
- Will you meet with me if I have nothing written?
- How will I get feedback?
- What progress do I need to make each semester?
- What happens if I don't finish in two years?
- How do I know if I am making good progress?
- Can you provide me with guidelines for how long this will take based on your experiences with other doctoral students?
- Can we establish a schedule to organise my work?
- Who has to evaluate my work?
- What are the characteristics of an acceptable dissertation proposal?
- What problems can I expect to encounter? (Brause, 2000: 63–4).

In the first term of my PhD I went away and read a series of papers and my supervisor and I would meet to discuss those papers so she could grapple with what I was really getting at. I'm very systematic and I think my supervisor is less systematic, so I suggested I did a work plan to cover each chapter and we'd meet to discuss each chapter in turn. That worked very well. Now she's very busy but I can always book in to see her. She's less strong on methodology but passionate about the subject matter.

Lorraine, PhD student, University of Eastfield.

As Lorraine suggests above, building a good working relationship is an important aspect of many postgraduate programmes. Other crucial roles and responsibilities of a supervisor include giving advice and guidance on realistic and achievable completion dates for the various stages of the project or research work. Your supervisor will probably be more aware than you of the time and effort required to develop and write-up substantive research-based work.

At a more formal level, it is the responsibility of your supervisor to formally and regularly (usually once or twice per year), inform the university of your progress. In addition, it is often the duty of your supervisor to ensure you receive information in relation to university requirements concerning the examination processes and procedures that relate specifically to your programme of study. In many larger departments or faculties this information is often issued to postgraduate students by the department or faculty research office.

STUDENT RESPONSIBILITIES

As part of the research for this text, we asked a number of supervisors, across a range of disciplines, to provide typical questions they might ask potential research students. Some of the questions that follow might appear obvious, but many of the supervisors indicated that a good number of their own research students might have difficulty in adequately or competently responding to such queries. It may be worthwhile, then, for the novice postgraduate research student, to develop answers to these questions in order to prepare for any initial supervisory meetings.

* Who do you consider to be the key authors in the field?

* Have you read my work in the area?

* What do you think of my work in the area?

* Why select me as a supervisor?

* Have you sought funding for your studies?

* How is your study likely to contribute to the body of knowledge?

* How is your study likely to contribute to our department/university research strengths?

* What difficulties do you anticipate with your intended research? How will you deal with these?

* Are you prepared to teach through your studies?

* What would you like to teach?

* How long will you take to complete your research?

* Do you intend to publish throughout your studies?

* Where do you intend to publish?

* Where else have you applied?

Not all researchers or supervisors work in the same way. It is important for students and supervisors to agree on the format and type of feedback that will best assist the development of the research student. Postgraduate students can often provide useful guidance on the approach to feedback that would best suit them. As Stephen highlights below, a clear articulation of the feedback required enables focused development and progression to take place on the part of the postgraduate learner.

> *I'm very used to being criticised and I work best when people really have a go at me and put me under pressure and tear apart my work. I don't really need support, whereas my supervisor is more interested in confidence-building, encouragement and support. So I'm always pushing him to be much more critical, to really tear my work apart. He's doing that much more now. Partly that's because as my work has progressed and become more substantive it's become more important to criticise it. We both recognise that it's a professional relationship and therefore nothing of what we say should be taken personally.*
>
> Stephen, PhD student, University of Southside.

STUDENT RESPONSIBILITIES

It is important to accept that students also have expected roles and responsibilities in the supervision process. In order to gain the most from meetings and exchanges between you and your supervisor, it might be worthwhile considering the following:

* During the initial stages of your relationship, outline clearly with tutors/supervisor(s) the scope and remit of the project or research work (thereby highlighting your interest in the subject, your level of understanding, and enabling you to take a lead on the direction and shape of your work).

* Exploring with the supervisor the type of guidance and feedback that is most helpful (some students prefer to receive informal and regular feedback on work submitted, whereas others prefer written comments on their draft work).

- Determining what other support is available within your university to complement that offered by your supervisor (for example, advanced literature review training and guidance may be available through your university library; support on using and applying advanced statistical techniques may be available through your IT or Computing department).

- Agreeing the format and length of supervision meetings (for example a short 20-minute meeting every two weeks and an hour-long review meeting every two months).

- Agreeing a timeline for your research or project work with your supervisor, clearly stating when the various stages of your work will be completed and outlining when your supervisor's input will be required.

- Preparing and circulating agendas, minutes and themes for discussion well in advance of supervision meetings.

- Providing regular reports of work completed and work-in-progress to enable your supervisor to provide focused and appropriate support and guidance.

(Adapted from Finn, 2005)

Managing the relationship

> *I think that what all postgraduates need to consider is that their supervisor's world does not revolve around them. [Supervisors] have many, many calls on their time – some more calls than others! In my experience I really had to fight (almost literally) to see my supervisor. He would not return my calls or emails and often wasn't in his office when his timetable indicated he was.*
>
> Sean, PhD student, University of Eastshire.

Sean's experience is not uncommon and relationships can be difficult to nurture and develop if students and supervisors do not, or rarely, meet. In addition, the transfer from undergraduate to independent postgraduate work can be difficult for some, as can the requirement to develop a professional working relationship with a supervisor – a typical situation described by Helen, below.

Throughout my undergraduate degree I had a fairly relaxed, informal, relationship with my tutors, but Pauline (my PhD supervisor) was much more formal from the beginning of our relationship. I am naturally a great worrier, so I prepared absolutely everything for our meetings – what we would discuss, how Pauline would assist, time frames for me giving her draft materials, feedback dates, etc. This wasn't how Pauline worked at all. So there was a bit of grappling to begin with, with us both establishing what we wanted and working out how this relationship was going to work. For the first two or three months I felt quite down about it. We'd have meetings but it would feel as though she was just saying 'go off and do this and come back and we'll talk about it.' It left me feeling that I wasn't going to get anywhere with my PhD. Plus she wasn't around much in the first term because she does a lot of consultancy work.

Then, after Christmas at the beginning of the second term, we had a cards-on-the-table meeting in which she said lots of nice things about me and I think the major issue is you want it all to be structured and that's the way you work but, I don't, so let's find a middle ground.' So we have done. She urged me to be more independent and have the confidence to go and do things to talk about at our set meetings. Since then it's got dramatically better. I feel we get on much better now.

Helen, PhD student, University of Westside.

Sometimes, and for the unfortunate few, the supervisor–supervisee relationship does not work. For some (academics and students alike), it is seen as a test of your resolve to continue studying despite the lack of any structured supervisory support. However, this is not a satisfactory state of affairs. When you as a postgraduate begin your studies, you should be made aware of practices or procedures used by your department, school or faculty to monitor and supervise the progress of postgraduates registered with them. Often, guidance or codes of practice are centrally determined by the university – departments, schools or faculties 'sign up' to these agreements. At the University of Leeds, many departments, schools and faculties produce detailed additional guidelines indicating appropriate treatment of registered postgraduate students. The Department of Statistics clearly specifies the number of meetings that should take place between supervisor and postgraduate research student.

> It is the joint responsibility of the supervisor(s) and student to agree a supervisory programme setting out the pattern, timing and style of supervision. The student will meet his/her supervisor on a regular basis to discuss progress and future plans. Usually there will be a minimum of twelve supervision meetings per year. Notes should be kept of all formal supervision meetings, with copies retained by the supervisor and student.
>
> (University of Leeds, Department of Statistics, Code of Practice for Research Degree Candidature, p. 1)

In addition to institutional and research council codes and guidance covering duties and responsibilities for students and supervisors, a growing number of other organisations, which typically fund postgraduate training, are producing their own guidance and procedural notes. The Wellcome Trust outline their interpretation of terms of good supervisory practice, thus:

- Institutions should ensure that appropriate direction of research and supervision of researchers is provided. Training in supervisory skills should be provided where appropriate.
- A code of responsibilities should be available for supervisors indicating, for example, the frequency of contact, responsibilities regarding scrutiny of primary data, and the broader development needs of research trainees.
- The need should be stressed for supervisors to supervise all stages of the research process, including outlining or drawing up a hypothesis, preparing applications for funding, protocol design, data recording and data analysis.
  (Wellcome Trust, 2002: 1)

Guidance notes are produced by institutions and funders to enable students and supervisors alike to clarify roles and responsibilities in their specific student–supervisor relationship. It is therefore very useful, in the early stages of the supervisory relationship, for students and supervisors to acquaint themselves with the relevant institutional or research-funder guidance.

KEEPING IN TOUCH WITH YOUR SUPERVISOR

Effective and regular communication or contact with supervisors is frequently advised in postgraduate research guidance. How often 'regular' means, however, is not always dictated. In most cases, it is left to you and your supervisor to determine the level and frequency of contact needed. For some, this may be a 20-minute meeting every month, and for others it may be less frequent face-to-face meetings but regular email communications. The crucial element here is to maintain communication throughout your whole programme of study. Your supervisor has the task of guiding you through your postgraduate journey – he or she cannot do that if you do not see them or communicate with them. To gain the most from your efforts, it might be helpful to structure your meetings in order to make the communication process more effective for you. This is an approach that has been successfully adopted by Charlotte.

I get on well with my supervisor as he works in a similar area to the one I'm interested in. He is also in charge of the directed reading for my Masters degree, so we see each other quite regularly (every week). It's important wherever possible to structure our meetings so that they can usefully inform the work I'm required to do for my dissertation.

Charlotte, ESRC 1 + 3 student, University College London.

To facilitate and encourage effective, worthwhile communication between you and your supervisor depends upon the personalities, backgrounds, interests, and approaches of both student and supervisor. Unfortunately, no one size fits all, but informative work has been published which indicates that the relationship and resulting communication is influenced by the roles adopted by both parties (Hockey, 1995; Hockey, 1996; Deem and Brehony, 2000; Delamont et al., 2004). While it is, therefore, inappropriate to suggest the same advice for managing each collaborative venture, Peter summarises some key issues and provides a number of reasonable expectations of the relationship.

To be good! To be supportive. It's when they are not supportive that they get criticised. They can demonstrate their support by listening and remembering what was said in previous meetings. And I suppose if they are going to be critical they have got to be positive at the same time. If you have a supervisor who is just talking about the problems of the research all the time, the student is going to feel de-motivated and won't move forward – you'll never get anywhere. There's no research that doesn't have problems.

A friendly approach is also useful. Sometimes they can be a bit too aloof. Asking a few questions about your personal life shows an interest and can help the supervisor and student bond a little. It can also enable you as a postgraduate to become less intimidated by your supervisor – getting to know them a little helps break down barriers.

I'd also expect a good supervisor to introduce you to relevant people in your area of study – that's how I got involved with the Interdisciplinary Centre here at the university. My supervisor chairs seminars and talks there and he said that it would be a good place for me to go and network.

Regular meetings are also important. With my supervisor, we have agreed to meet once a month. Sometimes, when we meet, I have certain action points and we agree to meet again to review

> *(Continued)*
>
> *these once I have completed them. Sometimes, I also give him something I've written and we then set a date to meet up once he has had a chance to read through it and develop some comments. Roughly though, we meet once a month. When we meet, I usually set the agenda for what we discuss – that's the way I said that I wanted to do it and he seems quite happy with that.*
>
> Peter, ESRC 1 + 3 student, University of Leeds.

Reference list, useful reading and websites

Blaxter, L., Hughes, C. and Tight, M. (1998) *The academic career handbook*. Buckingham: Open University Press.

Brause, R.S. (2000) *Writing your doctoral dissertation: invisible rules for success*. London: Falmer Press.

Cuthbert, R. (1996) *Working in higher education*. Buckingham: Open University Press/ Society for Research into Higher Education.

Deem, R. and Brehony, K.V. (2000) Doctoral students' access to research cultures – are some more unequal than others?, *Studies in Higher Education*, 25(2): 149–165.

Delamont, S., Atkinson, P. and Parry, O. (2004) *Supervising the doctorate: a guide to success*. Buckingham: Open University Press/SRHE.

ESRC (2005a) *ESRC Postgraduate studentships in the social sciences available in 2005: guidance notes for applications* (available online: http://www.esrc.ac.uk).

ESRC (2005b) *Postgraduate training guidelines 2005*. Swindon: Economic and Social Research Council.

Grix, J. (2001) *Demystifying postgraduate research: from MA to PhD*. Birmingham: University of Birmingham Press.

Hockey, J. (1995) Change and the social science PhD: supervisors' responses, *Oxford Review of Education*, 21(2): 195–206.

Hockey, J. (1996) Strategies and tactics in the supervision of UK social science PhD students, *Qualitative Studies in Education*, 9(4): 481–500.

Johnston, S. and Broda, J. (1996) Supporting educational researchers of the future, *Educational Review*, 48(3): 269–281.

Phillips, E.M. and Pugh, D.S. (2003) *How to get a PhD: a handbook for students and their supervisors* (3rd edn). Buckingham: Open University Press.

Quality Assurance Agency (1999) *Code of Practice for the assurance of academic quality and standards in higher education.* Section 1: Postgraduate research programmes. London: The Quality Assurance Agency for Higher Education.

The National Postgraduate Council (http://www.npc.org.uk).

The National Postgraduate Council (1995) Guidelines on Accommodation and Facilities for Postgraduate Research. Troon: The National Postgraduate Committee.

The UK grad programme. Managing your relationship with your supervisor. (http://www.grad.ac.uk).

Wellcome Trust (2002) *Guidelines on good research practice.* London: The Wellcome Trust.

9 Working with other researchers

Chapter overview

This chapter outlines the situations in which you may be required to work with others, and the reasons why this may be beneficial. Specifically, the chapter includes:

- The role of research in a university.
- Postgraduates and independent learners and researchers.
- Benefits of independent research/project work.
- The benefits of working with others.
- Places to meet other postgraduates.
- Online research groups and organisations.
- Setting up your own group.
- Tips for success when working with others.

The role of research in a university

Traditionally, universities have embraced two substantive purposes: to provide *teaching* for a range of students at a variety of levels, and to conduct *research* – broadly defined as pure or applied. Each of these purposes has been of mutual benefit to the other – results of research can inform our teaching, and teaching within a subject or discipline area can focus our expertise in a given area to the benefit of any subsequent research we may conduct. Research therefore has a crucial role to play in a university. Some commentators, analysts and even funders of research believe that research within specific areas is a specialised endeavour and, as such, should be reserved for the few. Recent initiatives and reports have suggested concentrating research by carefully selecting those institutions, departments and academics who are best placed to carry it out (Adams et al., 2000; Adams et al., 2002).

Through this process research excellence can be achieved. This approach is more prevalent in certain fields or disciplines (particularly the Natural Sciences), where critical mass in research effort and outputs is best achieved through clustering research within and between a limited number of (usually) large institutions.

An acknowledgement of the research environment in your field or discipline area will enable you to consider where and between whom your networking, research development and collaboration efforts should concentrate. Already, in Chapter 3 (Where to study and apply for funding), we have discussed how you can identify institutions that are active in research, determined by the level of output produced by academics. But it is often equally important to develop and nurture networks with other researchers (or novice academics). Networking or collaborating with other like-minded individuals has long been seen to enhance research effort and related outputs (Smith and Katz, 2000). This is so both within institutions (thereby facilitating optimum levels of interactions between researchers – often referred to as 'critical mass'), and across institutional, regional and national boundaries (helping researchers, academics and institutions to achieve national and international research/academic excellence through their combined collaborative efforts). This chapter outlines the various options available to postgraduates to develop research abilities through networking, negotiating and collaborating with other researchers and academics.

Independent researchers

BECOMING A RESEARCHER

For many, the shift from undergraduate to postgraduate study can be a major change to the way they experience higher education. Whilst undergraduates may rightly claim to be independent learners, at postgraduate level you are much more responsible for the direction, shape and development of your own learning. The crucial skills and experiences gained whilst studying as a postgraduate will enable learners to take advantage of a variety of careers following completion of their studies – not just those within the higher education sector. In work conducted for the Higher Education Staff Development Agency, careers advisers at the universities of Leeds, London, Newcastle and Wales (Swansea) have compiled interview- based case studies of the career paths of former academic researchers. It is clear from the example below from history student Mark, that the ability to work independently and develop skills of self-reliance – focused and honed as a postgraduate – are important in a whole host of work situations within and beyond higher education.

I enjoyed the research and using evidence to develop an argument. In particular, I enjoyed making use of several different archives and using interview as a research technique. ... I did not want to stay in academia and decided instead to obtain a professional qualification. ... The main parallels with academic research are using evidence to construct an argument and looking in different sources to find supporting information. ... The main difference is the amount of interaction with people – both clients and colleagues. ... In my current profession I use various skills that I gained as a researcher:

* Writing skills;
* The ability to read quickly, extract key information and deploy it succinctly in argument;
* Presentation skills;
* The ability to complete work to a deadline;
* The ability to organise one's own workload. (The Higher Education Staff Development Agency – Career paths of academic researchers; http://www.hesda. org.uk/subjects/rs/case.html accessed 29/3/04)

Working at postgraduate level requires that students quickly and effectively develop as self-sufficient, independent learners. Becoming an independent student can mean different things to different people. It can require determination, perseverance, humour, and an ability to rely on your own initiative to coordinate and manage your own professional development. We have discussed the importance of planning for your own development in Chapter 8 (Working with your supervisor), but what are the typical roles, responsibilities and functions of researchers or postgraduates? In background research during the development of this text, a number of students were asked to express what they understood to be the typical characteristics of students independently operating within their fields of enquiry.

Independent research – time to reflect

I've felt extremely supported as an independent student. My experience at this institution has included a lot of people making themselves available to me and helping me when I might have had any difficulties. One of the biggest changes for me, in

(Continued)

(Continued)

terms of becoming an independent student, has been the lack of emotional or leadership obligations that were present in the job I had before beginning my PhD. Outside the university [in the world of industry], things are always rushed – you have very little time and few resources to do things with. Here you've got the absolute luxury of being able to read whatever takes your fancy and see if it's got anything to do with your interests. So there's a more relaxed and reflective part of your brain that's really encouraged to get working. An example of how it all comes together is that at the end of last month I gave a presentation on my research. I had already given a similar talk two years ago as a practitioner in the area. This time, though, I was coming in as both a practitioner and a researcher and my presentation was much more solid. It was a much more reflective, thoughtful piece.

Sarah, ESRC 1 + 3 student, London School of Economics.

Independent research – networking

I want to expose my work to as many people as possible. If I can get it past five academics or researchers, then it's probably okay. People approach the same work in different ways and so when I expose my work to people who are not familiar with the topic or what I'm trying to say, they know if I'm not writing clearly enough. The ethos of the department is that everyone's very open: you can go to people and ask them questions. In reality, some are more willing than others: everyone is busy. Since I've focused my topic – I don't think I could have done it earlier – I've started to go to

(Continued)

(Continued)

conferences and workshops to meet specific people outside my university but in my specialism. They've been very helpful. I'm very much a believer in face-to-face contact. They see your face and remember who you are the next time you see them.

Adam, ESRC 1 + 3 student, University of Oxford.

Independent research – focused work

Working at postgraduate level enables you to really focus on your own work and plan your own study timetable. I still keep in contact with my tutors and I've had extra meetings with them just to discuss anything that may be relevant to my dissertation. I also meet up occasionally with other students but this is on a very informal basis to talk about my subject. I think that in the main, working at postgraduate level involves working alone because nobody else is really doing the same subject as you. This is great for me because I really enjoy working on my own – I enjoy seminars and talking to other people but I think research is something best done alone.

Stephanie, ESRC 1 + 3 student, Aberystwyth University.

As all of these case studies highlight, the notion of an independent researcher embraces a variety of issues and topics. For Sarah, a key to her independent study has been the opportunity to be reflective and analytical in her work – a luxury often denied her in her former life in industry. Adam's experiences indicated that he found value in networking, or sharing initial thoughts, with his colleagues. For others, such as Stephanie, independence in research includes a high degree of self-sufficiency in working alone, whilst recognising that others can provide focused assistance and guidance when required.

Other researchers

Whilst it is important to operate as independent and self-reliant researchers, it would be foolish to suggest that you should seek to complete your studies without making contact with your peers. Communicating and working with other post-graduates or researchers can be a valuable aspect of your studies. As Gareth and Jeff indicate below, others may have made, or be about to make, similar mistakes as you – it is therefore worthwhile to exchange experiences.

> *There's one really good reason to become involved with other postgraduates – they've made all the mistakes! They can tell you what not to do.*
>
> Gareth, ESRC 1 + 3 student, University of Edinburgh.

> *Contact with people who are going through the same thing is really useful because, actually, a problem shared is a problem halved. It's great when you talk to people who are further down the path of their PhDs. They can tell you about pitfalls you might face, they can tell you things like: 'In six months time, you will definitely feel like you are not getting anywhere with your work. It's normal to feel like that!'*
>
> Jeff, ESRC 1 + 3 student, University of Hull.

Postgraduate research colleagues can usefully provide feedback on your draft work (as indicated in Adam's networking example above), perhaps spotting errors or omissions that you, being too close to the material, cannot see. In addition, when working with academics, your fellow postgraduates can inform you as to the most 'prickly' members of staff, or the most eccentric – they might even suggest strategies for dealing with them. More experienced postgraduates (perhaps those in the later stages of their research) might be able to offer seasoned advice about what to expect in the different stages of your research journey. For example, how long progress meetings typically take, and when to shut up and just accept it if a senior professor criticises your work.

I think it is important to know a little about how the university works. If you need help, guidance or support, you can't underestimate working with other researchers, working with people who can provide contacts, people who are a year or two ahead of you and have made the same mistakes that you are about to make. They are also the ones who are likely to keep you sane. It's not a competition at postgraduate level. You can work quite well together and support each other.

Claire, ESRC 1 + 3 student, University of Birmingham.

Universities are typically huge organisations and obtaining (and understanding) all the procedural notes and guidance in relation to your programme of study can prove difficult. As Claire suggests, the collective interpretation of these can be shared through discussions with those in a similar position to yourself. Additionally, if postgraduate colleagues are conducting work in a broadly similar area to you, they may be able to offer useful guidance in selecting external examiners or academics who might be able to assist your work. In addition, working with other researchers need not be restricted to your own institution. As Peter outlines below, it is often beneficial to make contact with fellow researchers, following-up on material they have presented at conferences or published in academic journals.

A good way of building research competence and developing links with other researchers is to email them. For example, you might read some of their work and then make contact with them to comment upon it or seek further information. I am going to

(Continued)

(Continued)

New Zealand to carry out some of my work and that is purely down to reading someone's work and getting in touch with them to discuss it and seek further information. You know, normally you get an email address with the abstract of a piece you might read. I had a few questions I wanted to ask about the work done by this particular author so I emailed him and we discussed the issues electronically.

This approach is also fantastic for collecting conference information – I've often obtained lists of presenters at conferences and have emailed them for their abstracts or papers they presented. Often, they are more than happy to send you materials related to their work.

Peter, ESRC 1 + 3 student, University of Leeds.

Perhaps the most important aspect of working or communicating with other post-graduates is that they are useful support groups – keeping your spirits up when your work is criticised, your PC crashes, or your fieldwork is unavoidably delayed. That is not to say, though, that your networking and collaborative efforts should just be restricted to fellow postgraduates. Sarah, a PhD student based at the London School of Economics, believed that effective networking activities (within and outside her own institution) could enable her to consider other data sources, as she explains below.

You don't know what you don't know! I was aware that there must be swathes of fascinating stuff about my research area that I just had no idea about. So the first thing I did when I started my PhD was not only to associate with other postgraduates but to go off and find academics inside and outside my institution working in fields relevant to me. I went back to my

(Continued)

(Continued)

knowledge base from my previous employment and found out who these people were and where they worked. I simply sent out emails inviting them for a coffee. That provided me with contacts in Geography and the Development Institute at the London School of Economics and at Durham University. My impression is that academics are very keen to help people who are clearly enthusiastic about their topic and are very open to meeting up. Postgraduates should remember that academics are always looking to develop their own work, and if you've got something to offer them which is outside but relevant to their experience, they are often prepared to help you out.

Sarah, ESRC 1 + 3 student, London School of Economics.

THE BENEFITS OF WORKING WITH OTHERS

* Other postgraduates can provide feedback on your draft work.

* Your fellow postgraduates can tell you who to avoid.

* You can learn from each other's mistakes.

* You can share information on procedures and processes.

* You can support each other during low moments in your studies.

* You can build each other's confidence by sharing experiences.

In her substantive review work of doctoral students experiences, Rita Brause (2000) adds to these advantages of sharing experiences:

* They explain the details which somehow seem to escape the attention of the faculty.
* They help to figure out what is expected at different points in the process.
* They share their information about what happens at Vivas.
* They suggest some strategies for dealing with professors.
* They explain how they went about writing their 'literature review'.

- They tell you where to get useful university documents detailing the dissertation process.
- They help to pick up the pieces after your work has been criticized in front of your peers.
- They share their progress with you, helping you to learn from their experiences.
- They take time to celebrate with you when you have reached an important stage.
- They keep you focused when you become discouraged.
- They work with you in collecting and/or analyzing your data.
- They suggest how your ideas can be presented more clearly.
- They proofread your text.
- They seek your advice, learning from your experiences. (Brause, 2000: 71)

Upon first being introduced to fellow postgraduates, you will, no doubt, quickly establish areas and topics of mutual interest. However, to assist with potentially awkward initial meetings, there are a number of ice-breaking questions you might put to one another, including some of the following:

- How did you work with Professor Smith/Dr Green?

- What research strategies might you suggest I use/don't use?

- What particular problem areas have you thus far encountered with your research?

- How often do you meet with Professor Smith/Dr Green?

- Do you need to confirm appointments with them?

- What are Professor Smith/Dr Green like at keeping appointments?

- Are appointments with Professor Smith/Dr Green at times to suit you?

- Are Professor Smith's/Dr Green's comments on your draft work useful or overly critical?

- How long is the average supervision session and who sets the agenda?

- Are there any opportunities (or are you expected) to publish work with Professor Smith/Dr Green?

- What tips can you give me if things don't work out as I expected in my research?

- Is teaching expected of postgraduates in this department? If yes, what's the pay like?

- To supplement my income, where are the best paid teaching opportunities?

(Adapted from Brause, 2000: 73)

PLACES TO MEET: POSTGRADUATE SOCIETIES AND GROUPS

So where might you be able to ask your ice-breaking questions? Some university departments encourage postgraduates and researchers to organise discussions and support groups to enable students to network and collaborate on their research. In departments with small postgraduate numbers, or the individual postgraduate researcher, the University Postgraduate Society is often deemed to fulfil this role.

> *We have a postgraduate society here at Hull and we put together themes, for example focusing on first days out in the field, presenting your first paper, etc. – all sorts of topics to help postgraduates navigate through their research degree programme. They are quite informal events (usually with about six to eight people present), and we sit around with a glass of wine and discuss the theme of the day/evening. And what is really useful is that there are students there who are all at different stages of their PhDs – so you get lots of different perspectives on it.*
>
> Jeff, ESRC 1 + 3 student, University of Hull.

It is clear, from Jeff's example, that his experience of the Postgraduate Society is as a support group to aid the postgraduate journey, with group members offering guidance and support based upon their own shared and individual experiences. At the departmental level, Peter's group working experiences are more formal events, focusing upon discussions around a given theme or topic.

> *Within the department here we do something called 'PG Tips'. These are postgraduate talks (from those currently engaged in postgraduate research – so could be year 1 students or could be year 3 students), that are held every other week at lunchtime*
>
> *(Continued)*

(Continued)

for about an hour. The format of these is usually a 20-minute talk or presentation followed by discussion or questions. There are often five to ten people present. I've done two of these – they aren't just talks, they are more formalised discussion groups or seminars really. You put your name down to lead one and suggest the topic and provide some input to other postgraduates present on this. They are really useful in helping to develop presentation skills.

Peter, ESRC 1 + 3 student, University of Leeds.

Many universities have excellent Postgraduate Societies and support groups. For the few that don't, or that have inappropriate groups for your needs, you might consider starting your own group or community within your department, faculty or across the university. What might you need to consider? A starting point is to arrange an initial meeting with as many of your postgraduate colleagues as possible to 'test the water' for establishing a society or group. At such a meeting you should put forward your ideas and intentions for the group and ask others to do the same – perhaps brainstorming what everyone would like to get out of future meetings. If appropriate, you may be able to secure support and guidance for the society or group from postgraduate tutors and other academics. As Jeff and Peter indicate in their comments above, you may wish to structure your meetings around set themes and allow participants to lead on subjects/areas of interest to them. Perhaps suggesting a rotating Chair of the group or society may be an effective way to share the management of the group meetings? However and whenever your group decides to meet and work, the importance of these first tentative steps into networking and liaising with your fellow postgraduates/researchers cannot be underestimated. For many well-established academics, some of their most fruitful collaborations are as a result of networks developed whilst training as a researcher or postgraduate. These valuable networks therefore have the potential to provide some of the substance of an academic's cultural capital. Some discipline areas (particularly those in the broadly-based Natural Sciences) are more prone to networking and collaboration among and between their research staff, having long traditions of operating in such ways (Delamont et al., 2004: 29).

In recognition of the need to nurture and develop multi-institutional working, a number of organisations committed to research, through various, funded initiatives, has facilitated successful collaboration between researchers and academics. One example is the ESRC Research Seminar Competition. This annual event (summary information is provided below) seeks to assist those engaged in scholarly activity to share their ideas and develop useful working partnerships for future research activities.

ESRC Research Seminars Competition

The Economic and Social Research Council invites applications for the Research Seminars Competition 2004–5. Seminar Groups are multi-institutional groups of academic researchers, postgraduate students and non-academic users who meet regularly to exchange information and ideas with the aim of advancing research within their fields. Where appropriate, Seminar Group members should be drawn from industry, government departments and other relevant organisations as well as from academic institutions. We would particularly encourage Seminar Groups explicitly designed to bring together leading researchers from across disciplines to identify new research agendas or capacity-building priorities. We would encourage applications from existing ESRC Seminar Groups with demonstrable dynamism, where the ESRC remains the most appropriate funding source, as well as new groups.

Funding is available for UK higher education institutions and Independent Research Institutes (approved by the ESRC) to undertake these research seminars. For this year's competition, the ESRC expects to make approximately 40 awards of up to £15,000 each for a maximum period of two years.

Of the 200 applications received under last year's competition, 46 awards were made, which represents a success rate of 23%. The closing date for applications is Monday, 14 February 2005.

Source: The Economic and Social Research Council (http://www.esrc.ac.uk).

Face-to-face contact with other postgraduates and researchers is a useful way to discuss your work and seek advice on it from those in a similar position to you. However, more and more communication and collaboration between postgraduates is taking place virtually via email and the web. There are a number of services and facilities to support academics and researchers in their work, and whilst we do not intend to critique each and every one of them, two services of particular use include Researchtogether.com and the Connect service (see below). These resources, as do a number of similar services, allow academics and researchers to share their work with other like-minded people across and beyond the UK. Services such as these are, perhaps, useful starting points for those keen to develop their own research networks beyond the boundaries of their own institutions.

Researchtogether.com

Researchtogether is an internet-based service targeted primarily at researchers and academics operating in the HE environment. It has been developed by academics at Sheffield, and it has its base there.

Access to the basic service is free, once you've registered, and here you can find articles related to research, postgraduate study, networking events, etc. For a small charge (currently £10 per year), you can register for full access to the services provided. This includes services such as 'file safe' – a password-protected area that allows you to upload and download your work in progress to a secure area which can be read from anywhere with internet access. This is a useful service if you are conducting fieldwork away from your institution. User forums and expertise search facilities enable you to link up with other researchers and academics working in similar areas as your own. The Researchtogether service is an international service, so it may be possible to make national and international contacts in your area. As a way of disseminating and sharing your work, it is possible to 'post' material and add abstracts and keywords for other users to search through.

Source: Researchtogether.com (http://www.researchtogether.com).

Connect

Connect is the learning and teaching portal project funded by the HE Academy and the Joint Information Systems Committee (JISC). It's aim is to draw together, through one access point or 'portal', information on all aspects of teaching and learning. The project is an evolving service, but already has the following components available for use by researchers and academics:

(Continued)

- A funding opportunities database that allows users to identify opportunities for funding of projects and services related to learning and teaching. This includes tools for management of the content and for users to view and search the data through a variety of criteria, including sector, region, discipline and type of funding.
- An organisations database which lists UK agencies involved in quality enhancement of teaching and learning in both further and higher education. The database contains more than 100 entries and can be searched on a variety of criteria, such as sector, discipline, region or theme.
- A resources search facility which enables users to locate different learning and teaching support materials and resources from a wide range of sources. Searches are targeted at URLs specifically related to learning and teaching, and so return resources currently not accessible from other web searches.
- A discussion forum which includes a range of online tools and services to enable the more sophisticated management of virtual discussion events.
- Projects, a searchable database listing details of more than 1,000 learning- and teaching-related national projects.

Source: Connect (http://www.connect.ac.uk).

Research groups

One way of securing detailed, relevant information and data for your project/ research is to join a research group of similar individuals as yourself who have the same or vaguely similar research interests. Reasons for joining, or indeed starting, research groups vary. Nick, a postgraduate student from Oxford, provides a useful summary below, based upon his own experiences.

[Nick organises a seminar series in the department, open to external speakers, on 'classroom-based research']

I wanted to do that because there weren't a lot of seminars around that were about classrooms and there are so many

(Continued)

(Continued)

experts around the department: the teacher educators all do classroom-based research [and] there's at least five PhD students doing some also. I also thought it would be a nice way to get my name known to people. I got to write to outside academics and invite them to give seminars and that was really good because I suppose it's a self-esteem thing. My name's not really out there yet; I'm not in huge numbers of journals but I want people to know me. I guess it's good for my CV as well. It started when I asked Kathy [Sylva, Chair of the Research Committee] and she said 'yes' and gave me £150 to get things off the ground. I had to draw up a list of potential speakers who reflected a lot of different subjects and fields. It's a huge amount of work – more than I ever anticipated – arranging dates and dealing with dates that clash, hotel bookings, travel expenses, publicity and worrying about whether or not people will come along. But it's all worth it to be the Chair of a seminar that lots of important and senior people from inside and outside the department have turned up to.

Nick, ESRC 1 + 3 student, University of Oxford.

Research groups can provide fantastic support for your work, broadening the exploration and examination of issues usually beyond the physical boundaries of your department or institution. As a result of the increasing use of the internet by academics and researchers, many such groups now 'meet' in a virtual sense, but there still remain a number of groups who utilise the 'real time' meeting to good effect. The British Educational Research Association (BERA) have a number of special interest groups (SIGs) that arrange semi-formal meeting sessions at regular intervals through the year. These SIGs, in a similar way to meetings you may organise with research groups in your own institution, will develop agendas for meetings and raise issues of interest to members. The major benefits of becoming a member of a research group, in addition to working more locally with other researchers, is that your work is introduced to a wider audience, you are introduced to different perspectives on issues related to your work, and you see how other researchers, from other institutions, work and operate – all important considerations for postgraduate study and beyond.

SEARCHING FOR GROUPS

Your supervisor or postgraduate tutor may be able to offer guidance in seeking out appropriate research groups to support your studies. They may be members themselves, and as such can provide an insight into their workings, politics, and the quality of materials and ideas discussed or debated. Conferences are also useful events through which to identify suitable research groups – some events now set time aside within the programme for identified groups to meet. If they don't, keynote speakers or other presenters may be able to provide guidance during key networking times – such as coffee and lunch breaks. Conference organisers will gladly tell you of events supported or promoted within the main conference and they may even be able to guide you to other events that also enable researchers to work and communicate their ideas in this way (we provide some other useful tips and guidance on how to get the most out of conferences later in this chapter – see pages 214–15).

The internet enables access to a wide range of interest and research groups so finding one that is appropriate for your work might prove to be a lengthy exercise. The Social Sciences Information Gateway (SOSIG) provides a coordinated entry site to a range of internet-based resources for those engaged in Social Science research work. It receives funding and support from the ESRC and Joint Information Systems Committee, and is hosted through the Institute for Learning and Research Technology at the University of Bristol. A simple search for issues relating to central and local government provides a number of returns, including details of the Centre for Local and Regional Government Research, based at Cardiff University. Included within this site is a 'forum' facility whereby those interested in discussing local and regional government issues can make contributions and network with others.

The Social Science Information Gateway (SOSIG)

What is SOSIG?
SOSIG is a freely available internet service which aims to provide a trusted source of selected, high-quality internet information for students, academics, researchers and practitioners in the Social Sciences, Business and Law. It is part of the UK Resource Discovery Network.

SOSIG Internet Catalogue
The SOSIG Internet Catalogue is an online database of high-quality internet resources. It offers users the chance to read descriptions of resources available over

(Continued)

(Continued)

the internet and to access those resources directly. The Catalogue points to thousands of resources, and each one has been selected and described by a librarian or academic. The catalogue is browsable or searchable by subject area.

Social Science Search Engine
This is a database of over 50,000 Social Science Web pages. Whereas the resources found in the SOSIG Internet Catalogue have been selected by subject experts, those in the Social Science Search Engine have been collected by software called a 'harvester' (similar mechanisms may be referred to as 'robots' or 'Web crawlers'). All the pages collected stem from the main internet catalogue. This provides the equivalent of a Social Science search engine.

Social Science Grapevine
Grapevine is the 'people-oriented' side of SOSIG, offering a unique online source of career development opportunities for Social Science researchers in all sectors. Grapevine carries details of relevant training and development opportunities from employers and training providers. Researchers can also make their CVs available online which are freely accessible to all visitors to the site. Grapevine's Likeminds section provides a forum for the exchange of ideas and information about potential research opportunities and partnerships. If you want to find contacts in your field, you can also check the Social Science departmental database.

Source: Social Sciences Information Gateway (SOSIG) (http://www.sosig.ac.uk/about_us/what_is.html) (Accessed 26/9/04).

There are a host of organisations that support or coordinate internet-based groups or forums. For example, within the broad area of 'education', the British Educational Communications and Technology Agency (BECTA) supports a wide range of email discussion groups related to various aspects of education. One example is the Special Educational Needs Coordinators (SENCOs) forum (http://lists.becta. org.uk/mailman/listinfo/senco-forum). This forum is a service provided for SENCOs and others (including researchers) involved with supporting children with special educational needs. Joining internet-based groups can be as simple as subscribing to the group through email (as is the case with many of the BECTA-supported groups/forums), or may involve completing a registration form.

Examples of networking/discussion events include those hosted by the Society for Research into Higher Education (SRHE). The event detailed below was recently promoted by the research organisation, with the aim of bringing together those interested in the subject of student learning. Professors Ainley (University of Greenwich) and Murphy (University of Nottingham) coordinated the event which enabled attendees to get together and learn from each other with a view to developing related research and other work. Such events are excellent opportunities for postgraduates to listen to the views of others, explain their own work and develop useful working relationships and networks with other researchers or academics operating within the same or similar areas. Many discussion networks or forums such as the ones promoted by SRHE, BERA and other subject or discipline groups are open to both members and non-members (although the costs of attending for non-members are usually higher than for members).

A networking event for researchers and academics

Tuesday 22 June 2.00 pm to 5.00 pm
SRHE, 76 Portland Place, London W1B 1NT

Convenors: Professor Patrick Ainley, University of Greenwich for SRHE
Professor Roger Murphy, Nottingham University for BERA

Open to all interested in or working in this area of research into what students learn, their wider experiences and the anthropology of student life to compare the value of study at different Higher Education Institutions.

Are today's students learning more or less or something different compared with the recent past? Or does what they learn depend, as ever, on what and where they study? So does it make sense to assert that there ever was a common culture of 'higher' education? And what could be 'higher' – as compared to 'further' – about it? Can it survive commodification by fees? In short, are today's students tomorrow's knowledge workers in a brave new information economy, or is this what has been called 'The Bamboozling of a Generation'?

Scholars and researchers in this country and elsewhere are increasingly concerned with these questions and various projects have made a start towards answering them. This meeting will be an opportunity for us to get together and learn from each other with a view to taking the work forward.

Cost of the meeting is £10 for SRHE members (either individual or corporate) and £15 for non-members. Coffee and tea will be available throughout the afternoon.

Source: The Society for Research into Higher Education (http://www.srhe.ac.uk).

An innovative way in which postgraduates, researchers and academics can work together to establish areas for potential research is through a 'sand pit' event. Sand pits are intensive discussion forums (usually lasting a day or two) where free-thinking and brainstorming about a subject or issue is encouraged in order to delve deeper into the problems on the group's agenda. An example of a sand pit event, promoted by the Engineering and Physical Sciences Research Council (EPSRC) and the Economic and Social Research Council (ESRC) is provided below. Some links are now being developed with other funding agencies to develop similar initiatives.

A sand pit for ideas

The focus of this sand pit is to explore ways of better understanding the causes of the UK's productivity problem. This sand pit will be led by an academic Director, whose role will be to define the topic and facilitate discussions at the sand pit event. For each topic, a pre-determined amount of research funding is made available, with the aim of developing an adventurous multidisciplinary research programme. Topics to be considered include:

- Novel methods for modelling productivity and its determinants, especially at the micro-level in both manufacturing and service sectors and the public and private domains.
- Methods for modelling the interactions between macro-economic policy drivers and micro-level activities within organisations (or sub-units within organisations), to take account of population, selection and individual effects.
- Better understanding of the role of factors other than labour and capital.

Source: The Engineering and Physical Research Council (http://www.epsrc.ac.uk/Content/CallsForProposals/2005CallForIDEASTopics.htm) (Accessed: 14/1/05).

SETTING UP YOUR OWN GROUP

If, following your investigations, you conclude that no suitable group(s) exist in relation to your work, you may wish to set up your own group. In Nick's example (see page 20 above), he felt that other groups did not discuss the central issue of his research interest – classroom-based research – so he set about developing his own research group. This can be a time-consuming but very rewarding activity to undertake –

rewarding in the sense that you will be developing and enhancing your networking skills, and also discussing and debating topics of direct relevance to you and your work.

As a starting point in developing your group, you may wish to gauge the potential for membership of the group by speaking with fellow researchers in your own institution and others (for example, at conferences and training events). If the reaction is positive (i.e. others would be interested in joining or contributing), you can then move on to the organisation of the group. Perhaps begin by collecting the contact names, addresses and, more helpfully, email addresses of all interested parties and arrange a mutually convenient time and place to meet. This might not be as easy as it sounds due to problems caused by conflicting timetables, fieldwork duties, teaching commitments and other logistical difficulties. A solution might be to suggest a range of dates and times and decide upon the one that most colleagues can make. As with Nick's example above, it is often easier for the organiser of a research group to organise a meeting at his or her host institution (you may decide at your first meeting to rotate the location of future meetings between group membership institutions). As guidance provided for working with others (earlier in this chapter) indicates, a great deal of working and communication that currently takes place between postgraduates is now online and virtual. Drawing upon the services provided by organisations such as 'Connect' and 'Researchtogether', you may well be able to develop collaborative links with other researchers and develop an online research group. Much of the guidance for starting your own institutional postgraduate society (detailed earlier) applies to starting your own research group, as do the benefits of working and collaborating with your peers.

ATTENDING CONFERENCES

Attending conferences is an effective way of networking with others, sharing ideas about your work and keeping up to date in your chosen field of study. Your supervisor or tutor should be able to suggest some useful conferences for you to attend, but they will probably encourage you to search out relevant conferences for yourself. Checking postgraduate noticeboards at your institution is a good way to make yourself aware of upcoming events. Journals and some newspapers (*Guardian Education*, *Times Higher Education Supplement*, etc.) also provide details of forthcoming conferences. Through membership of your various research groups, you may have access to mailing lists in discipline or subject areas. Joining or subscribing to these lists will enable you to access information about relevant events in your research area.

It may be the case that you cannot attend a conference you are particularly interested in. In such a situation it may be worthwhile asking a colleague who is attending to collect a copy of the conference proceedings for you or, if this is costly, perhaps you can borrow theirs? If colleagues are also not attending, you can contact the conference organisers directly, and ask for the conference proceedings to be forwarded to you in due course – although some conference organisers charge for this to cover the costs of producing hard copies of materials presented. However, in order to disseminate information as widely as possible, many conference organisers now publish proceedings on the internet shortly after the conference has taken place.

Remember that there is much more to conferences than the papers presented at them. They are key networking events, useful advice-seeking venues, and can provide you with insights – during breakout sessions, intervals and meal breaks – of what researchers and academics are currently working on in your area.

Finally, just because something is presented at a conference does not *necessarily* mean it is good (although particularly poor conference papers should have been rejected at the review stage). Conference papers are usually reports on work in progress or initial, tentative, findings of research work. As such, they afford you insight into what is happening now in your area. For many, they are not meant to be carefully polished pieces of work; rather they are (often) useful explorations of what your colleagues are currently working on.

GETTING THE MOST OUT OF CONFERENCES

Conferences can provide excellent opportunities to meet new people and discuss ideas of relevance to your own research work. However, many people (the author of this text included) sometimes find making useful contact with others at such meetings difficult. However, there are a number of strategies and approaches you can employ to mitigate this:

- You can present a paper which introduces you (through your presentation), to a variety of people quickly and effectively. Those interested in your work may even approach you, following the session, to discuss aspects of it with you.

- Attend all or as many of the paper presentations as you can. By getting out there into the thick of it you are going to come into contact with many more people than if you just attend the odd session.

- By asking an interesting (and related) question to a presenter during the 'any questions' section of their session you will make yourself known (to the presenter at least) as being interested in what they have said. You may have a chance to discuss their material further during coffee or meal breaks.

- Utilise the resources already available to you. Ask your supervisor or colleagues from your host School, Department or institution to make the introductions for you. Most good tutors or supervisors will do this anyway.

- When nurturing a relationship with a new contact, try not to be too controversial in the things you say. Don't be *too* eager to let others know your views. Rather listen to what they have to say and make reasoned comments that respect their viewpoints.

- It is often useful to make some attempt to speak with the person next to you at a session. Introduce yourself and ask about their interests in the paper being presented.

- In readiness of new introductions, have your 'cocktail party' summary of your research well-planned in advance. This should be a short, perhaps two-sentence, summary of what your interests and research activities currently are.

- Having lunch with different people each day of the conference can be an informal way of getting to know others and what their interests are.

- After-conference drinks in the bar certainly relax the situation, but remember that moderation is helpful. You will need to have a reasonably clear head to remember the salient points of what people do and their research interests.

Having spent some considerable time (probably) at conferences making contact with others, it is crucial that you maintain and nurture fruitful and potentially fruitful relationships:

- Always follow-up on contacts made. If you offer to forward a working paper, then do so (as soon as possible) following the end of the conference.

- If you have exchanged email or contact addresses, it is useful to send a follow-up message to particularly useful contacts thanking them for their comment, discussion or guidance. If you need to access these people in the future, they will (often) remember such touches and be more likely to respond positively to any requests for assistance.

- If you did not get the chance to fully discuss an area of interest to you with your contact, suggest that you do this over the phone or via email. Or perhaps, if logistics and resourcing allow, offer to visit them at a mutually convenient time at their institution.

Tips for success

When you are working with other academics on a project, it's very useful to know what they want or expect out of the relationship. Their priorities may be different from yours. It is helpful to know who you are up against!

Professor Green, University of Northside.

Professor Green's comments indicate the importance of understanding the remit and scope of any collaboration in which you may become involved. If you intend to pursue an academic career, it will be almost impossible to work in isolation on all of your research activities. Working or collaborating with others increasingly forms part of the work of academics and postgraduate researchers.

WORKING WITH OTHERS – SOME GUIDANCE NOTES

The general guidance provided in this chapter is relevant when developing and nurturing working relationships with others. Experience and evidence collected from others as part of the research for this text highlights the following areas:

* When working with others, have clear outlines of responsibilities (preferably written and agreed at the outset of the collaborative endeavour) – these might prevent confusions and arguments emerging during the research as to who is responsible for what.

* Others may not have the same reasons for collaborating as yourself, so try to understand your collaborators and recognise that their objectives may not be exactly the same as yours.

* Try to be clear about the allocation of tasks within the collaboration – utilise yours (and others') strengths by deploying suitable collaborators to the areas of the research/project that most closely match their skills/expertise.

* If there is physical distance between collaborators, regular communication (through email, telephone, face-to-face contact or written correspondence) is crucial to facilitate the effective implementation of the research/project work.

* Remember that today's effective collaboration might lead to future collaborations with fellow researchers and academics.

Reference list and useful reading

Adams, J., Cook, N., Law, G., Marshall, S., Mount, D., Smith, D.N. and Wilkinson, D. (2000) *The role of selectivity and the characteristics of excellence – report to the Higher Education Funding Council for England; a consultancy study within the Fundamental Review of Research Policy and Funding.* Bristol: HEFCE.

Adams, J., Jackson, L., Law, G., Mount, D., Reeve, N., Smith, D.N. and Wilkinson, D. (2002) *Maintaining research excellence and volume – a report to the Higher Education Funding Councils for England, Scotland and Wales, and for universities UK*. Leeds: Evidence Ltd.

Brause, R.S. (2000) *Writing your doctoral dissertation*. London RoutledgeFalmer.

Deem, R. and Brehony, K.V. (2000) Doctoral students' access to research cultures – are some more unequal than others?, *Studies in Higher Education*, 25(2): 149–165.

Delamont, S., Atkinson, P. and Parry, O. (2004) *Supervising the doctorate: a guide to success*. Buckingham: Open University Press/SRHE.

Johnston, S. and Broda, J. (1996) Supporting educational researchers of the future, *Educational Review*, 48(3): 269–281.

Rugg, G. and Petre, M. (2004) *The unwritten rules of PhD research*. Buckingham: Open University Press.

Smith, D.N. and Katz, S. (2000) *Collaborative approaches to research – report to the Higher Education Funding Council for England; a consultancy study within the Fundamental Review of Research Policy and Funding*. Bristol: HEFCE.

West, M.A. (2003) *Effective teamwork: practical lessons from organisational research*. London: Blackwells.

Wisker, G. (2001) *The postgraduate research handbook: succeed with your MA, MPhil, EdD and PhD*. London: Palgrave.

10 Career planning

Chapter overview

This chapter summarises a number of issues related to career planning for post-graduates and those seeking to develop an academic career. Specifically, the chapter includes:

- Gaining experience in academia.
- Planning your career development.
- Options in academia – research and teaching.
- Tips for academic success.

There are a variety of employment routes available to you once you have completed your studies. You may decide to remain in academia, to teach or carry out further research work, or you may, as Caroline outlines below, decide to move out of higher education and into the 'real world'.

> *I've enjoyed my time at university conducting my postgraduate research work, but I don't wish to stay here and pursue an academic career. I find the environment very politically charged. Having this qualification (a PhD) will be extremely useful in the real world outside academia – it shows that I have advanced skills in research work. That's worth a lot.*
>
> Caroline, PhD student, University of Westside.

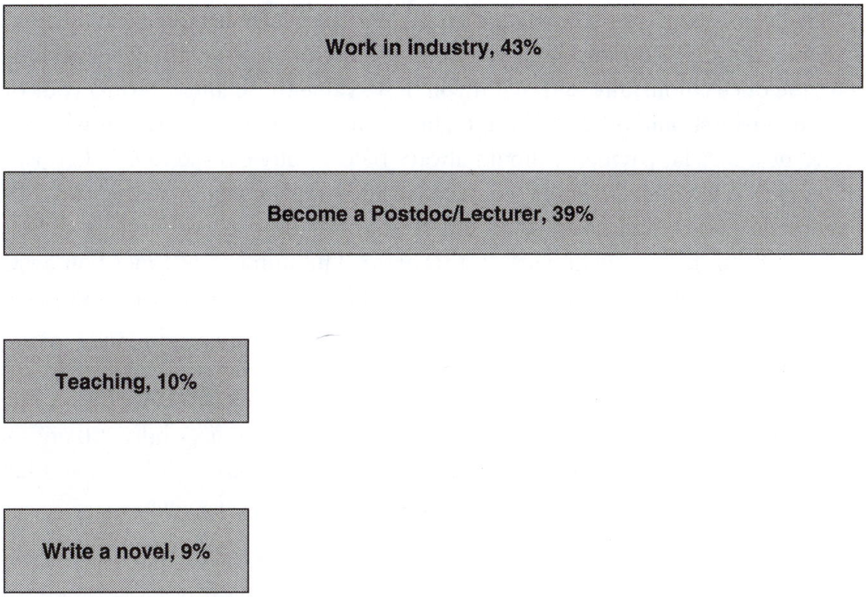

Work in industry, 43%

Become a Postdoc/Lecturer, 39%

Teaching, 10%

Write a novel, 9%

FIGURE 10.1 **What do you want to do after your PhD?**

Source: FindAPhD.com (http://www.findaphd.com/students/pollresults.asp)
(Accessed: 11/10/04)

Gaining experience

For many engaged in advanced level (particularly PhD) study, the preferred option is to remain in higher education and pursue an academic career – and that is the focus of this chapter. Entering the academic ranks can be difficult and competitive. As discussed earlier in Chapter 5 (finding your feet – the culture of academia), universities are peculiar places with cultures, conventions and understandings that may differ from those found in other work environments. Developing a profile in such an environment is important if you are to have any chance of being made aware of employment and other career development opportunities, and of being able to take advantage of them. Supervisors, tutors, peers and institutional or departmental websites (where the jobs are first advertised before appearing in the academic press) are useful places to start out if you are interested in staying on at your institution. Offering to conduct work for free (in order to gain experience) is another useful way of maintaining good links and contacts with your academic/research community. However, beware! There are still some unscrupulous colleagues out there who will gladly use your free knowledge and expertise whilst having no intention of recommending you for that junior academic post or post-doctoral fellowship. A colleague once colourfully said that if you don't value (in financial terms) your own time, then why should others? Undertaking such development work, for which you receive no financial payment, should always be carefully considered. What 'value' is it to you? Will you make more 'contacts' in academia by taking on the work? Will you broaden your skill base? Is it something you find interesting? Is there an opportunity to develop paid work in this area? The number of times you answer 'yes' to these questions should help you to decide whether taking on the work is a good idea or not.

Teaching experience and the acquisition of teaching duties are a valuable part of many postgraduate programmes, and they are crucial elements for those interested in pursuing an academic career. Pursuing teaching duties whilst still engaged in postgraduate study can be demanding, but the rewards, as both Peter, and Janet Cowper (1996) explain, can benefit your own personal development.

Shortly after I started my postgraduate programme, I was assigned a group of first-year undergraduates – working as a demonstrator for their practicals. This was quite good experience in learning the technique of explaining things to others and certainly helped to focus and hone my own teaching and explaining skills. Teaching provides some very valuable preparatory work for my viva.
Peter, ESRC 1 + 3 student, University of Leeds.

Inevitably, experience of teaching will feed back into all areas of a postgraduate's life, including their research and dissertation work. Moreover, the increased academic confidence and communication skills acquired through successful teaching experience will be significant personal gains for any postgraduate tutor. (Cowper, 1996: 26)

In their research work examining the postgraduate learning experience, Harland and Plangger indicated that teaching duties and responsibilities added considerable value to the professional development of postgraduates in a number of ways. The development and testing of ideas, facilitated by teaching, enables students to develop valuable transferable skills as well as providing a place to rehearse arguments and enter into a dialogue with a non-judgemental audience (Harland and Plangger, 2004: 80).

Other ways of developing as a researcher or academic, as discussed in Chapter 9 (working with other researchers), includes attending and presenting at conferences. In recognition of this development need, a number of funding organisations provide assistance to those engaged in scholarly activity. A recent example of this is the conference grants initiative funded by The Royal Society.

The Royal Society: Conference grants

The Royal Society conference grants support UK-based scientists either to present their own paper/poster or to chair a session at an overseas conference.

Subjects covered include all areas related to the Sciences, that is the disciplines in which the Society will elect researchers to the Fellowship of the Royal Society.

Applicants must have a PhD, or extensive experience at an equivalent level, by the date of conference. Applicants in the final year of their PhD can submit an application. If successful, the award will only be given subject to the confirmation of his or her PhD at the time of the conference.

Funding is for the first ten days of a visit where conference participation is the main or sole purpose of visit. Auxiliary visits to scientific institutions can be included up to a maximum of ten days, although the total duration of the visit can be longer.

Applicants can claim for their airfare, subsistence of up to £60 per day, and registration fees of up to £300.

Closing dates for applications are: 1 March, 1 June, 1 September, 1 December. Results are usually available within eight to ten weeks of the closing date and applicants are notified by email whether they have been successful or not. Conference grant holders will need to submit a final report by logging into e-GAP after returning from the conference.

Source: The Royal Society (http://www.royalsoc.ac.uk).

The use of personal development plans

On any programme of study it is important to organise and structure your studies in a way that will enable you to effectively monitor and map out your own progress along your postgraduate research journey. As Maureen indicates below, planning includes structuring your writing plans as well as other aspects of your professional development. Increasingly, postgraduate programmes have elements within them that are dedicated to personal development – helping students to identify what skills and knowledge they need to develop in order to complete their degree satisfactorily or pursue their intended career.

Reporting on your work at postgraduate level is no mean feat. If you think about it, up until this point the longest piece of writing a typical undergraduate student will have submitted will be no longer than about 6,000 words. At postgraduate level you have to structure and plan for a much larger project and research work – and that includes planning for all of the associated writing tasks (drafting work, structuring outlines, developing chapter frameworks, collating and presenting your information or data). With all of this going on, you need a very clear framework for writing up. This requires careful and deliberate planning, with appropriate chunks of time set aside throughout the programme to ensure that you complete your work within the allotted time frame.

Maureen, ESRC/CASE student, University of Leeds.

In their postgraduate guidance, the Economic and Social Research Council recognise the importance of the budding researcher or academic identifying key academic skills and nurturing their development. In addition, they detail a range of generic and transferable skills, the acquisition of which will be crucial for post-graduate researchers, who are charged with more proactively managing their research careers. To enable researchers to flourish and develop in a constantly changing work environment, ESRC guidance suggests skill development in:

* researching and retrieving information on opportunities for employment and continuing personal and career development through the use of new technology;
* networking and negotiation;
* critical self-awareness and evaluation of personal and career development needs;
* self-reliance in career planning and decision-making; and
* self-promotion and marketing. (ESRC, 2005: 23)

The range of subject-specific skills outlined by ESRC (and other research funding organisations) were discussed in Chapter 2 (Developments in postgradu-ate study). As part of your structured career planning, it might be useful to reflect upon this guidance and incorporate elements of it into your plan.

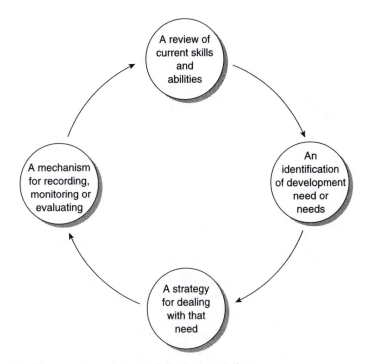

FIGURE 10.2 **The structure of personal development plans**

Part of the process of development and planning may involve postgraduates agreeing a plan for their research with their supervisor, department and/or institution, and recording this 'plan' within a broader personal development plan (PDP). Many institutions provide frameworks for PDPs and these can vary in their scope and the level of prescribed detail. Most formal plans are structured around:

• a review of current skills and abilities;

• an identification of development need or needs;

• a strategy for dealing with that need; and

• a mechanism for recording, monitoring or evaluating the effectiveness of the training or development undertaken.

Many interpret this as a cyclical process, where one element of the 'plan' builds upon its predecessor, as suggested in Figure 10.2.

A useful practical example of a personal development plan outline is the one used at City University for postgraduate students within the Centre for Professional Development and Innovation (see below). These forms are used by work-based students to help determine and frame their own learning and development on their programmes of study.

Personal development plans – an example

 **City University**
London

The University for business and the professions

Centre for Professional Development and Innovation

School of Arts

Professional development plan proforma

This plan serves the same purpose as a course programme does for a more conventional course. It allows you to create your own unique programme of study that meets your personal and professional interests and goals.

Use this proforma as a working document initially. Your professional development tutor will provide help and guidance at learning set and individual meetings. By the end of the Spring term you will need to present it more formally for agreement by City University and your employer.

The planning process helps you to work out and agree:

- where you are now
- where you want to be
- your route to getting there
- how you will know that you have got there
- planning your time

Your name:
Your Professional Development Tutor:
Date for review:
Date this plan was agreed with my employer:
Date this plan was agreed by City University Board:

Where you are now

This section helps to determine your current situation.

What experience do you have? What professional and academic qualifications do you have?

....

....

(Continued)

....

....

What are your current weaknesses and strengths and how can the programme of study help build and develop these?

....

....

....

....

Where do you want to be

This section helps you to identify what your professional goals are and how studying can help.

What are your professional and personal goals? Think about some of the work we have done at the development centres. How can a programme of study help you meet these? What benefits will studying on this programme bring you and your organisation? What is preventing you/your organisation from achieving your goals? How can these be mitigated or addressed/overcome?

....

....

....

....

What level of qualification are you aiming for? We have listed the possible qualifications in the appendix.

....

....

....

Your route to getting there

In this section you will provide a detailed action plan, determining what and how you are going to learn.

The first step is to determine your learning goals – derived from the work you have done above on your strengths, weaknesses, qualification objectives and professional goals.

(Continued)

(Continued)

What specifically are you setting out to learn? List your learning objectives in order of importance so that you can begin to develop a time frame. Over the course of the programme what are realistic and manageable learning goals? How will you manage these effectively? What are the milestones?

....

....

....

....

The second step is to decide what learning activities, strategies and resources you will use. The Professional Development Programme provides you with lots of options, including seminars, workshops, online materials, tutorials and action learning sets, work-based assignments and projects (see appendix). *Which ones will you use in order to help you to achieve your learning and qualification goals? What else might you do, e.g. in-house training programmes, taking on new job responsibilities, work-shadowing, find a mentor, etc.? What timescales will you impose on your learning activities? See appendix for an example action plan chart.*

....

....

....

....

How you will know that you have got there
This section will specify the evidence you will provide to prove that you have achieved your learning goals.

What work-based projects will you put forward for assessment? You may want to draw upon specific reports and plans produced for work or undertake a group assignment with your action learning set. You will need to agree with the help of your professional development tutor what exactly your assessed projects will be. The requirements for the Award are given in the appendix and relate to the type of qualification you want to undertake.

....

....

....

....

(Continued)

What kind of criteria will you use to assess your own learning? You are asked to keep a reflective learning log and at the end of your programme of study to produce an evaluative report on your learning experience. For example, What can I do better now than before? How can I demonstrate that learning has taken place? Have I got additional/further responsibilities or duties as a result of learning? What new skill, knowledge or experience have I gained? Do my colleagues/peers support my claims for learning achievement?

....

....

....

....

Planning your time

This section helps to work out a timetable for action.

What timescales will you impose on your learning activities? At first you need to start thinking about what time of the day and week you can set aside for study and for work-based assignments. How will they integrate with your current work?

....

....

....

....

Assessing your plan

Before implementing your plan you may wish to assess its value with reference to the following questions:

- What will you know or understand that you didn't before?
- Is your plan directly linked to your identified learning needs?
- How will your professional activities show what new skills/knowledge you have gained?
- Does your plan represent the learning you wanted to do?
- Will your plan help you in your work or in the understanding of a subject related to your work?
- Overall will the result of your plan justify the effort involved?

Source: City University, CPDI Work-Based Learning Programmes 2003–04

Should you decide to construct a development plan for your own studies, what else might usefully be included in it? In addition to any institutional guidance you may have access to through your supervisor, school or department, an informative document is the Joint Statement of the Research Council's/AHRB's Skills Training Requirements for Research Students (Metcalfe et al., 2002). This document identifies the key skills that postgraduate research students would be expected to develop during their research training. Skill areas are divided into seven themes: research skills and techniques; research environment; research management; personal effectiveness; communication skills; networking and teamworking; and career management. Chapter 2 (Developments in postgraduate study) details the full criteria associated with each of the skill areas. Completing the form provided as Table 2.1 (see page 24) may help you to identify your immediate and longer-term research needs.

I had a little bit of difficulty thinking about planning for the whole of my studies. After all, its three years, full-time, of solid work! My supervisor had seen the Joint Statement issued by the Research Councils and we discussed its content. Some of the areas within it were completely new to me. We hadn't really covered them much on my Masters programme. Perhaps we should have done. I found the skill areas incredibly useful really. If I want to become a reasonable researcher it's important that I have these skills.

John, PhD student, University of Southside.

Options in academia

RESEARCH

As part of any plans you may have to remain in academia, you should consider whether or not you wish to pursue a research-based career or a typical academic career. Key differences between research and typically academic careers, which include a core element of teaching, relate to security and pay. Traditionally, research posts in universities have been short-term contracts (a contract of a year or more is considered good, and many contracts are of shorter duration); pay for researchers is lower than comparable work conducted by traditional academics (university teaching staff are employed on the academic payscale). This being so, any postgraduates seeking to pursue a career in academia tend to apply for academic posts in attempts to gain security of position and favourable rates of pay. Opportunities do exist, however, for postgraduates to continue to develop their research and project skills once they have completed their programmes of study. Two excellent examples are available from the British Academy and The Leverhulme Trust (see below). Both of these schemes, and many others promoted by other research funding agencies, seek to support the continued development of research activities by those recently completing (usually postgraduate) university programmes of study.

The British Academy – Postdoctoral Fellowships

Postdoctoral Fellowships in the Humanities and Social Sciences

Up to 37 British Academy Postdoctoral Fellowships are offered, tenable for three years from autumn 2005, in a UK university or other institution of higher education. This scheme is designed to enable outstanding scholars who have recently completed their PhDs (or expect to do so by 30 June 2005) to pursue independent research and obtain teaching experience in any field of Humanities or Social Sciences.

Source: The British Academy (http://www.britac.ac.uk/funding/guide/pdfells.html).

The Leverhulme Trust – Early Career Development Fellowships

Closing Date: 15 March 2005

The Leverhulme Trust has available approximately 30 Fellowships to be offered in 2005. Their aim is to provide career development opportunities for those with a proven record of research who do not hold, or have not held, a full-time established academic post in a UK university or comparable institution in the UK.

Applicants should be, or have recently been, a member of the UK academic community and intend to remain so. They should also normally be under age 35 and hold an awarded doctorate or have equivalent research experience at the time of taking

(Continued)

(Continued)

up the award. Applications from those over 35 will be considered if they began their academic studies at a later age than usual or have had a career change/break. Those registered for a doctorate may apply only if they have submitted their doctoral thesis by the closing date, and confirmation of this will be required as part of the application procedure.

Fellowships, which are for 24 months, can be held at universities or at other higher education institutions in the UK and all fields are eligible and should be taken up between the beginning of the 2005/06 academic year and 1 May 2006.

The Trust will contribute 50% of each Fellow's total salary costs up to a maximum of £19,000 per annum; the balance is to be paid by the host institution.

Source: The Leverhulme Trust (http://www.leverhulme.ac.uk).

Postdoctoral fellowships and early career fellowships are extremely prestigious awards, which are made to postgraduates displaying exceptional research and academic potential. Competition for awards is fierce as the schemes are usually offered on a national competition basis. Less competitive (as a result of their more localised competition) are university fellowships. A number of university departments, schools or faculties offer a limited number of these on an annual basis. Details of these are usually published on university websites and in the education press (such as *Guardian Education* and the *Times Higher Education Supplement*).

TEACHING

Academic teaching careers in universities usually begin with a junior lecturer post or, as is becoming increasingly common, a teaching fellow post. In almost all universities, lecturer posts consist of three areas of work: a teaching load, administrative duties (such as module or programme leader, chairing exam boards, etc.), and research. This is not generally the case for teaching fellow posts. This variant on the lecturer post has emerged in recent years to combat the increasing numbers of students in universities who require contact time with teaching staff. The role of teaching fellow usually consists of a combination of teaching and administration of that teaching – research activity is not often part of the post. If you desire a career in teaching, then becoming a teaching fellow may be for you; if you wish to conduct research *and* teach, then the most appropriate option is to secure a position as a lecturer.

Many current postgraduates, who are charged with teaching duties in addition to their own research or project work, enjoy some of the attributes of teaching fellows and research assistants, as Peter summarises below.

A number of postgraduates in my department teach at undergraduate level. I suppose we are viewed as hybrids of teaching fellows and research assistants, because we are involved with teaching whilst also conducting our own research work. We get the best of both worlds really. An issue with typical teaching fellows is that they are employed just to do the teaching, whereas the problem with research assistants and research officers is that they only conduct their research work and perhaps don't interact with the department as much as PhD students do.

Peter, ESRC 1 + 3 student, University of Leeds.

A lecturership for those beginning their academic career typically includes some teaching (usually a heavier load than that assigned to a senior lecturer) and some course or programme responsibilities. As university departments and schools expand and develop new areas of provision, their needs for new teaching and research stock also increases. The advertised posts below display a number of typical roles and duties of junior academics beginning a university teaching and research career. Also indicated as part of these posts are the key skills required of applicants. You should consider, within your career plan, how you can develop these skills. Are there any opportunities to work with senior colleagues to develop these skills? Does your department or school provide training in these areas that you can undertake?

University of Leicester – Lecturer A/B in Criminology, Department of Criminology

Main purpose of the post

The post-holders will be responsible to the Head of the Department of Criminology and will undertake research, teaching, administration and other activities supporting the development of the department and enhancing its reputation, both internal and external to the university. Key skills required for the post include:

(Continued)

(Continued)

- Excellent academic qualifications relevant to Criminology/Criminal Justice, including a postgraduate qualification, or be engaged in or approaching completion of a PhD. Excellence in published work and a proven ability to produce quality research publications is essential, except in the case of a new lecturer where such potential must be clearly demonstrated. A proven record of experience in higher education would be advantageous.
- Ability to initiate and produce high-quality research and to publish either in peer-reviewed journals or with well-established book publishers.
- Evidence of quality research from a more experienced candidate and/or evidence of strong research potential from a less experienced candidate at the commencement of their career.
- Ability or potential to generate external funding (through research grants, contracts and other sources) to support research programmes.
- Ability to teach postgraduate and undergraduate students in lectures, seminars and tutorials, as well as occasional short study schools for distance-learning students.
- Ability to initiate curriculum developments and to take responsibility for the effective and efficient delivery of required teaching programmes.
- Good effective communication (oral and written) and presentation skills.
- Ability to liaise successfully with mature students, often with significant professional responsibilities, who are seeking to contextualise themselves intellectually and enrich their careers.
- Good interpersonal skills.
- Ability or potential to initiate work independently as well as part of a team on research and teaching programmes.
- Competency in IT and familiarity with a computerised environment, and an awareness of its relevance for teaching and research.

Source: University of Leicester (http://www.le.ac.uk/personnel/jobs/) (Accessed 19/1/05).

Royal Holloway, University of London – Lecturer in Economics, Department of Economics

Main purpose of the post

The main responsibilities of the post are: researching and publishing, at the international level of distinction; high-quality undergraduate and postgraduate teaching, including supervisors; actively contributing to the intellectual life of the department, including regular participation in departmental seminars; and contributing to the international standing of the department by presenting papers at other universities and conferences.

Key skills required for the post include

- First-class degree from top university or compensating strengths.
- Excellent PhD completed, or within 1 year of completion.
- Strong likelihood of publications in top Economic journals during probationary period.
- Strong analytical skills.
- Teaching experience desirable.
- Strong communication skills.
- Willingness to develop own career.

Source: Royal Holloway, University of London (http://www.rhul.ac.uk/Personnel/JobVacancies.htm).

Most lecturer positions in universities are structured around the following levels (progression through the levels equates to more senior posts and associated higher salaries): Lecturer A, Lecturer B, Senior Lecturer, Professor. Progression through these levels can take considerable time and is dependent upon a varying mix of teaching experience, administrative experience and often the amount and quality of publications produced (this is particularly so for the transfer from Senior Lecturer to Professor). A fuller discussion of the different roles and responsibilities of various teaching staff in universities is provided in Chapter 5 (Finding your feet – the culture of academia).

Tips for academic success

Throughout the development of this text, a wide range of fellow academics, post-graduates and researchers were consulted to explore their views and understandings of working in a UK university. Their comments, advice and guidance have shaped the text considerably, and the following 'key tips' in academic career planning and management have emerged. Those wishing to pursue an academic career could do much worse than considering the following:

* Make efforts as soon as possible into your academic careers to seek your own research project funding. This can be for quite small pots of funding initially – your efforts can continually grow from bidding experience. Securing research contracts will also aid your promotion prospects.

* Try to publish in respected journals. Target the ones that receive the most citations for the articles they publish. If you are aiming to promote yourself and your own work, and reach a wider audience/readership, this will be crucial.

* Network. Network. Network. Attend seminars, go to conferences, join special interest groups. Make sure you are out there mixing with other researchers and fellow academics. Many opportunities for academic advancement occur through networking with others.

* Join professional bodies associated with your discipline area, or those that encompass a variety of disciplines (such as the Higher Education Academy). Opportunities for advancement may emerge through these sources also.

* Regularly scan the employment sections of relevant publications. In education a good source is the *Times Higher Education Supplement*. Identify the ones that cover your discipline area and keep an eye on the jobs that are available and the types of skills they require. This information may suggest areas for your own skill development if you wish to angle your career in a certain employment direction.

* Learn from the experts. Speak with your fellow academics and friendly professors (yes, there are some out there!). Ask them how they did it and what specific advice, tips and guidance they can give to you.

Reference list and useful reading

Blaxter, L., Hughes, C. and Tight, M. (1998) *The academic career handbook*. Buckingham: Open University Press.

Blaxter, L., Hughes, C. and Tight, M. (1998) Telling it how it is: accounts of academic life, *Higher Education Quarterly*, 52(3): 300–315.

Brown, S. and Race, P. (2002) *Lecturing: a practical guide*. London: RoutledgeFalmer.

Cowper, J. (1996) Postgraduate training: an education for all, in D. Allan (ed.), *In at the deep end: first experiences of university teaching*. Lancaster: Unit for Innovation in Higher Education/Times Higher Education Supplement. pp. 25–37.

Delamont, S. and Atkinson, P. (2004) *Successful research careers: a practical guide*. Buckingham: Open University Press/SRHE.

ESRC (2005) *Postgraduate training guidelines 2005*. Swindon: Economic and Social Research Council.

Harland, T. and Plangger, G. (2004) The postgraduate chameleon, *Active Learning in Higher Education*, 5(1): 73–86.

Metcalfe, J., Thompson, Q. and Green, H. (2002) *Improving standards in postgraduate research degree programmes*. Bristol: Higher Education Funding Council for England.

Ramsden, P. (2003) *Learning to teach in Higher Education*. London: RoutledgeFalmer.

Reece, I. and Walker, S. (2003) *Teaching, training and learning: a practical guide*, (5th edn). Sunderland: Business Education Publishers.

Robson, E. (2003) The interview hurdle to postgraduate studies and the job market, *Journal of Geography in Higher Education*, 27(3): 349–354.

Publishing opportunities

Chapter overview

This chapter explores the opportunities for postgraduates to publish. Specifically, it includes:

- Reasons to publish.
- What to publish.
- Where to publish.
- Preparing your publication.
- The peer review process.

Why should you publish?

The pressure to publish is a prevalent feature of academic life, as Stephanie articulates below – what some academics have jovially referred to as a 'publish or die' philosophy. But should postgraduates, in the initial stages of their academic careers, be under this or similar pressure? There are certainly advantages associated with publishing your work, as this chapter discusses below.

This year, through the research training programme, we've really had it drummed into us that we should be publishing, especially from the Careers Department, which said that without publications we'd find it hard to get work. So I have been thinking

(Continued)

(Continued)

a lot about publishing. My supervisor has said, though, that it's something I shouldn't rush into too soon because in a few years time, when my writing style has improved, I might look back at what I'd published and wished I'd waited. This is the best advice I think I've been given.

Stephanie, ESRC 1 + 3 student, Aberystwyth University.

DISSEMINATION OF FINDINGS

Most of us want to share the exciting results of our work with others – and the even braver among us want critical feedback, comment and analysis of what we have discovered. Publishing allows this to take place. Sharing or disseminating our work with others opens our material (for better or worse) to wider professional scrutiny. It enables other researchers working in the same, or similar, fields to examine our work. Through publishing, our work is deemed to have reached an acceptable professional standard. Publishing research informs and facilitates communication about it – having read your interim results, a fellow academic may cite your work in his or her own material or contact you for clarification or comment on work in which he or she is currently engaged.

A key aim of publication is to contribute to the body of knowledge in the field. Most avenues of publication open to postgraduate researchers demand that the work you submit for publication is both original and adds to the collection of scholarly literature in the field. Postgraduate researchers engaged in doctoral study will already be aware of the need for their work to provide an original contribution to the field or discipline in which it is based. Providing an original contribution to the field enables researchers and fellow academics to develop a reputation and recognition in the field. Through publication, recognition will usually be national, and it is increasingly becoming international. Most respectable academic publications have an international audience. Again, through publication, your work will become more widely known.

In terms of communicating the message and general content of your research work, certain aspects of publication are particularly useful. Wherever you publish your work, it will usually result in the transfer of information and knowledge about your work to a wider audience than those associated with your own institution.

TO GET A JOB

Without doubt, and for better or worse, publishing your work enables other postgraduates, researchers, academics and policymakers to become familiar with your research or project work. It identifies you within a discipline area and can facilitate communication and networking with similar professionals working within the same field of study. In doing this, you will be better placed (through your networks) to become aware of actual opportunities or potential opportunities for future work within that environment. A list, or developing a track record, in publishing proves your academic credentials to potential employers. For one, it proves that you can articulate your ideas, results or findings in writing and to an acceptable professional standard. University departments, with an eye on the next Research Assessment Exercise, will be keen to appoint staff with established publication records, as both Peter and Yo indicate below.

> *If you want to get into academia what you have written (and had published) is very important because within universities they measure a lot of your success on how much you've published and where you've published. For me, I think it is important to publish my work in a journal that is accessible to the people I am researching.*
>
> Peter, ESRC 1 + 3 student, University of Leeds.

> *I think it is commonly accepted that if you want an academic career, then you have to have published. If you want someone to offer you a job, then you have to have a bibliography to your name.*
>
> Yo, ESRC 1 + 3 student, University of Lancaster.

In their excellent text on developing academic research careers, Sara Delamont and Paul Atkinson (2004) indicated that whilst published journal articles and papers do not provide immediate cash returns for the researcher (and we can reasonably include postgraduates here), they do have a longer-term financial value. The academic, if that is what postgraduates wish to become, who publishes regularly and in good-quality journals, compared to ones who do not, will secure rapid promotion up the academic pay scale. Delamont and Atkinson suggest that this difference between an academic who remains a lecturer and one who is promoted rapidly to senior lecturer can result in an income-earning difference (based on 2002 pay scales) of £140,000 (Delamont and Atkinson, 2004: 47).

OTHER FACTORS

The act of writing, redrafting, submitting, resubmitting, and writing some more actually improves your skill and ability to write succinctly and appropriately for different types of audience. If you find this hard to believe, think back to the first research proposal you submitted for a dissertation or PhD study – would you frame and discuss concepts, approaches, methodologies and research tools in the same way now you have undertaken part of your research journey? As you read more, and write more, your writing will improve.

Credibility with students can be a difficult thing to achieve, but through writing about and publishing your work, your academic credibility will be enhanced. Students also recognise that to publish work requires skill and exceptional standards in writing. When teaching, tutoring or supervising students, it adds greater authority to what you say if you have published work within the area. Although writing for publication can be very hard work (this text will have gone through numerous drafts, redrafts and heated arguments over its content before it reaches you), it can be very rewarding. To see your work in print for the first time is something academics don't easily forget.

The ability to publish your work, and to continue doing so, is obviously dependent upon your ability to write to an appropriate professional standard. For some, this comes easily; for others, including the author of this text, it takes considerable practice. Practising and developing the craft of academic writing can be achieved through participation in a number of writing activities. Blaxter, Hughes and Tight (1998) classify the various types of academic writing according to three stages of the academic career: initial career, middle career and later career.

In the initial career stage, in which most postgraduates will find themselves, you may gain valuable writing experience by:

* turning elements of your dissertation or thesis into monographs or journal articles;

* making applications for research funding; or

* developing teaching materials or seminar programmes.

In your middle career, you may be required to:

* review articles written by your peers;

* provide written commentaries for a role as an external examiner; or

* produce single-or joint-authored texts.

In later career writing, your skills will continue to develop through:

* the delivery of guest lectures;

* the development of policy papers or reviews; and

* the provision of expert opinions (Blaxter, Hughes and Tight, 1998: 140).

In short, your skills as a writer will never and should never, be complete. As you write more, you will learn more about the craft of academic writing.

In her summary of the needs or desires to publish, Abby Day (1996) lists many of the reasons above and assigns them to four main themes:

Because I have to – academics believe that in order to remain a part of the academic community they must also contribute to its body of knowledge through publication.

Because I want to get ahead – those who publish are in demand and therefore progress their careers. Those who publish in respected journals are themselves respected.

Because I need to learn through others – publishing your work affords you entry to a community of fellow authors. Working alongside your peers like this, and networking with them at various events, facilitates your continued professional development.

Because I need clarity – writing about something helps you to clarify your own thoughts and beliefs about it. Writing enables a structured progression to our arguments to emerge.

Where to start

In terms of academic status, the refereed journal article in a well-respected journal is difficult to beat, but what makes such journals well respected? There are a variety of selection tools to draw upon when deciding the quality of a journal. The main ones seem to be: word of mouth and citation rates or impact factors.

WORD OF MOUTH

Your peers, academic colleagues and supervisors or tutors will all have suggestions of where to publish your work. They may provide informal guidance, or insider knowledge if they are members of a journal's editorial review panel, as to the type of language or tone to use when enquiring about submission to a journal. They may also know of up-coming journal special issues specifically related to your area of research. David, below, has some useful advice on this.

If you want to develop a publishing profile, it's a good idea to speak with your research tutor or supervisor first. They can help assess your writing abilities and possibly suggest suitable journals for your work. It is clear that you get the most recognition for publishing in the really big international journals, but these are often ones everyone is going for, so competition to get your material published is going to be quite stiff. Initially, you may have more success in targeting some of the journals that are a little less prestigious. My supervisor suggested this to me and I was successful in getting my first piece published this way.

David, PhD student, University of Southside.

If your work impacts upon a variety of subject areas, as Yo's does (below), it will be extremely beneficial to conduct some background research into the remit and scope of the journals you intend to approach. It may also be useful to explore if your university provides central support or training sessions for those wishing to publish their work – a good number of university Staff Development or Training Units now provide excellent support for the budding academic writer.

I am working with my supervisor on this but to a large extent it would depend upon the subject matter of the paper. Social Sciences is such a disparate area that there are very specialised journals in particular sub-areas of subjects. It also depends on the quality

(Continued)

(Continued)

of the paper as well as the subject matter. Some journals only publish empirical research, some focus on policy issues, etc. I know quite a lot about that, and there are people available here at Lancaster who could help with that. In addition, there are actually courses available as part of the Faculty Research Training Programme on how to get published. These are offered to PhD students as advanced courses or programmes in their second and third years. I also have some useful texts on the subject. But there is always a trade-off with publishing. You have to find the time to get the papers or publications together. Trying to find the time to do that when it's not directly counting towards your PhD can be difficult.

Yo, ESRC 1 + 3 student, University of Lancaster.

In addition to actively seeking advice from academic colleagues, it is also helpful to observe *their* favoured publication outlets through an examination of their own publication lists. Staff pages on university and departmental intranets are ideal sources of this type of information.

For a number of postgraduates, the publication of a journal article is the end point of a structured process to formal publication. For example, as Kelly highlights below, the journey to article publication may begin with a testing of your ideas, frameworks, explanations, etc. at a research seminar or conference. Whilst other, particularly PhD, students viewed publication as preparatory work for their final thesis submission, as indicated by Sarah below, almost all of those consulted during the development of this text agreed that this helped shape and focus ideas about a research subject.

My department has given us a rough rule of thumb for an idealistic and realistic pattern of publication based upon the following. In the first year try to get something into an online or student journal, or present something at a departmental seminar session or conference. Then use this as a stepping stone in

(Continued)

(Continued)

your second year where you want to try to send something to a printed journal and perhaps present something at a national conference. It is quite structured. I think they said that, by the time you finish, if you can have a couple of good quality publications in quite respected journals that would benefit your progression.

Kelly, ESRC 1 + 3 student, University of Manchester.

I think publishing is important because it helps you to keep your ideas fresh. It also allows you to communicate your work with others, potentially getting their feedback on it. It's also far easier to pull everything together at the end because you will have written some of it up through publishing.

Sarah, ESRC 1 + 3 student, University of Sheffield.

CITATION RATES AND IMPACT FACTORS

In a number of discipline areas, particularly those within the broadly defined areas of Science and Engineering, substantial value is placed upon citation rates and journal impact factors (the methodology for the calculation of impact factors is detailed in Chapter 6 on reading and searching for information, see page 141). This is a key selection tool used by academics when considering where to submit their journal articles. As a result, the submission rate for such journals is high and the opportunity to publish successfully, particularly for novice academics, is considerably lower than it would be for journals with fewer citations rates.

Other routes to publication

The range of publication options available to postgraduates, researchers and academics is wide and varied, and includes:

* academic journals;

* book reviews;

* single-authored texts;

* jointly authored texts;

* book chapters;

* edited texts;

* conference papers and conference proceedings;

* consultants' reports;

* discussion papers;

* monographs;

* the internet;

* newspapers and popular journals; and

* professional journals.

Whilst some of these publication formats are more difficult to achieve than others, it may be beneficial to target some of the easier options to gain experience of academic writing. Dan, below, suggests that providing book reviews is a great way for novice writers to develop their skill.

A good start on the publishing journey is to write a book review. This gets you noticed and introduces you to the discipline. You need to be careful with this kind of thing, though, and make sure it has some relevance to your research or PhD work. That way you will get most out of the experience: a publication to your name and literature source to add to your own work's reference list or bibliography.

Dan, ESRC 1 + 3 student, University of Edinburgh.

It is clear that one of the most popular and substantive forms of publication, especially in academia, is the journal article or paper. A cursory glance through any library catalogue will confirm that there are a huge number of academic journals dedicated to a variety of academic areas of study. Each of these has specific remits, which are usually printed on the inside-back cover of the journal, detailing subject coverage and content. These statements are crucial guides. For example, the journal *Active Learning in Higher Education* focuses upon practitioner HE-based research (see the journal statement below). By contrast, *The Journal of Higher Education Policy and Management* has a more broadly defined remit, and encourages potential authors to discuss preliminary ideas with the editorial team prior to a full-paper submission.

Active Learning in Higher Education: Notes to contributors

Active Learning in Higher Education focuses on all aspects of developments, innovations and good practice in higher education teaching and learning worldwide. The journal includes accounts of research by those active in the field of learning and teaching in HE, and overviews of topics, accounts of action research, outputs from subject-specific project teams, case studies, information and communication technologies (C&ITs) and theoretical perspectives.

The Journal of Higher Education Policy and Management

The *Journal of Higher Education Policy and Management* (*JHE*) welcomes contributions. The Journal prefers papers to be no longer than 5,000 words. *JHE* also invites short comments, reports and book reviews. The editors are happy to discuss with authors initial ideas and to review preliminary outlines and drafts of possible contributions.

It might seem obvious, but initial attempts to publish your work should focus upon the things you know best. Usually, for postgraduates this includes recent dissertation or thesis work, or other activities related to project or research work. As a result of your intense engagement with this subject matter, you will be more confident reporting upon it in the format of a journal article or research paper. Suitable and popular elements of your research or project work, which you may seek to publish formally, could include the following: your review of the literature surrounding your work; a presentation of the findings or conclusions of your work; or an analysis of the methodological considerations of conducting such research or project work in your discipline area. Of course, your research work will very likely require tweaking, reworking and tailoring to complement the remit of the publication(s) you wish to target, but at least you will already have the foundations in place (your dissertation or thesis work) from which to build your potential publications.

Other routes to getting your work into print, or gaining more experience of developing work for publication, include becoming involved with the production of a textbook or a journal. Both of these routes, particularly working on a new journal (as discussed below), typically involve more work on the part of the postgraduate, researcher or academic than a journal article.

WORKING ON A BOOK

There are essentially four ways to publish your work in book form:

* the single-authored text;

* the jointly authored text;

* the edited text; and

* the contribution of a chapter or chapters within a text.

The responsibility for the content and shape of the work in a single-authored text lies solely with the one author. This is a considerable undertaking as most academic texts average at around 80,000 words (slightly less than the average PhD thesis), and many of the leading academic publishers require manuscripts to be delivered within approximately one year from the signing of contracts. In addition, the academic book market is extremely competitive, and publishers need to be convinced of the need for your book. To assist with this, many publishers provide guidance for those who wish to develop their work into a textbook. Book proposals submitted to publishers should therefore take the following structure:

Title   The suggested title of the text and a summary rationale as to why it is needed.

The readership   An indication as to who will need the book and whether or not this is a sizeable market.

Existing or competing texts   An honest appraisal of existing or competing texts. This demonstrates that you are aware of the market and where your text is placed within that market (i.e. as a study guide, a reader, or a core text for specific degree programmes).

Background   An explanation of why you are writing the book and why you are qualified to write it, including a list of your other publications, if any, and the research work you have already carried out in relation to the subject matter of the text. (This section can be linked to the 'Title' or 'Readership' sections above.)

Key characteristics   A key sentence or two that can explain and promote your book to non-experts.

Book outline   A chapter-by-chapter summary of the text, indicating its content and coverage.

Length   The intended length of the proposed book so that publishers can estimate their production costs.

Distinctive features   What are the unique selling points (USPs) of the book? What makes it different from other books, and therefore makes it saleable?

Author details   Your contact details.

Essentially, the same procedure is followed for jointly authored and edited texts, except the workload (by agreement between the authors) is usually shared. A word of warning is necessary here for those of you considering jointly writing or editing a text. Most publishers insert into the contract a broad statement indicating that the authors (or editors in the case of an edited collection) are responsible for the production of the text. This can mean that once a contract has been signed, one of the writing parties (or the editor in the case of an edited collection) can be left to write more than his or her agreed share of the work, whilst other authors sit back, do nothing, and wait for the book to be published. Unfortunately, this is not an uncommon occurance. Therefore choose your co-authors wisely and, if necessary, gain separate written agreements(s) from them, indicating which parts of the text they will write.

An example of the typical content of a book proposal is provided below. This one is based upon the outline prepared by Birmingham and Wilkinson for the textbook *Using research instruments: a guide for researchers* (RoutledgeFalmer, 2003).

Book proposal: *Using research instruments: a guide for researchers*

This text will base its user-friendly style on that of the *Researcher's toolkit: the complete guide to practitioner research.* It will be practically rather than academically based, thereby making it accessible to a broad range of potential readers. These will include those who would find guidance in constructing, using and analysing research instruments as part of their work/studies helpful. Specifically, these include:

- Undergraduates: particularly those learners engaged in marketing or business-related programmes of study, where survey and market research work forms a major part of their course.
- Work-based learners: who are required (either as part of their job or for study purposes) to develop, use and analyse research instruments. This group would include teachers and other professional groups, such as those involved in nursing or the police.

Readership
Target group: undergraduates
The practical nature of the text indicates that it will be relevant and useful to a wide variety of potential readers. In addition to the two key readership groups identified for the previous *Researcher's Toolkit* text (nurses and teacher trainers), this text will also be of particular relevance to undergraduate learners engaged in business-related programmes of study. Many of these programmes have core modules which focus on market research and evaluation activities utilising the research instruments detailed in the proposed text.

Specifically in terms of market, available data indicate that there are a large number of undergraduates in subjects related to education. 1998/99 data indicate that 62,960 students were enrolled in courses (either full-time or part-time) broadly defined as education undergraduate programmes. When ranked, the Manchester Metropolitan University provided the largest number of full-time undergraduate places (see attached HESA data). It is intended that, where possible, the proposed text will tailor itself to the provision offered by these high-ranking institutions. Programme materials will be sought to facilitate this.

An exploration of the market in terms of Business and Administrative Studies shows that, using 1998/99 figures, 19 institutions have more than 2,000 full-time

(Continued)

undergraduates enrolled on programmes broadly covering business-related studies (see Table 2). As a proportion, business and administrative studies students represent almost 12% of the total full-time undergraduate population in the UK. It is intended that, where possible, the proposed text will tailor itself to the provision offered by the high-ranking institutions listed in the attached analysis of recent HESA data. To gauge the suitability of the text, key reviewers have been identified from these institutions. Details of these referees are provided at the end of this proposal.

Target group: work-based learners
Again, the practical basis of the text will be of great use to work-based learners who may not have time to wade through traditional research texts which tend to focus on theory at the cost of practical relevance. Figures for work-based learners are more difficult to determine than undergraduates. However, one indicator of the size of this market is the number of part-time postgraduates (these are more likely to be learners from the professions studying on a part-time basis to fit in with work commitments). Recent HESA data show that a number of institutions have large populations of part-time, postgraduate students. In terms of Business and Administrative Studies, almost all of the institutions in the top ten ranking have over 1,000 part-time postgraduates (see attached analyses of HESA data).

Required knowledge
The combined substantial experience of the authors of the proposed text leads them to believe that many students have a limited knowledge of approaches to research and the correct use of research instruments. Therefore, this text will be written in a jargon-free way (similar to its predecessor the *Researcher's toolkit*) and key terms will be defined throughout the text.

Existing books in the area
There are many research methods books available, focusing on the markets identified above. However, few provide detailed sample material. The unique feature of the proposed text is that it will contain complete examples of research instruments used by practising researchers, rather than the decontextualised sections from research instruments that many texts employ. For example, the text will contain approximately 6–8 examples of questionnaires used by the authors in their own research work. Comparator texts include:

(Continued)

(Continued)

Research methods in education, Cohen, L., Manion, L. and Morrison, K. (2000) London: Routledge

Questionnaire design, interviewing and attitude measurement, Oppenheim, A.N. (1992) London: Pinter Publishers

Real world research: a resource for social scientists and practitioner-researchers, Robson, C. (1993) Oxford: Blackwell

Doing your research project: a guide for first-time researchers in education and social sciences, Bell, J. (1999) Buckingham: Open University Press

Background

The plan for this text has been informed by the substantial experience of both of the authors in developing and using many research instruments as part of their professional work. In essence, the text is a workbook of 'real' examples of research instruments which readers can modify for their own particular research projects. Readership will focus upon those new to research (work-based learners, undergraduates in nursing and other areas where use of research instruments has not been fully developed or covered by other texts). The proposed work will also be of use to practising researchers as a resource or file of typical instruments available.

Drawing on substantial knowledge and experience as researchers operating in the field, this text will provide examples of research instruments used in actual research projects. In order to respect copyright issues, permissions will be sought where necessary, but also slight changes will be made to examples given in order to protect the privacy of those concerned. Where permissions will be difficult to obtain, generic examples of appropriate research instruments will be provided.

The text will build upon the user-friendly style used in the previous work, *The Researcher's toolkit: the complete guide to practitioner research*. In particular, it will develop the chapter 'Research Instruments' to incorporate a substantial number of actual instruments.

(Continued)

Soundbite

A practical rather than academic text, written by a partnership with over a decade of active research experience to draw upon. This text acts as a workbook of 'real' examples of research instruments, which readers can modify for their own particular research projects. The book is suitable for work-based and undergraduate 'researchers'.

Outline

Each chapter within the text will begin with a detailed summary indicating what will be covered. In addition, appropriate references and further reading lists will be provided at the end of each chapter to guide the reader to literature of specific interest covered in that chapter.

Five chapters will be dedicated to exploring the main research instruments: questionnaires, observation schedules, interview schedules, focus groups and content analysis.

Chapter 1: Questionnaires

This chapter will explore the many types of questionnaire available to researchers. Issues relating to phrasing questions, the appropriateness of tone used, Likert and other measurement scales will be highlighted. Specifically, this chapter will include:

- Framing questions (how to ask difficult questions, avoiding ambiguity, ideal question word length, order of questions)
- Designing questionnaires (layout, use of routing, ideal page length)
- Piloting (establishing a suitable sample group)
- Analysing responses (simple tabulations, advanced statistical techniques, analysing qualitative responses)
- Web-based questionnaires (unique design issues, analysis advantages)
- 6–8 examples of 'real life' questionnaires

Chapter 2: Observation schedules

Observation schedules are used as a tool to facilitate the observation process in a number of settings: for example, meetings, presentations, classroom and role-play activity. Schedules vary considerably in the scope of the interactions between participants they cover and the level of detail. This chapter will embrace all forms of observation schedules. Specifically, it will include:

(Continued)

(Continued)

- Negotiating access to the setting (who should you approach? what permissions do you require?)
- Participant/non-participant observation (advantages and disadvantages of both methods)
- Recording your observations (documenting your observations, types of observation schedule to use – Flanders Interaction Analysis and other models, other methods such as audio/video)
- Analysing the observations (tools available, statistical analysis, presenting results)
- 6–8 examples of 'real life' observation schedules

Chapter 3: Interview schedules
Generally, interviews can be one of a number of types: structured, semi-structured or unstructured. This chapter will cover the many styles used and their effectiveness in collecting research information. Specifically, the chapter will cover:

- Devising suitable questions to ask in an interview situation (which questions are acceptable? are the questions necessary? can other sources corroborate the responses?)
- Developing a schedule (is the interview going to be structured, semi-structured or unstructured? which questions should come first? how long should the interview be?)
- The interview itself (seating plans, body language)
- Analysing the data (statistical techniques, using computer analysis packages)
- Presenting the results (tabulations, narratives)
- 6–8 examples of 'real life' interview schedules

Chapter 4: Focus groups
What makes a focus group discussion different from other kinds or types of interview? This chapter will discuss this and other issues, such as the role of the researcher in focus group interviews. Specifically, the chapter will cover:

- What is a focus group (why is it different from other types of interview? when should a focus group be used?)
- What skills are required to conduct a focus group effectively (does it require much training? what makes a good/bad focus group?)
- Recording the process (organising the responses)

(Continued)

- Analysing the data (using statistical and other techniques)
- Examples of 'real life' focus group topics and the resulting notes

Chapter 5: Content analysis
What is the place of content analysis in the wider research project? This chapter discusses using content analyses as a foundation for your research. It provides examples of the effective use and application of content analysis and explores its place within the broader research process. Specifically, the chapter will include:

- Defining content analysis (how the term and concept has evolved)
- Different approaches to content analysis (frequency counts, concepts)
- Recording/analysing the data
- Examples of 'real life' content analyses

Length

It is expected that the length of the book should reflect its user-friendly and accessible style and therefore should be around 160 pages in length, using a similar page size and layout format as *The researcher's toolkit: the complete guide to practitioner research*. We anticipate using diagrams, activity boxes, summary charts, etc., as the issues under discussion demand. To reflect the style of the text it is anticipated that each chapter will have at least one summary, 2 activity boxes and a number of diagrams.

Distinctive features

- A practical, jargon-free guide to the most appropriate use of research instruments, written in such a way as to instil confidence in even the most inexperienced of researchers.
- A relevant and timely alternative to other research methods texts, informed as much as possible by the content and structure of existing programmes of study in the UK higher education sector.
- A reliable and sure-footed text which contains, wherever possible, actual examples of proven research instruments that have been piloted, revised and utilised in their final form by practising social and educational researchers during their involvement with a range of prestigious and far-reaching research projects, sponsored by, among others, ESRC and DfES.

(Continued)

(Continued)

Authors
(see attached summary CVs)

Referees
(see attached suggested referee contact information)

WORKING ON A JOURNAL

Another option for those interested in developing their academic profile is to become involved as a reviewer or editorial assistant on a current journal, or to become involved with the production of a new one. Leading academic publishers are always interested in developing their portfolio of journals, although they generally seek to liaise with established academics in order to develop their range of outputs. Given this, it might be useful to factor the future potential development of a journal within your career development plan (see Chapter 10 on career planning). Alternatively, it might be possible to work with senior colleagues who have more experience of publishing and reviewing academic work, offering to help with editorial work on current journals, or offering to provide support with the development of new journals in your shared areas of expertise. Supervisors and research tutors are often useful colleagues with whom to develop ideas for journals.

Typical proposals for journals include similar elements as those for book proposals described above, although they usually focus around the following:

Title   A suggested title for the journal.

Aims and scope   A statement of the aims and remit of the journal. Who is it aimed at? What intellectual level is required of readers? Which discipline or subject areas is it targeted at? Will the journal be national or international in its remit (many publishers favour the latter as this broadens the potential market)?

Background/rationale   What gap does the proposed journal fill? Why is it needed? How will the proposed journal add to and complement the currently available journals in the area? Is there a need for published material in this area? Can you secure enough material to publish in the journal?

Editorial structure   Have you secured appropriate editors to coordinate the academic content of the proposed journal? If the journal is international, have you secured the involvement of international scholars? How will the administration of the journal be achieved? Will your institution supply support and resourcing for this?

Format and level   What will be the general format of the papers accepted for this journal (theoretical, practical, mixture of both)? Will the journal have other features, such as proposed special issues, opinion pieces, book reviews. How many issues will there be annually?

The market   Who will purchase or subscribe to the journal? How many subscriptions would you envisage? Do you envisage academic libraries subscribing to this journal?

A number of postgraduates and other tutors or supervisors choose to produce jointly authored journal articles to promote the postgraduate's research or project work. Such collaborations are common and often result in submissions that are more readily accepted by journals than their solely postgraduate-authored counterpart. Nick, below, found this a successful way to ensure that his work made it into print, whilst also benefiting from his supervisors considerable experience.

> My supervisor and I have had two papers published up to now, in *Discourse and Society* and *Visual Communication*, and another one we've just submitted. What happens is I write and she acts like an editor and gives me advice on restructuring things and tightening up the argument. She gives me a lot of free reign and I have the confidence to express my views. She has a lot of confidence in me and has told me she has never found anyone she could write with before. We're a partnership: I tend towards a creative type of writing; she knows that but she's a more formal writer and so we strike a nice balance between the two. I think that's why we've had success up to now and why we'll continue to have success.
>
> Nick, ESRC 1 + 3 student, University of Plymouth.

THE REVIEW PROCESS

As a result of increasing competition to publish work with them, most journals have guidance notes that are issued to those charged with reviewing articles for submission (often referred to as the review panel). A range of criteria may apply to each article (common criteria are provided below). Reviewers are also asked to rate the article on a sliding scale.

- Does the piece satisfy the broad aims/remit of the journal?

- Has the author published before?

- Is the piece written in an appropriately professional way?

- Does the piece add to the body of knowledge in the field/area?

- Have acceptable research methods/approaches been used?

- Are analyses conducted in an acceptable way?

- Has other similar work been conducted?

- Has the piece generic interest/wider implications?

- Are assertions/conclusions clearly backed up by evidence?

Rate on a scale from 1 to 5, where 1 = very poor, and 5 = excellent. Then, in your judgement, should we: (a) accept the piece without revision or amendment, (b) accept the piece with minor revisions/amendments (please indicate the areas you believe should be revised), (c) ask for major revision/amendment and re-submission, (d) reject the piece.

Acceptance of the piece without the requirement for any changes is rare. More common is an acceptance of the piece subject to minor revisions suggested by the reviewers. However, rejection is also common for many journal articles submitted for consideration. Most require some reshaping or rewriting before they are deemed to reach the appropriate journal standard. Consider the fictional example overleaf (although it is based upon a real review of a submitted paper). This rejection letter includes fairly reasonably and constructive feedback. It identifies elements of the paper that require improvement or clarification and encourages the author to rewrite the paper for re-submission or consideration elsewhere.

Most skilled journal editors will ensure that those who submit work for potential publication will receive suitable and reasoned critical feedback, as the example shows. It would be a mistake to believe that only more senior academics secure success every time they submit a piece for publication. Those who think this should read Malcolm Tight's lively review of the academic peer review process – an analysis which examined the review and assessment procedures of a range of academic journals with some interesting results (Tight, 2003).

Sean Briggs
University of Westfield
Westferry Campus
Westfield
WF3 4HR

February 2005

Dear Sean,

Thank you for submitting your article entitled 'Negotiating access in the IT age' to the *Journal of Information Technology and Schooling*. I am sorry for the slight delay in responding to your requests for feedback, but I am now pleased to say that I have received comments from the two reviewers of your article – these are enclosed with this letter. I regret to inform you that the article has not been accepted for the journal as it is currently written.

As you will see from the attached feedback, the reviewers have made considerable detailed notes on your submission. However, the key issues appear to be as follows:

- Given the length of the article (8,000 words), the reviewers both indicated that the focus of the piece should be made much clearer to guide the reader through its content.
- Some of the content is unnecessary as this is merely reporting work already published in the journal.
- You draw some interesting conclusions from the data you have collected. As such, you should make your methodology section much clearer and provide more detail in relation to the construction of the research instruments you have used.
- Both reviewers clearly indicated that the paper had some interesting and new material to share with the wider community, but both also felt that the preparation of the manuscript was not adequately developed to merit the data being published. As a result, both agreed that the paper should be redeveloped and considered for publication again once all areas raised by the reviewers had been addressed.

Based upon the recommendations of the reviewers, we were therefore unable to accept your paper for publication at present. However, I do hope you will consider re-writing elements of your paper and re-submit it to us or another appropriate journal.

Yours sincerely

Alan Capshaw
Editor

Reference list and useful reading

Barrass, R. (1995) *Students must write: a guide to better writing in coursework and examinations.* London: RoutledgeFalmer.

Barrass, R. (2002) *Scientists must write: a guide to better writing for scientists, engineers and students.* London: Routledge.

Barrass, R. (2002) *Writing at work: a guide to better writing in administration, business and management.* London: Routledge.

Becher, T., Henkel, M. and Kogan, M. (1994) *Graduate education in Britain.* London: Jessica Kingsley Publishers.

Black, D., Brown, S., Day, A. and Race, P. (1998) *500 tips for getting published: a guide for educators, researchers and professionals.* London: Kogan Page.

Blaxter, L., Hughes, C. and Tight, M. (1998) *The academic career handbook.* Buckingham: Open University Press.

Brause, R.S. (2000) *Writing your doctoral dissertation.* London: RoutledgeFalmer.

Burns, T. and Sinfield, S. (2003) *Essential study skills: the complete guide to success at university.* London: Sage.

Cuthbert, R. (1996) *Working in higher education.* Buckingham: Open University Press/ Society for Research in Higher Education.

Day, A. (1996) *How to get research published in journals.* Aldershot: Gower.

Delamont, S. and Atkinson, P. (2004) *Successful research careers: a practical guide.* Buckingham: Open University Press/SRHE.

Phillips, E.M. and Pugh, D.S. (2003) *How to get a Ph.D: a handbook for students and their supervisors.* Third edn. Buckingham: Open University Press.

Tight, M. (2003) Reviewing the reviewers, *Quality in Higher Education*, 9(3): 295–303.

Wilkinson, D. and Birmingham, P. (2003) *Using research instruments: a guide for researchers.* London: RoutledgeFalmer.

Annotated bibliography

Throughout the research phase of this text, and as a result of teaching experience in the various areas related to its content, a considerable number of textbooks and associated resources – targeted at the postgraduate student market – have been consulted. Presented here, organised by chapter heading, is a carefully selected and annotated list of currently available textbooks that may support your own studies and professional development. This list is not meant to be exhaustive; rather it is indicative of resources that have been useful in developing this text.

Chapter 2: Developments in postgraduate study

Brause, R.S. (2000) *Writing your doctoral dissertation: Invisible rules for success.* RoutledgeFalmer, London. £15.99

Rita Brause's text draws upon a range of data sources to provide a book that discusses the entire doctoral process in a lively and engaging way. Focus groups and question-naire data collected from doctoral students adds value throughout the work. Contents include: comparing a dissertation to a long term paper; jumping through hoops, going on a journey: personal metaphors for the process; the stages in writing a dissertation: an overview; pithy insights and suggestions for success; preparing for your study; creating your setting and identifying your dissertation topic and research questions; forming your dissertation committee; your dissertation committee: roles and respon-sibilities; creating a professional setting with student colleagues; developing a productive setting; writing your dissertation proposal.

Brown, T. (2003) *Providing for the postgraduate market.* Troon: The National Postgraduate Committee of the UK.

This report, conducted on behalf of the National Postgraduate Committee, explores what some universities are doing to support postgraduate learners within their institutions. It also examines the impact upon university communities of developing exclusive facilities for postgraduates.

Delamont, S., Atkinson, P. and Parry, O. (2000) *The doctoral experience.* Falmer Press, London. £75 (hardback)

Drawing upon research work funded through the Economic and Social Research Council, this text analyses and discusses research data collected from a variety of academic and research students based at a range of British universities. Chapters unpack the doctoral experiences of academics and students, and in doing so they explore the exchange and application of educational and academic knowledge. References are made to the work of other professional groups in order to compare the culture of academia. Throughout the text, vignettes and case studies illustrate the reality of the key issues raised.

Chapter 3: Where to study and apply for funding

Darwen, J., Bell, E. and Goodlad, S. (2002) *National survey of postgraduate funding and priorities*. Troon: The National Postgraduate Committee of the UK.

Report on a national survey of students, exploring issues such as what factors do students consider in deciding to pursue postgraduate study? How are postgraduate students funded through their courses, and what are the implications of these funding mechanisms? How many postgraduate students undertake paid work, what sort of work do they do and why, and what impact does this have on their study (if any)? What are the future career plans of postgraduate students, and what factors do they take into account in making these plans? Does debt accrued as a student have any effect on these plans? Provides useful and informative context for those thinking about applying for postgraduate study in the UK.

Graves, N. and Varma, V. (1997) *Working for a doctorate: a guide for the humanities and social sciences*. Routledge, London. £14.99

This guide offers practical advice on the doctoral process. It includes helpful case studies of student experiences as well as material focusing on the cultural and process aspects of studying for a PhD.

The Guardian university guide (2005) £14.99 and
The Times good university guide (2005) £15.99

Both of these guides are primarily targeted at those considering undergraduate programmes of study. However, they contain extremely useful summary data relating to teaching, research and resourcing of UK universities.

Prospects (2004) *Prospects postgraduate funding guide 2004/05*. Prospects. (http://www.prospects.ac.uk) £4.99

This annual guide provides focused advice and guidance in relation to securing funding from employers and other sponsors, detailed information on available loans and their terms and conditions, and other sources of finance available to assist post-graduate study.

Chapter 4: Developing proposals

Blaikie, N. (2000) *Designing social research: the logic of anticipation*. Polity Press, Cambridge. £18.50

A general text detailing the mechanics of social science research. Of particular use for postgraduate students are the descriptions and analyses of research approaches and proposal designs in the first part of the text. All of the key social science research approaches and tools are thoroughly discussed by relating them to appropriate applications. Contents include: preparing research proposals and research designs; designing social research; research questions and objectives; strategies for answering research questions; concepts, theories, hypotheses and models; sources and selection of data; methods for answering research questions; sample research designs.

Punch, K. (2000) *Developing effective research proposals*. Sage, London. £16.99

An excellent, short text dealing with the proposal development and writing process. The book deals with both qualitative and quantitative proposals and includes detailed examples of each. Contents include: the proposal – readers, expectations and functions; a general framework for developing proposals; some issues; methods; writing the proposal; tactics.

Chapter 5: Finding your feet – the culture of academia

Blaxter, L., Hughes, C. and Tight, M. (1998) *The academic career handbook*. Open University Press, Buckingham. £21.99

An excellent text for those thinking about pursuing an academic career. The text details the traditional and emerging career options for would-be and newly appointed academics. Written by a well-established writing team, the text covers such areas as starting an academic career, networking, teaching opportunities (including tutoring and supervision), researching, writing, and managing yourself and other academics. The authors draw upon a wealth of additional material to emphasise the points they make, as well as providing 'hints' and 'tips' for success. Contents include: academic careers, networking, teaching, researching, and managing and developing your career.

Burton, S. and Steane, P. (2004) *Surviving your thesis*. Routledge, London. £16.99

This edited volume comprehensively covers the research journey and will be of use and relevance to undergraduates and postgraduates alike. There is sufficient detail within the text for a broad readership to obtain some useful guidance and assistance from its content. Links to helpful websites and further reading suggestions are also provided within key sections of the text. The unique cultural and social elements of UK universities are not covered in detail within the text, however, as the writing team are academics from institutions outside the UK.

Cuthbert, R. (1996) *Working in higher education*. Open University Press/SRHE, Buckingham. £22.50

In three substantive parts, this book explores the workers, the work and the work context of higher education. In examining the work, the text provides an analysis of employment types and rights, and the nature of an academic career. The 'work' section examines disciplinary similarities and differences, and managing academics. The 'work context' section unpacks notions of autonomy, culture and professional status. For students within higher education, this text will provide useful context and background information to the operation and function of UK universities. Contents include: academic staff: information and data; managing the employment relationship in higher education: *quo vardis?*; does it pay to work in universities?; which of us has a brilliant career? Notes from a higher education survivor; new liberty, new discipline: academic work in the new higher education; professors and professionals: on changing boundaries; managing how academics manage; works committees; geographical transitions; just like the novels? Researching the occupational cultures of higher education; which academic profession are you in?; autonomy, bureaucracy and competition: the ABC of control in higher education; all work and no play?

Chapter 6: Reading and searching for information and seeking advice
Burns, T. and Sinfield, S. (2003) *Essential study skills: the complete guide to success at University*. Sage, London. £14.99

Of particular use and relevance to those returning to higher education following some time away. Contents include: how to learn and study; how to organise yourself for study; how to research and read academically; how to use the overview; how to pass exams; how to learn creatively; how to build your confidence; how to succeed in group work; how to prepare better assignments; how to be reflective.

Fairbairn, G.J. and Fairbairn, S.A. (2001) *Reading at University*. Open University Press, Buckingham. £14.99

An introductory text designed to help learners develop effective skills in information management and analysis. Of particular use to those learners returning to university who wish to refresh their skills in this general area. Contents include:

reading as communication; developing reading skills and disciplines; reading as research; organising and planning your reading.

Rumsey, S. (2004) *How to find information: a guide for researchers*. Open University Press, Maidenhead. £16.99

A thorough and accessible text written by a senior librarian with substantial experience of conducting information searches. A wide range of tools and techniques are discussed, including common search conventions, accessing online databases and using the internet. Contents include: formats of information sources; identi-fying the information need; the online searching process; citation searching; using the world wide web for research; evaluation of resources; citing references; intellectual property and plagiarism.

Chapter 7: Managing your time, academic writing and presenting your work

Becker, L. (2004) *How to manage your postgraduate course*. Palgrave, London. £12.99

Becker provides general tips and guidance concerned with the overall management of a postgraduate course. This is particularly suited to traditional Masters students, rather than those undertaking PhD study, who may require more specialised and focused guidance. Coverage includes: assessing your skills base; managing your course; teamworking and networking; presenting ideas; writing up research work.

Phelan, P.J. and Reynolds, P.J. (1995) *Argument and evidence: critical thinking for the social sciences*. Routledge, London. £70 (hardback)

The development of clear and reasoned approaches to the evaluation of arguments/evidence are put forward in this text. This reference guide might be useful for those postgraduates eager to develop and articulate arguments and supporting rationales within their work. Contents include: argument and evidence; context, convention and communication; an informal analysis of arguments; patterns of reasoning; establishing validity; critical analysis in practice and assumptions; evidence and what counts as evidence; presenting and summarising evidence; furthering knowledge; probability and uncertainty; probability theory applied; estimation and reliability; testing hypotheses.

Potter, S. (2002) *Doing postgraduate research*. Sage, London. £16.99

A practical edited collection of materials that embraces the postgraduate research process. Particularly useful elements include sections on planning research investi-gations. Contents also include: getting going; the writing process; undertaking a topic review; using computers in research; responsibilities, rights and ethics; the examination process and the *viva*.

Van Emden, J. and Becker, L. (2004) *Presentation skills for students*. London: Palgrave. £11.99

A short and accessible guide to preparing and making presentations to a variety of audiences, including preparing materials for seminars, tutorials and more formal conference presentations and papers to academics. Specific contents include: personal development: speaking to an audience; delivery and non-verbal communication; using visual aids; speaking as part of your course; speaking as part of a group.

Wisker, G. (2001) *The postgraduate research handbook: succeed with your MA, MPhil, EdD and PhD*. Palgrave, London. £14.99

A useful and, in places, detailed text providing guidance for those embarking on a postgraduate journey. It is perhaps more relevant for Masters level learners, rather than those embarking on the research element of PhD study. Useful, generic sections include: choosing your supervisor; developing proposals; managing your studies and planning your work; writing up and preparing for the *viva*.

Chapter 8: Working with your supervisor

Delamont, S., Atkinson, P. and Parry, O. (2004) *Supervising the doctorate: a guide to success* (2nd edn). Open University Press/SRHE, Buckingham. £19.99

Based upon their considerable combined knowledge of supervising doctoral students, the three authors of this text offer insights into the process from the supervisor's point of view. They discuss a range of issues and topics associated with the supervision process, including: negotiating and agreeing the parameters of the supervisor–supervisee relationship; what a supervisor should expect from the role; how to manage students and their work; giving appropriate and helpful feedback. These and other areas are discussed in some detail and emphasised through the use of colourful vignettes and case studies. Although targeted at those undertaking the role of supervisor, much of the coverage will be of interest to the postgraduate student who is keen to develop and nurture this important relationship.

Grix, J. (2001) *Demystifying postgraduate research: from MA to PhD*. University of Birmingham Press, Birmingham. £9.99

A very accessible text that discusses a variety of topics and issues of relevance to postgraduate learners. Much of the coverage relates to PhD students but there is enough generic material to be of use and relevance to other postgraduate learners. Particularly useful, and crisply written, are sections on the supervision and *viva* processes, and the mechanics of conducting postgraduate research. Coverage also includes: the nature of doctoral research; dealing with the literature and critically reviewing it; methods of research and investigation.

Phillips, E.M. and Pugh, D.S. (2003) *How to get a PhD: a handbook for students and their supervisors* (3rd edn). Open University Press, Buckingham. £17.99

One of the most popular texts for postgraduate students, offering seasoned advice based upon the authors' substantive experience of working with postgraduate students. A particularly accessible chapter covers the supervision process, offering guidance and support to the student who seeks to get the most out of this relationship. Contents include: becoming a postgraduate; getting into the system; the nature of the PhD qualification; how not to get a PhD; how to do research; the form of a PhD thesis; the PhD process; how to manage your supervisor; how to supervise; the formal procedures; how to survive in a predominantly British, white, male, full-time academic environment; the limitations of the present system.

Chapter 9: Working with other researchers

Rugg, G. and Petre, M. (2004) *The unwritten rules of PhD research*. Open University Press, Buckingham. £17.99

This text attempts to investigate areas of the PhD process that other books do not. It does this admirably in places by, for example, offering reasoned interpretations of the university system within which PhD students must operate and work. Procedural notes, tips and guidance are offered throughout. Particularly useful sections, missing from most other texts, include elements on networking, developing academic papers and their different types, the *viva* process, making presentations, and getting the most out of conferences.

West, M.A. (2003) *Effective teamwork: practical lessons from organisational research*. Blackwells, London. £15.99

Although focused upon industrial organisational research, this text will be useful for postgraduate researchers seeking to develop their teamwork and collaborative working skills. Coverage includes: creating teams; building and leading teams; participating in teams; supporting team members; creative problem-solving; dealing with team conflicts.

Chapter 10: Career planning

Brown, S. and Race, P. (2002) *Lecturing: a practical guide*. RoutledgeFalmer, London. £19.99

An accessible and user-friendly text for those undertaking teaching duties for the first time. Coverage includes: the place and types of lecture; effective use of voice and body language; facilitating effective learning; using lecturing tools; working with groups; ensuring quality in lectures.

Ramsden, P. (2003) *Learning to teach in Higher Education*. RoutledgeFalmer, London. £22.99

This user-friendly text presents the reader with a range of tools and techniques that are important considerations for those wishing to be successful in university teaching. The book is split into three substantive sections which deal with learning and teaching, designing learning, and evaluating the quality of provision offered. Specific chapter coverage includes: ways of understanding teaching; approaches to learning; learning from the student perspective; theories of teaching in higher education; teaching strategies for effective learning; evaluating the quality of higher education; what it takes to improve university teaching.

Reece, I. and Walker, S. (2003) *Teaching, training and learning: a practical guide* (5th edn). Business Education Publishers, Sunderland. £26.50

An excellent and thoroughly practical guide to teaching and training in post-compulsory education. Contents include: an introduction to teaching; student learning; teaching strategies and learning styles; learning aids; planning for teaching and learning; communication, assessment and evaluation of the learning experience.

Chapter 11: Publishing opportunities

Black, D., Brown, S., Day, A. and Race, P. (1998) *500 tips for getting published: a guide for educators, researchers and professionals*. Kogan Page, London. £15.99

A very useful and accessible pocket guide to approaching publishers and getting your work in print. Contents include: targeting the right journal; making your research publishable; using the literature search effectively; finding the right voice; style points; improving your 'hit rate'; responding to referees' feedback; dealing with rejections.

Rubens, P. (2000) *Science and technical writing: a manual of style*. Routledge, London. £17.99

An innovative text dealing with the complexities of technical writing and presentation. This guide helpfully takes readers through the stages of translating technical information, and the transfer from paper-based to electronic presentation of work. Contents include: audience analysis and document planning; writing for non-native audiences; grammar, usage and revising for publication; punctuating scientific and technical prose; using acceptable spelling; incorporating specialised terminology; using numbers and symbols; using quotations, citations and references; creating indexes; creating non-textual information; creating useable data displays; designing useful documents.

Thomson, A. (2001) *Critical reasoning: a practical introduction* (2nd edn). Routledge, London. £12.99

An aid to developing arguments and critical thinking and reasoning skills. Contents include: analysing reasoning: recognising reasoning and identifying conclusions; argument indicator words; recognising argument without argument indicator words; identifying conclusions; judging whether a passage contains an argument; summary: is it an argument?; evaluating reasoning; evaluating the truth of reasons and assumptions.

Woods, P. (1999) *Successful writing for qualitative researchers*. RoutledgeFalmer, London. £14.99

For students engaged in qualitative research, this innovative text provides useful structures and approaches to explore and examine your data. In addition, guidance is provided on getting your work into print. Specifically, contents include: getting started and keeping going; a standard approach to organisation; alternative forms of writing; style; editing; collaborative writing; writing for publication.

Appendix 1   Postgraduate views

During the summer and early autumn of 2004 interviews were conducted within university schools and departments, coffee shops, bars, student unions and the odd corridor to establish and discuss the issues of importance to learners as they progress upon their postgraduate programme of study. As a result of the considerable input of all of those interviewed, this text is enlivened and enriched with real-life accounts of what it is like to be a postgraduate learner within a British university. During extremely busy periods, all interviewees gladly gave up their time to answer questions relating to their study and university experiences. As part of each interview, the discussion focused upon the student's specific research/study area. For further information, and to embellish and contextualise individual quotes used within the text, brief summaries of these areas are provided below.

Claire, ESRC 1 + 3 student, University of Birmingham 'Societal security in Kyrgyzstan'

This research will contribute to conceptual and policy debates on new security thinking. The empirical focus of the study will be the comparison of security perceptions among different identity groups within Kyrgyzstani society. This project will develop the concept of societal security, enhancing the existing framework to ensure operability and counter current criticisms. Thanks to the diversity of intersecting identity groups in Kyrgyzstan, it is possible to take a reflexive approach to the concept and its development through the use of empirical data. The second purpose of the research is to provide a more differentiated picture of security issues in Kyrgyzstan and the wider region, highlighting the conflicts and interdependencies of referent objects and actors. By using the framework provided by the concept of societal security, it is envisaged that a better understanding of dynamics and processes can be gained, while avoiding the imposition of western theoretical and policy preconceptions that continue to skew perceptions of the Central Asian region. Claire can be contacted via cxw861@bham.ac.uk.

Sarah, ESRC 1 + 3 student, University of Sheffield 'The effect of question format and repetition within interviews on young children's eyewitness testimony'

Sarah completed her first degree in Social Anthropology in 1985, continued with a PGCE, taught in primary schools both in England and in Switzerland and had three children. During the last four years of teaching Sarah studied for a Psychology degree with the Open University, after which she applied to do her current

M.Res/PhD at Sheffield. Sarah has recently completed a study into the effect of repetition and question format within a single interview on young children's eyewitness responses. Sarah is especially interested in the patterns of change in responses to questions and repetitions, which she will pursue in subsequent research. At present Sarah is analysing police transcripts to assess the effect of question repetition in recorded interviews.

Peter, ESRC 1 + 3 student, University of Leeds 'Interventions for male violence against women'

Peter is conducting research work at Leeds which seeks to explore interventions for male violence against women. He will be using a psychoanalytic approach to look at the life stories of male perpetrators of domestic violence while trying to fit that in with UK and New Zealand policies of responses to male violence against women.

Anna, ESRC 1 + 3 student, University of Manchester 'ICT and not-for-profit organisations'

Following completion of her MSc at the University of Hull, Anna worked for a not-for-profit organisation which specialised in the marketing and city regeneration of Hull. In July 2003 she was awarded an ESRC 1 + 3 scholarship and in September 2003 began an MSc in Marketing at UMIST. Anna's MSc dissertation at UMIST was based on the use of the internet and ICT by not-for-profit organisations, a research focus she continues to explore through the remainder of her PhD programme.

Charlotte, ESRC 1 + 3 student, University College London 'The impact of loss of cultural heritage on identity and knowledge transmission in Djenné, Mali'

Charlotte's current research themes include an examination of whether European notions of cultural heritage preservation are relevant in an African context. There is considerable debate at the moment among heritage conservation practitioners about the best way of preserving and documenting cultural knowledge in order to guarantee its transmission. UNESCO's concept of culture has been criticised by many in the heritage field. At the same time, there does not seem to be any clear idea of what an alternative, non material-centric, non Euro-centric, multi-vocal approach to heritage preservation would look like. This work seeks not only to assess the success of heritage protection policies but also to have a close look at what this success means to different parties involved.

Dan, ESRC 1 + 3 student, University of Edinburgh 'Identity in contemporary South African society'

Following the completion of a Geography degree at Oxford University, Dan moved to the Centre of African Studies, University of Edinburgh, on a 1 + 3 ESRC scholarship. His research is a consideration of the location of coloured identity in contemporary South African society. By investigating different notions of identity across generations and between socio-economic groups within the coloured community, processes of formal and informal education will be placed within the shifting social environment of South Africa. Changing concepts of identity across these groups will be analysed regarding the influence of intellectuals in the formation and maintenance of identity in South Africa, and its relationship with wider political debates on race and identity both nationally and globally.

Francesca, ESRC 1 + 3 student, Fitzwilliam College, University of Cambridge 'Beyond the ideal: bourgeois mothering in Victorian Lancashire'
Francesca's research investigates the historical geography of motherhood and mothering in Victorian Lancashire. It has two foci: an investigation of the ideal of motherhood through literature, art, engravings; and an investigation of women's lived experience of mothering through women's diaries and letters. To explore these two areas, Francesca's work will compare the conceptions of the ideal of motherhood with women's experience of mothering in Victorian Rochdale. This will be facilitated through a qualitative analysis of women's letters to one another and their private diaries (searching for key themes such as experience of childbirth, nurturing, maternal feelings). Demographic comparator statistics for the area of investigation will be sought from the 1881 census.

Gareth, ESRC 1 + 3 student, University of Edinburgh 'Personality traits, health behaviours and health status outcomes'
Gareth's research proposal for his ESRC application was effectively an extension of project work conducted during his final year undergraduate degree programme, but also a refinement. In that project he had looked at relationships between personality traits and sexual risk-taking behaviours, spurred by his work in the HIV prevention voluntary sector. A central issue Gareth wishes to explore within his PhD work is that if general health behaviours 'cluster' together (co-occur) in the general population (e.g., smokers also tend to drink, people who use dental floss also tend to use sun cream), then the behaviours may share underlying psychological causes.

Ian, ESRC 1 + 3 student, University of Manchester 'Business Improvement Districts in New Labour's urban neo-liberalisation project'
Ian specialises in urban political geography. Recent projects and working papers have focused upon the politics of urban regeneration and gentrification; place marketing; urban entrepreneurial politics; and the relationship between New Labour and neo-liberalisation. He recently completed a MA dissertation on the evolution of public–private partnership working in Liverpool. He is now beginning a PhD study on the imposition of Business Improvement Districts in city centres throughout the

UK, their role in New Labour's urban neo-liberalisation project and their material and discursive North American origins. His research website is at www.iancook.cjb.net and his contact email address is i.r.cook@postgrad.manchester.ac.uk

Stephanie, ESRC 1 + 3 student, Aberystwyth University, 'A comparative study of the effects of unemployment in the South Wales and Great Northern coalfields during the economic depression of the 1930s'
During the final year of her undergraduate degree in 2003 Stephanie decided to pursue postgraduate study because of her intense interest in her dissertation research topic. Discussions with tutors led to her application to the ESRC for the 1 + 3 funding as Stephanie's historical interest clearly fell within economic and social history. Stephanie's research explores the effects of mass unemployment through an examination of how household means-testing affected the unemployed, their families and wider society during the 1930s.

Nick, ESRC 1 + 3 student, University of Plymouth, 'Rhetorical and argumentative skills of police officers'
Having previously trained as an artist and sculptor, Nick graduated from the University of Plymouth in 2002 with a first degree in Social and Organisational Studies. After winning ESRC funding for a PhD and completing an MSc with distinction in social research, he began his PhD with the School of Psychology in October 2003. As a social constructionist and discourse analyst, his PhD work is concerned with the rhetorical and argumentative skills of police officers as they set about the 'doing' of policing. He continues to write and research on 'racism' and minority groups, especially 'asylum seekers', and is committed to exploring and extending discourse analysis to include visual imagery. His contact email address is nlynn@plymouth.ac.uk

Lewis, ESRC 1 + 3 student, University of Oxford, '1980s UK governments and market failure'
Following completion of his first degree with the London School of Economics, Lewis became very interested in the interaction between economists and policy-makers. His MSc course at Oxford has enabled him to further these interests as his dissertation focused upon economic policymaking in the 1980s. He continues to explore this area for his PhD work. Lewis can be contacted via his email address: lewis.allan@trinity.oxford.ac.uk

Jeff, ESRC 1 + 3 student, University of Hull, 'Educational disaffection among working-class adolescents'
After gaining a first in Sociology and Social Anthropology at Hull, Jeff was awarded ESRC 1 + 3 funding for a PhD in Anthropology. Based on a comparative cultural

analysis of English and Irish education, it primarily focuses on the disproportionate under-achievement found among young people from less advantaged socio-economic backgrounds. An MSc thesis on teachers and the 'new work order' has been followed by long-term ethnographic fieldwork carried out in school-based settings located in the Northeast of England and Southern Ireland. Chicago School urban anthropology and the subsequent critical interventions of Paul Willis, as well as the current work of Stephen Ball, and his development of Foucault's ideas inform the research.

Philip, ESRC 1 + 3 student, University of Liverpool, 'Sustainable communities: the cultural contribution of transport'

Philip has a professional background in cartography and photogrammetry. Prior to undertaking his PhD he worked at Ordnance Survey headquarters in Southampton for nine years and was promoted three times, reaching the grade of Mapping & Charting Officer. He returned to full-time education in 1998 and graduated with a degree in Cultural Studies from Sheffield University in 2001. During this time, Philip became involved in voluntary community work. In 2002, after completing the first year of a postgraduate course in Town and Country Planning, he decided to submit a PhD proposal looking at the pivotal role of transport in building sustainable communities. Philip's work explores the contention that improvements to transport networks could significantly improve the results of metropolitan community and economic regeneration programmes.

Kelly, ESC 1 + 3 student, University of Manchester 'Justice in community? Locating the bases for a new politics of community'

Kelly began her research work at Manchester in 2002 by studying for an MA in Political Theory, and throughout this programme of study she refined her PhD research area. The principal motivation of her work is a concern with the ethical implications of political boundaries of all kinds for those included and excluded from the relevant communities. Through close analysis of recent normative political theory and its consequences for understanding community at both a practical and conceptual level, she seeks to construct a framework which adequately considers how the implied communities should be treated in ethical action and policy.

Yo, ESRC 1 + 3 student, University of Lancaster, 'Falling exclusions: have pupils with Special Educational Needs benefited?'

Yo's work seeks to investigate the current extent and trend of exclusions of pupils with special educational needs (SEN) in the context of recent falls in the overall level of recorded exclusions. The high proportion of excluded pupils identified as having SEN has been repeatedly highlighted by previous research studies, but many of these reports were conducted before official statistics began to show a fall in exclusions in response to the government target set in 1998. This PhD research work will seek to provide reliable data on the current extent and trend of such exclusions.

Miranda, ESRC 1 + 3 student, University of Surrey, 'Drug-assisted rape and sexual assault: an investigation'

Miranda completed her MSc in Forensic Psychology in 2003. As part of the MSc programme she conducted research into perceptions of sexual relationships between adults and adolescents. Drawing upon some of this work, Miranda began her PhD in September 2003 with a focus on drug-assisted rape and sexual assault. The main aim of Miranda's work is to build a picture of the crime, its perpetrators and victims, and how and where it is committed. Her research is being conducted in close collaboration with Surrey and Derbyshire police forces with the intention that her findings will inform future police investigations, police training and crime prevention strategies. You can contact her at m.horvath@surrey.ac.uk or find out more about her research at http://www.surrey.ac.uk/SHS/fpac/

Maureen, ESRC/MRC student, University of Leeds, 'Beliefs about stroke: how do couples negotiate a shared understanding?'

The aim of Maureen's research is to gain an understanding of how couples comprehend and respond to illness, using stroke as an example, and how they negotiate changes in their lives in response to it. To date, research has generally focused on how either the patient or the carer adapts following stroke. This research therefore brings together two strands of research which have generally been considered in isolation, to focus on the couple, not the individual. This work will contribute towards an understanding of the processes involved in shaping health beliefs and how these affect adaptation to this chronic illness, and thus accords with the ethos of the government's 'expert patient' initiative. The research applies psychological theory to place the couple's beliefs within the framework for understanding recovery from and adaptation to this medical condition. Thus this research is clearly interdisciplinary, incorporating medical, psychological and social factors.

Pete, ESRC/CASE student, University of Leeds, 'Neighbourhood profiling and classification for community safety'

The aim of Pete's research is to analyse the relationships between spatial patterns of crime and anti-social behaviour, crime prevention schemes and a new classification of neighbourhoods in Leeds. The primary objective is the design and construction of this new neighbourhood classification for community safety. This is done using a cluster analysis of variables drawn from national datasets, such as the 2001 census and Nomis, and local data collected and maintained by the various members of the Leeds Community Safety Partnership, who are the CASE collaborator. The memberships of the different classes of neighbourhood are then examined to identify the extent to which similar neighbourhoods have similar crime profiles. The extent to which this is, or is not, the case is then analysed against macro-level spatial histories of neighbourhood regeneration in Leeds and micro-level details of specific types of crime prevention/reduction intervention.

Peter, PhD student, University of Oxford, 'ICT in educational settings: a comparative analysis'

Peter is currently engaged in the early stages of a part-time DPhil in Educational Studies at the University of Oxford. He is seeking to explore what influence or effect new-generation software has on pupils' engagement with their subject? How do pupils, in using software, approach the tasks set for them by their teachers? What is it that pupils actually do with software? The essence of Peter's research will be to capture and make available for scrutiny and assessment by means of audio- and video-recordings the ways in which students and teachers produce the ordinary activities in which they engage during the course of those aspects of their educational lives in which the very latest information and communications technology plays an increasingly profound role.

Alexej, ESRC 1 + 3 student, University of Wales, Aberystwyth, 'Explaining globalisation: an analytical framework'

Originally from Germany, Alexej graduated from the London School of Economics with a degree in international relations and history in 2002. He then joined the Department of International Politics at the University of Wales, Aberystwyth, where he was awarded a research-track Masters degree in 2003; he expects to complete his PhD by September 2006. From January to July 2005, Alexej will also be a Visiting Scholar in the School of International Relations at the University of Southern California, Los Angeles. His doctoral thesis deals with the problem of how to define and explain a complex process like globalisation, arguing that many dominant social science approaches are limited in their ability to define or explain globalisation due to the problematic nature of their underlying philosophy of social science.

Nick, ESRC 1 + 3 student, University of Oxford, 'Investigating how pupils interpret their Geography learning experiences and their conceptions of the subject'

Nick's DPhil study attempts to explore the nature of pupils' conceptions of geography and how they relate to the way they interpret their learning experiences, work on, and value tasks in Geography lessons. The study involves six case pupils, two from each of three schools. Techniques used include observation, post-lesson interviews, self-directed photography, concept mapping, and researcher-led probes using photographs and a series of geographical questions. The research aims to contribute to knowledge of the nature of pupils' subject conceptions, as well as detailing ways in which pupils construct meaning in their learning experiences. Nick hopes to conduct more research with pupils in other school contexts in the future.

Sarah, ESRC 1 + 3 student, London School of Economics, 'Societies investing in street children'

Sarah's PhD research aims to improve understanding of how governments approach and deal with children who live on the streets. This topic emerged from a combination of Sarah's empirical concerns arising during 15 years of work as a leader of civil society organisations which deliver quality services to street children in Latin America, and her theoretical interests pursued in a master's degree in Public Policy (Princeton University, USA) and a second master's degree in Social Policy research (London School of Economics). Her research is interdisciplinary, drawing heavily on sociological and social policy literature on the construction of childhood and social exclusion. She is currently undertaking case-study fieldwork in Mexico, exploring how policies for urban children in Puebla City are formulated, and how resulting interventions are experienced by children living on Puebla's streets.

Michelle, ESRC 1 + 3 student, University of Cambridge, 'What are you looking at! Prisoner self-narratives, social-information processing and prison violence'

Michelle's research examines whether prisoner self-narratives, their life stories, bias social-information processing in such a way as to encourage and promote fights and assaults in prison. She will be paying particular attention to themes of masculinity and shame, within their self-narratives, to determine whether these themes bias the cues prisoners encode, the interpretations they form and the behavioural solutions they generate in response to a situation.

Adam, ESRC 1 + 3 student, University of Oxford, 'Time as an aspect of social exclusion: the social exclusion of working lone mothers in the UK'

Adam returned to Oxford University for the 1 + 3 after completing a PPE degree there as an undergraduate. The DPhil research looks at the impacts which paid employment has on the time resources of lone mothers in the UK. The research is framed conceptually within the social exclusion literature and uses the notion of citizenship to reconfigure social exclusion. The resource of time is introduced as an element of social exclusion alongside financial and other resources. Empirically, the research then analyses the impacts which paid employment has on the time use of working lone mothers through quantitative analysis of the 2001 UK Time Use Survey, interviews with lone mothers and non-participant observation in a Job

Centre. The research aims to extend the policy focus of New Deal for Lone Parents through highlighting important ways that working generates new temporal forms of exclusion for lone mothers. Adam can be contacted about his research at adam.whitworth@socres.ox.ac.uk

Dan, ESRC/CASE student, University of Leeds, 'Multi-level, integrated classifications based on the 2001 census of population and neighbourhood statistics'

Dan's project aims to develop general purpose classifications of households, neighbourhoods (output areas), wards, local authorities and to link the classifications at different levels together. The outputs from this project will be a set of classifications which will be made available to users via both the ONS website (http://www.statistics.gov.uk) and the academic website (http://www.census.ac.uk) (maintained by the Census Dissemination Unit of the MIMAS service of Manchester Computing). The student and supervisors will develop a series of papers outlining the classification methods and a comprehensive description of the classes in collaboration with ONS.

Liz, ESRC/CASE student, University of Leeds, 'Gender equality and career progression in science: managing work and family life on fixed-term contracts'

Liz's PhD was originally registered part-time and in Law at the University of Leeds. In 2002 she successfully applied, with the help of colleagues in Sociology, for an ESRC CASE award to start in the following year. She therefore left Law in September 2003 and registered as a new PhD student with the Sociology Department. Between January 2003 and September 2003 Liz worked full-time as a research assistant on a European Union funded project (MOBISC – the link project for the CASE award) and linked her PhD into the project. Since September 2003 she has continued to work on the project as a paid research assistant for one day a week and has linked her work and PhD together with the aim of producing deliverables both for the PhD and for the project. Liz was aware that this 'linked' PhD was not the traditional way of going about doctoral research and training in the Social Sciences, and benefited from support and advice provided by colleagues at the university (who had knowledge and experience of PhD completions using this method).

Appendix 2   Higher degree qualifications obtained in the UK, 1995–2002

Source: Higher Education Statistics Agency – Higher Education Statistics for the UK (1994/95–2001/02)

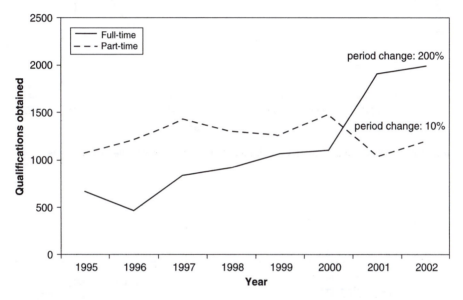

Total higher degree qualifications obtained in the UK – Medicine and Dentistry

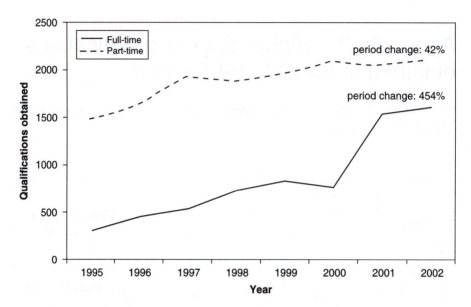

Total higher degree qualifications obtained in the UK – Subjects allied to Medicine

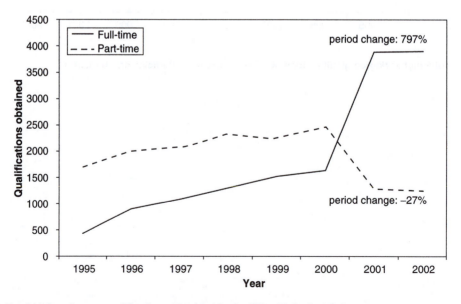

Total higher degree qualifications obtained in the UK – Biological Sciences

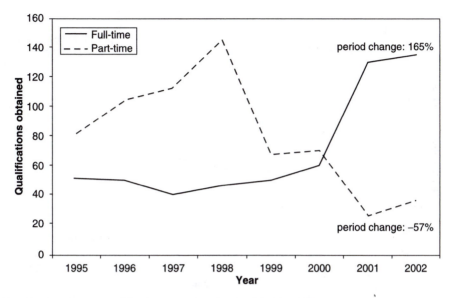

Total higher degree qualifications obtained in the UK – Veterinary Sciences

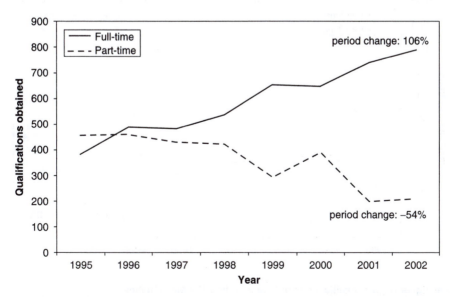

Total higher degree qualifications obtained in the UK – Agricultural and related subjects

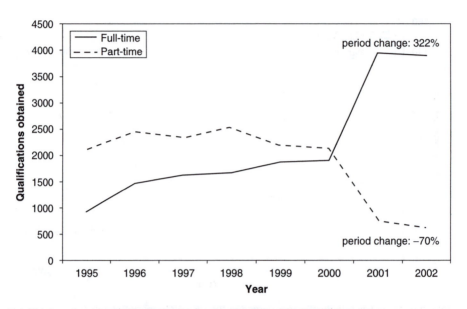

Total higher degree qualifications obtained in the UK – Physical Sciences

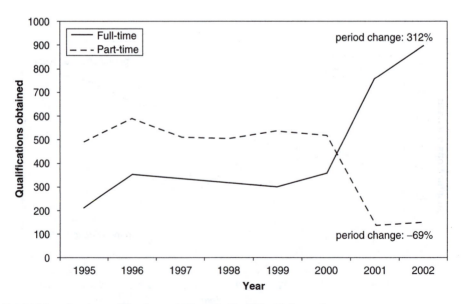

Total higher degree qualifications obtained in the UK – Mathematics

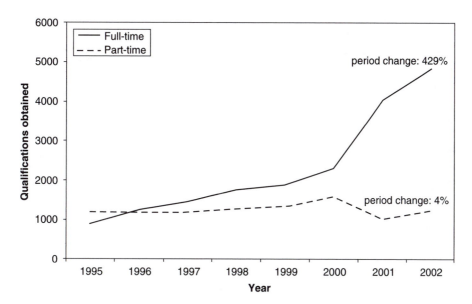

Total higher degree qualifications obtained in the UK – Computer Science

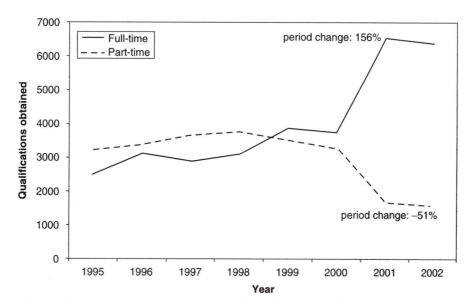

Total higher degree qualifications obtained in the UK – Engineering and Technology

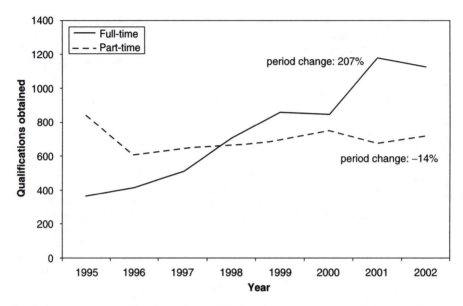

Total higher degree qualifications obtained in the UK – Architecture, Building and Planning

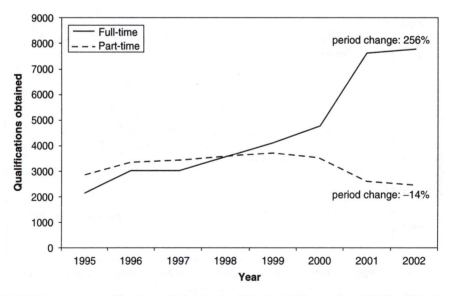

Total higher degree qualifications obtained in the UK – Social, Economic and Political Studies

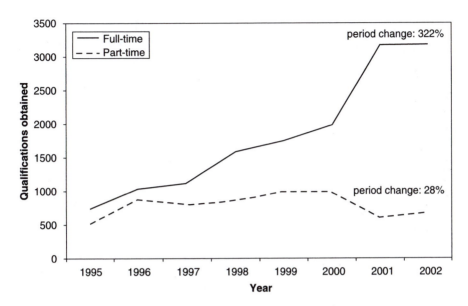

Total higher degree qualifications obtained in the UK – Law

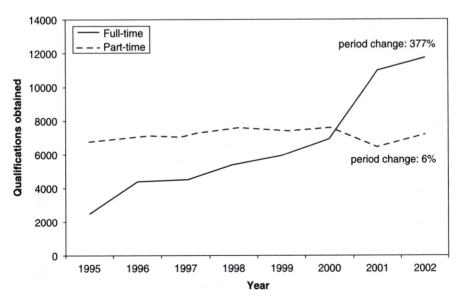

Total higher degree qualifications obtained in the UK – Business and Administrative Studies

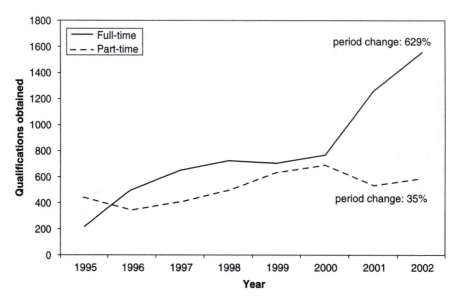

Total higher degree qualifications obtained in the UK – Librarianship and Information Science

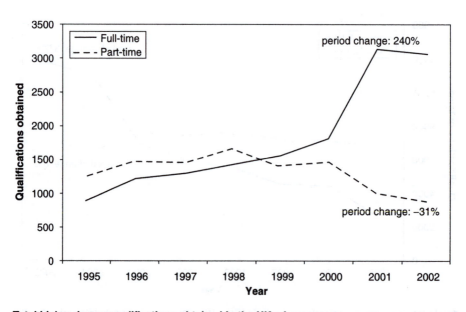

Total higher degree qualifications obtained in the UK – Languages

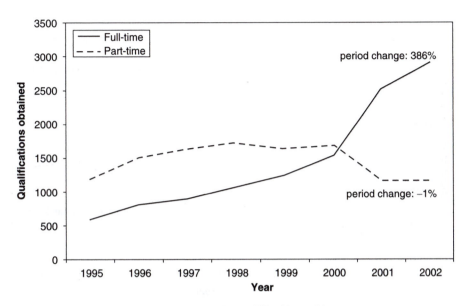

Total higher degree qualifications obtained in the UK – Humanities

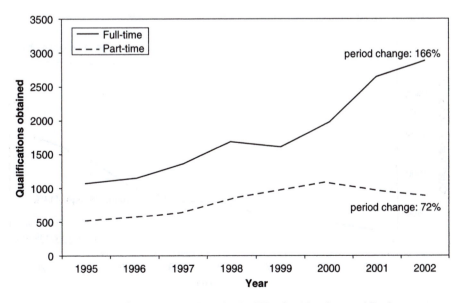

Total higher degree qualifications obtained in the UK – Creative Arts and Design

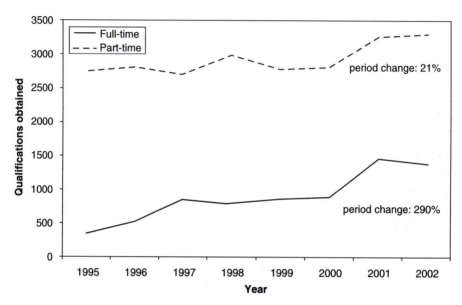

Total higher degree qualifications obtained in the UK – Education

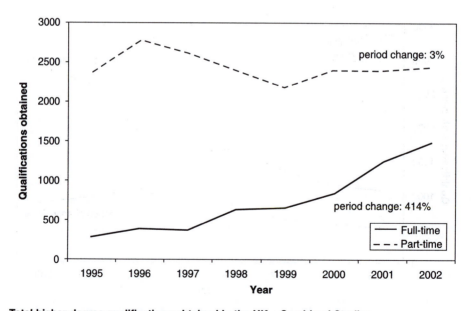

Total higher degree qualifications obtained in the UK – Combined Studies

Appendix 3   Top 10 institutions by research income, 2003

Source: Higher Education Statistics Agency – Finance Record 2002/03

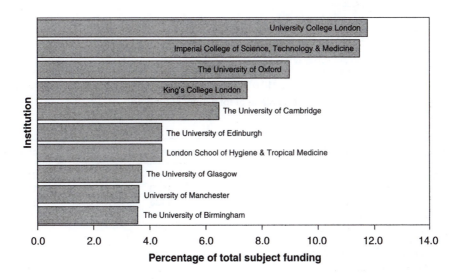

Subject area: (1) Clinical Medicine	Income £(000s)	% of total
University College London	88361	11.8
Imperial College of Science, Technology & Medicine	86157	11.5
The University of Oxford	67575	9.0
King's College London	56226	7.5
The University of Cambridge	48591	6.5
The University of Edinburgh	33258	4.4
London School of Hygiene & Tropical Medicine	33228	4.4
The University of Glasgow	27982	3.7
University of Manchester	27184	3.6
The University of Birmingham	26854	3.6

Subject area: (1) Clinical Medicine

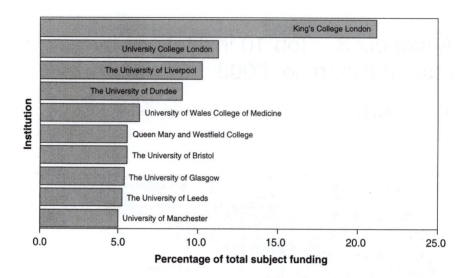

Percentage of total subject funding

Subject area: (2) Clinical Dentistry	Income £(000s)	% of total
King's College London	2962	21.2
University College London	1580	11.3
The University of Liverpool	1436	10.3
The University of Dundee	1262	9.0
University of Wales College of Medicine	886	6.3
The University of Bristol	778	5.6
Queen Mary and Westfield College	778	5.6
The University of Glasgow	756	5.4
The University of Leeds	735	5.2
University of Manchester	700	5.0

Subject area: (2) Clinical Dentistry

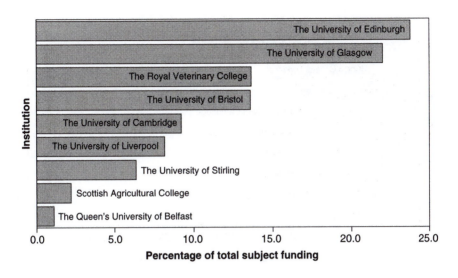

Subject: (3) Veterinary Science	Income £(000s)	% of total
The University of Edinburgh	7475	23.8
The University of Glasgow	6919	22.0
The Royal Veterinary College	4288	13.6
The University of Bristol	4278	13.6
The University of Cambridge	2899	9.2
The University of Liverpool	2570	8.2
The University of Stirling	1999	6.4
Scottish Agricultural College	691	2.2
The Queen's University of Belfast	342	1.1

Subject: (3) Veterinary Science

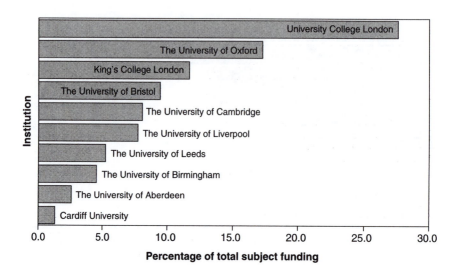

Percentage of total subject funding

Subject: (4) Anatomy and Physiology	Income £(000s)	% of total
University College London	13823	27.6
The University of Oxford	8656	17.3
King's College London	5835	11.7
The University of Bristol	4730	9.4
The University of Cambridge	4034	8.1
The University of Liverpool	3863	7.7
The University of Leeds	2622	5.2
The University of Birmingham	2270	4.5
The University of Aberdeen	1303	2.6
Cardiff University	672	1.3

Subject: (4) Anatomy and Physiology

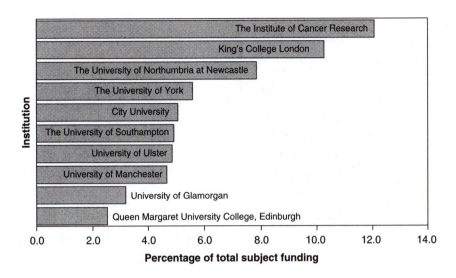

Percentage of total subject funding

Subject: (5) Nursing and Paramedical Studies	Income £(000s)	% of total
The Institute of Cancer Research	3399	12.1
King's College London	2889	10.3
The University of Northumbria at Newcastle	2208	7.8
The University of York	1570	5.6
City University	1424	5.1
The University of Southampton	1386	4.9
University of Ulster	1367	4.9
University of Manchester	1312	4.7
University of Glamorgan	900	3.2
Queen Margaret University College, Edinburgh	713	2.5

Subject: (5) Nursing and Paramedical Studies

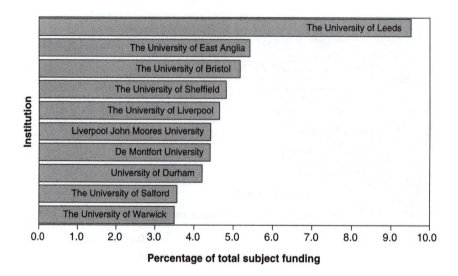

Percentage of total subject funding

Subject: (6) Health and Community Studies	Income £(000s)	% of total
The University of Leeds	2494	9.5
The University of East Anglia	1423	5.4
The University of Bristol	1358	5.2
The University of Sheffield	1265	4.8
The University of Liverpool	1221	4.6
Liverpool John Moores University	1161	4.4
De Montfort University	1159	4.4
University of Durham	1104	4.2
The University of Salford	934	3.5
The University of Warwick	917	3.5

Subject: (6) Health and Community Studies

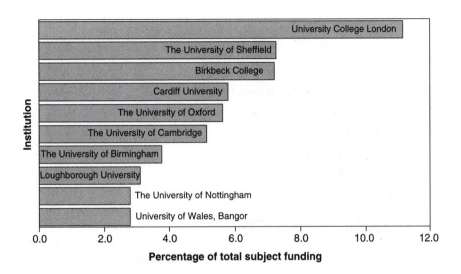

Percentage of total subject funding

Subject: (7) Psychology and Behavioural Sciences	Income £(000s)	% of total
University College London	5257	11.2
The University of Sheffield	3415	7.2
Birkbeck College	3395	7.2
Cardiff University	2724	5.8
The University of Oxford	2650	5.6
The University of Cambridge	2420	5.1
The University of Birmingham	1710	3.6
Loughborough University	1463	3.1
The University of Nottingham	1315	2.8
University of Wales, Bangor	1314	2.8

Subject: (7) Psychology and Behavioural Sciences

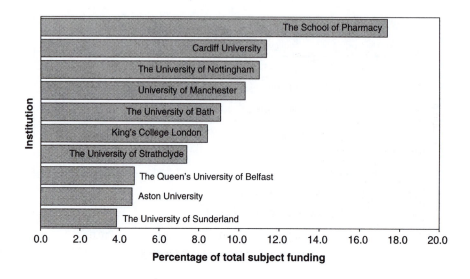

Percentage of total subject funding

Subject: (8) Pharmacy	Income £(000s)	% of total
The School of Pharmacy	3943	17.4
Cardiff University	2580	11.4
The University of Nottingham	2495	11.0
University of Manchester	2339	10.3
The University of Bath	2062	9.1
King's College London	1911	8.4
The University of Strathclyde	1677	7.4
The Queen's University of Belfast	1076	4.7
Aston University	1051	4.6
The University of Sunderland	875	3.9

Subject: (8) Pharmacy

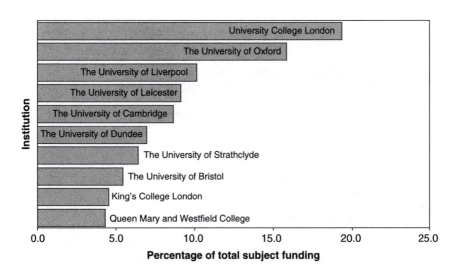

Percentage of total subject funding

Subject: (9) Pharmacology	Income £(000s)	% of total
University College London	4252	19.3
The University of Oxford	3483	15.8
The University of Liverpool	2227	10.1
The University of Leicester	2008	9.1
The University of Cambridge	1902	8.7
The University of Dundee	1526	6.9
The University of Strathclyde	1410	6.4
The University of Bristol	1199	5.5
King's College London	1000	4.5
Queen Mary and Westfield College	948	4.3

Subject: (9) Pharmacology

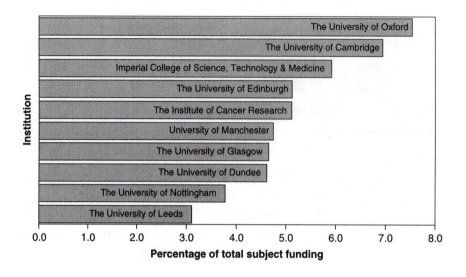

The University of Oxford
The University of Cambridge
Imperial College of Science, Technology & Medicine
The University of Edinburgh
The Institute of Cancer Research
University of Manchester
The University of Glasgow
The University of Dundee
The University of Nottingham
The University of Leeds

Institution

Percentage of total subject funding

Subject: (10) Biosciences	Income £(000s)	% of total
The University of Oxford	29332	7.5
The University of Cambridge	27057	7.0
Imperial College of Science, Technology & Medicine	23030	5.9
The University of Edinburgh	19935	5.1
The Institute of Cancer Research	19906	5.1
University of Manchester	18450	4.7
The University of Glasgow	18105	4.7
The University of Dundee	17940	4.6
The University of Nottingham	14724	3.8
The University of Leeds	12113	3.1

Subject: (10) Biosciences

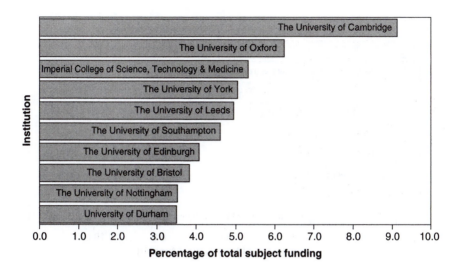

Subject: (11) Chemistry	Income £(000s)	% of total
The University of Cambridge	11123	9.1
The University of Oxford	7596	6.2
Imperial College of Science, Technology & Medicine	6484	5.3
The University of York	6158	5.1
The University of Leeds	6030	4.9
The University of Southampton	5615	4.6
The University of Edinburgh	4972	4.1
The University of Bristol	4672	3.8
The University of Nottingham	4294	3.5
University of Durham	4266	3.5

Subject: (11) Chemistry

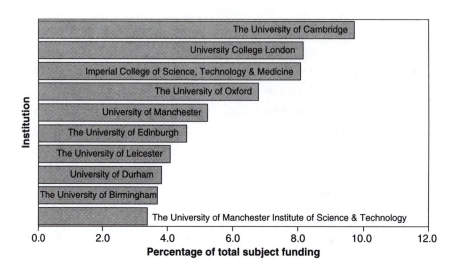

Percentage of total subject funding

Subject: (12) Physics	Income £(000s)	% of total
The University of Cambridge	15291	9.7
University College London	12852	8.2
Imperial College of Science, Technology & Medicine	12713	8.1
The University of Oxford	10690	6.8
University of Manchester	8228	5.2
The University of Edinburgh	7208	4.6
The University of Leicester	6433	4.1
University of Durham	6009	3.8
The University of Birmingham	5822	3.7
The University of Manchester Institute of Science & Technology	5333	3.4

Subject: (12) Physics

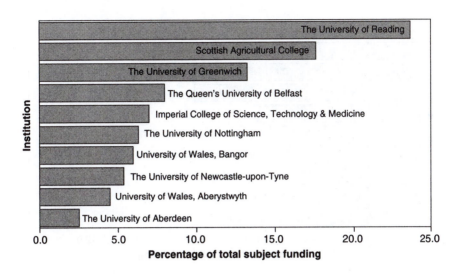

Subject: (13) Agriculture and Forestry	Income £(000s)	% of total
The University of Reading	7694	23.6
Scottish Agricultural College	5732	17.6
The University of Greenwich	4315	13.3
The Queen's University of Belfast	2594	8.0
Imperial College of Science, Technology & Medicine	2275	7.0
The University of Nottingham	2049	6.3
University of Wales, Bangor	1942	6.0
The University of Newcastle-upon-Tyne	1744	5.4
University of Wales, Aberystwyth	1466	4.5
The University of Aberdeen	820	2.5

Subject: (13) Agriculture and Forestry

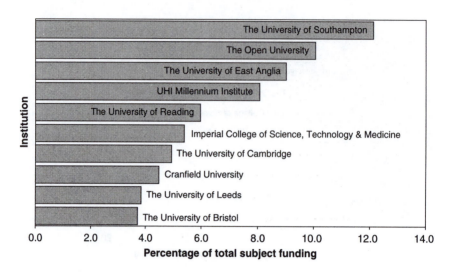

Institution

Percentage of total subject funding

Subject: (14) Earth, Marine and Environmental Sciences	Income £(000s)	% of total
The University of Southampton	10270	12.1
The Open University	8515	10.1
The University of East Anglia	7624	9.0
UHI Millennium Institute	6825	8.1
The University of Reading	5048	6.0
Imperial College of Science, Technology & Medicine	4554	5.4
The University of Cambridge	4171	4.9
Cranfield University	3803	4.5
The University of Leeds	3248	3.8
The University of Bristol	3144	3.7

Subject: (14) Earth, Marine and Environmental Sciences

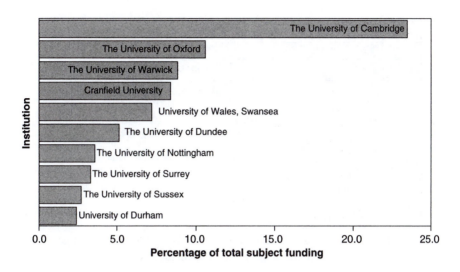

Percentage of total subject funding

Subject: (16) General Engineering	Income £(000s)	% of total
The University of Cambridge	16563	23.4
The University of Oxford	7479	10.6
The University of Warwick	6255	8.9
Cranfield University	5935	8.4
University of Wales, Swansea	5095	7.2
The University of Dundee	3633	5.1
The University of Nottingham	2527	3.6
The University of Surrey	2331	3.3
The University of Sussex	1922	2.7
University of Durham	1698	2.4

Subject: (16) General Engineering

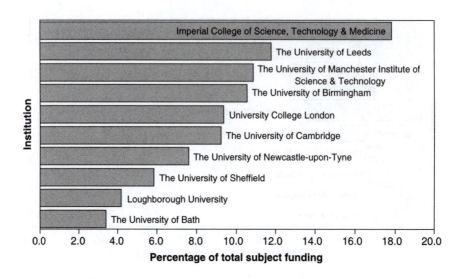

Percentage of total subject funding

Subject: (17) Chemical Engineering	Income £(000s)	% of total
Imperial College of Science, Technology & Medicine	4162	17.8
The University of Leeds	2747	11.8
The University of Manchester Institute of Science & Technology	2538	10.9
The University of Birmingham	2462	10.5
University College London	2185	9.4
The University of Cambridge	2153	9.2
The University of Newcastle-upon-Tyne	1772	7.6
The University of Sheffield	1366	5.9
Loughborough University	976	4.2
The University of Bath	796	3.4

Subject: (17) Chemical Engineering

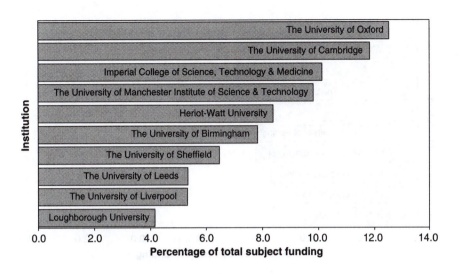

Percentage of total subject funding

Subject: (18) Mineral, Metallurgy and Materials Engineering	Income £(000s)	% of total
The University of Oxford	5424	12.5
The University of Cambridge	5121	11.8
Imperial College of Science, Technology & Medicine	4380	10.1
The University of Manchester Institute of Science & Technology	4244	9.8
Heriot-Watt University	3628	8.4
The University of Birmingham	3392	7.8
The University of Sheffield	2802	6.5
The University of Leeds	2316	5.4
The University of Liverpool	2305	5.3
Loughborough University	1802	4.2

Subject: (18) Mineral, Metallurgy and Materials Engineering

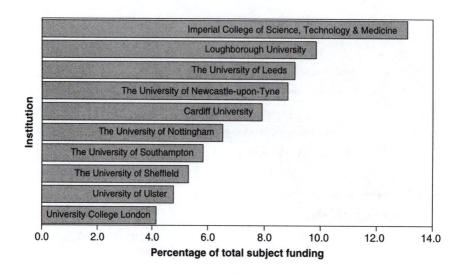

Percentage of total subject funding

Subject: (19) Civil Engineering	Income £(000s)	% of total
Imperial College of Science, Technology & Medicine	4154	13.1
Loughborough University	3122	9.8
The University of Leeds	2881	9.1
The University of Newcastle-upon-Tyne	2797	8.8
Cardiff University	2508	7.9
The University of Nottingham	2068	6.5
The University of Southampton	1845	5.8
The University of Sheffield	1681	5.3
University of Ulster	1514	4.8
University College London	1319	4.2

Subject: (19) Civil Engineering

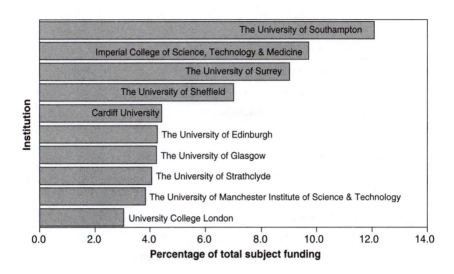

Percentage of total subject funding

Subject: (20) Electrical, Electronic and Computer Engineering	Income £(000s)	% of total
The University of Southampton	11880	12.1
Imperial College of Science, Technology & Medicine	9553	9.7
The University of Surrey	8861	9.0
The University of Sheffield	6887	7.0
Cardiff University	4350	4.4
The University of Edinburgh	4197	4.3
The University of Glasgow	4171	4.2
The University of Strathclyde	4002	4.1
The University of Manchester Institute of Science & Technology	3784	3.8
University College London	2999	3.1

Subject: (20) Electrical, Electronic and Computer Engineering

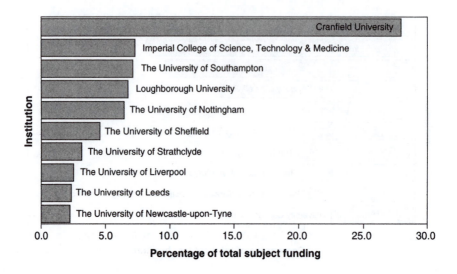

Subject: (21) Mechanical, Aero and Production Engineering	Income £(000s)	% of total
Cranfield University	26238	27.9
Imperial College of Science, Technology & Medicine	6837	7.3
The University of Southampton	6700	7.1
Loughborough University	6331	6.7
The University of Nottingham	6053	6.4
The University of Sheffield	4288	4.6
The University of Strathclyde	2973	3.2
The University of Liverpool	2376	2.5
The University of Leeds	2244	2.4
The University of Newcastle-upon-Tyne	2139	2.3

Subject: (21) Mechanical, Aero and Production Engineering

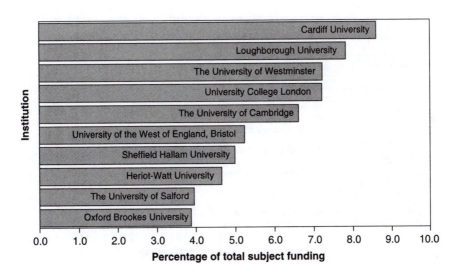

Subject: (23) Architecture, Built Environment and Planning	Income £(000s)	% of total
Cardiff University	1853	8.6
Loughborough University	1682	7.8
The University of Westminster	1553	7.2
University College London	1552	7.2
The University of Cambridge	1423	6.6
University of the West of England, Bristol	1129	5.2
Sheffield Hallam University	1074	5.0
Heriot-Watt University	1001	4.7
The University of Salford	850	3.9
Oxford Brookes University	834	3.9

Subject: (23) Architecture, Built Environment and Planning

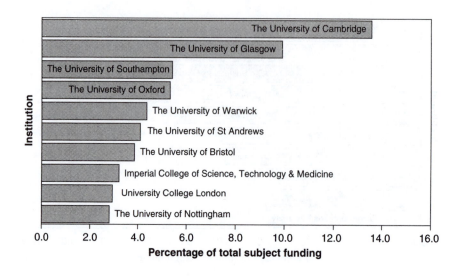

Subject: (24) Mathematics	Income £(000s)	% of total
The University of Cambridge	4604	13.6
The University of Glasgow	3361	9.9
The University of Southampton	1841	5.4
The University of Oxford	1810	5.3
The University of Warwick	1477	4.4
The University of St Andrews	1389	4.1
The University of Bristol	1307	3.9
Imperial College of Science, Technology & Medicine	1093	3.2
University College London	998	2.9
The University of Nottingham	956	2.8

Subject: (24) Mathematics

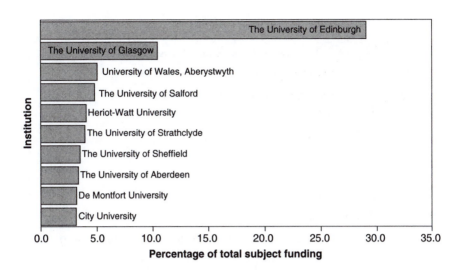

Subject: (25) Information Technology and Systems Sciences	Income £(000s)	% of total
The University of Edinburgh	5591	29.0
The University of Glasgow	2008	10.4
University of Wales, Aberystwyth	972	5.0
The University of Salford	926	4.8
Heriot-Watt University	783	4.1
The University of Strathclyde	762	4.0
The University of Sheffield	677	3.5
The University of Aberdeen	644	3.3
De Montfort University	613	3.2
City University	608	3.2

Subject: (25) Information Technology and Systems Sciences

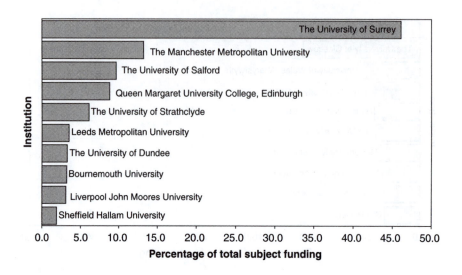

Percentage of total subject funding

Subject: (26) Catering and Hospitality Management	Income £(000s)	% of total
The University of Surrey	440	46.1
The Manchester Metropolitan University	126	13.2
The University of Salford	92	9.6
Queen Margaret University College, Edinburgh	84	8.8
The University of Strathclyde	58	6.1
Leeds Metropolitan University	34	3.6
The University of Dundee	32	3.4
Bournemouth University	31	3.2
Liverpool John Moores University	30	3.1
Sheffield Hallam University	19	2.0

Subject: (26) Catering and Hospitality Management

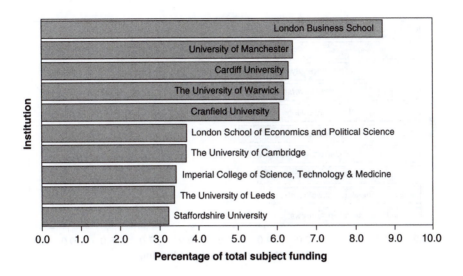

Percentage of total subject funding

Subject: (27) Business and Management Studies	Income £(000s)	% of total
London Business School	4137	8.7
University of Manchester	3043	6.4
Cardiff University	2993	6.3
The University of Warwick	2938	6.2
Cranfield University	2879	6.1
London School of Economics and Political Science	1755	3.7
The University of Cambridge	1751	3.7
Imperial College of Science, Technology & Medicine	1626	3.4
The University of Leeds	1603	3.4
Staffordshire University	1534	3.2

Subject: (27) Business and Management Studies

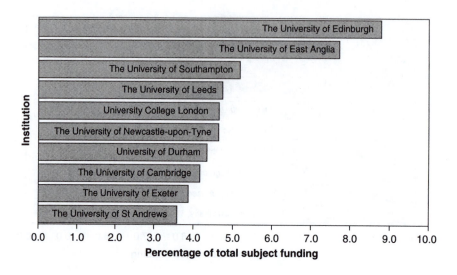

Subject: (28) Geography	Income £(000s)	% of total
The University of Edinburgh	2056	8.8
The University of East Anglia	1808	7.7
The University of Southampton	1212	5.2
The University of Leeds	1109	4.7
University College London	1089	4.7
The University of Newcastle-upon-Tyne	1086	4.6
University of Durham	1017	4.3
The University of Cambridge	976	4.2
The University of Exeter	907	3.9
The University of St Andrews	841	3.6

Subject: (28) Geography

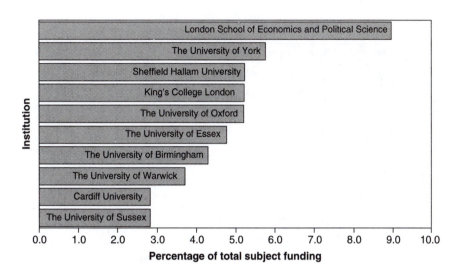

Percentage of total subject funding

Subject: (29) Social Sciences	Income £(000s)	% of total
London School of Economics and Political Science	10745	9.0
The University of York	6919	5.8
Sheffield Hallam University	6273	5.2
King's College London	6265	5.2
The University of Oxford	6244	5.2
The University of Essex	5719	4.8
The University of Birmingham	5147	4.3
The University of Warwick	4450	3.7
Cardiff University	3382	2.8
The University of Sussex	3382	2.8

Subject: (29) Social Sciences

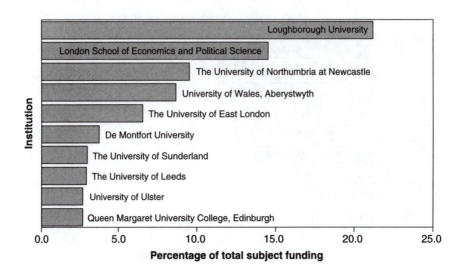

Subject: (30) Librarianship, Communication and Media Studies	Income £(000s)	% of total
Loughborough University	945	21.2
London School of Economics and Political Science	648	14.5
The University of Northumbria at Newcastle	424	9.5
University of Wales, Aberystwyth	387	8.7
The University of East London	292	6.5
De Montfort University	166	3.7
The University of Sunderland	132	3.0
The University of Leeds	130	2.9
University of Ulster	120	2.7
Queen Margaret University College, Edinburgh	120	2.7

Subject: (30) Librarianship, Communication and Media Studies

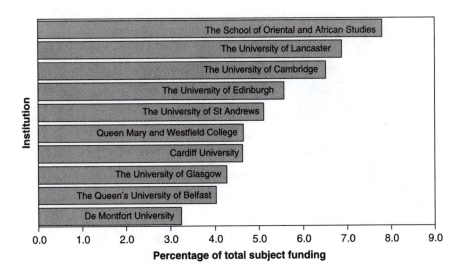

Percentage of total subject funding

Subject: (31) Language-based Studies	Income £(000s)	% of total
The School of Oriental and African Studies	904	7.8
The University of Lancaster	798	6.9
The University of Cambridge	756	6.5
The University of Edinburgh	646	5.6
The University of St Andrews	593	5.1
Queen Mary and Westfield College	539	4.6
Cardiff University	536	4.6
The University of Glasgow	495	4.3
The Queen's University of Belfast	466	4.0
De Montfort University	375	3.2

Subject: (31) Language-based Studies

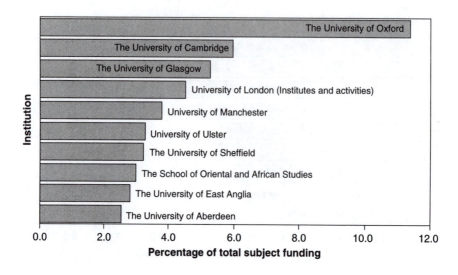

Percentage of total subject funding

Subject: (32) Humanities	Income £(000s)	% of total
The University of Oxford	3019	11.4
The University of Cambridge	1582	6.0
The University of Glasgow	1401	5.3
University of London (Institutes and activities)	1198	4.5
University of Manchester	1006	3.8
University of Ulster	870	3.3
The University of Sheffield	856	3.2
The School of Oriental and African Studies	796	3.0
The University of East Anglia	747	2.8
The University of Aberdeen	676	2.5

Subject: (32) Humanities

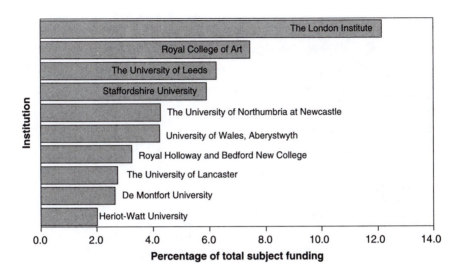

Percentage of total subject funding

Subject: (33) Design and Creative Arts	Income £(000s)	% of total
The London Institute	1576	12.2
Royal College of Art	965	7.4
The University of Leeds	811	6.3
Staffordshire University	765	5.9
The University of Northumbria at Newcastle	555	4.3
University of Wales, Aberystwyth	549	4.2
Royal Holloway and Bedford New College	423	3.3
The University of Lancaster	356	2.7
De Montfort University	345	2.7
Heriot-Watt University	262	2.0

Subject: (33) Design and Creative Arts

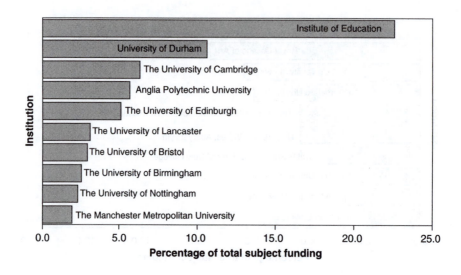

Percentage of total subject funding

Subject: (34) Education	Income £(000s)	% of total
Institute of Education	11610	22.6
University of Durham	5468	10.6
The University of Cambridge	3260	6.3
Anglia Polytechnic University	2920	5.7
The University of Edinburgh	2624	5.1
The University of Lancaster	1606	3.1
The University of Bristol	1507	2.9
The University of Birmingham	1322	2.6
The University of Nottingham	1211	2.4
The Manchester Metropolitan University	1017	2.0

Subject: (34) Education

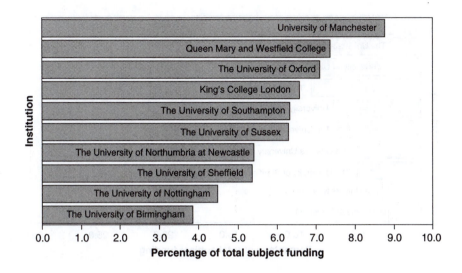

Percentage of total subject funding

Subject: (35) French, Spanish and German Modern Languages	Income £(000s)	% of total
University of Manchester	219	8.8
Queen Mary and Westfield College	184	7.4
The University of Oxford	177	7.1
King's College London	164	6.6
The University of Southampton	158	6.3
The University of Sussex	157	6.3
The University of Northumbria at Newcastle	135	5.4
The University of Sheffield	134	5.4
The University of Nottingham	112	4.5
The University of Birmingham	96	3.8

Subject: (35) French, Spanish and German Modern Languages

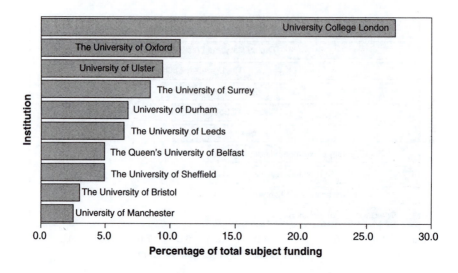

Percentage of total subject funding

Subject: (36) Other Modern Languages	Income £(000s)	% of total
University College London	628	27.2
The University of Oxford	248	10.7
University of Ulster	218	9.4
The University of Surrey	196	8.5
University of Durham	156	6.8
The University of Leeds	149	6.5
The Queen's University of Belfast	114	4.9
The University of Sheffield	114	4.9
The University of Bristol	70	3.0
University of Manchester	59	2.6

Subject: (36) Other Modern Languages

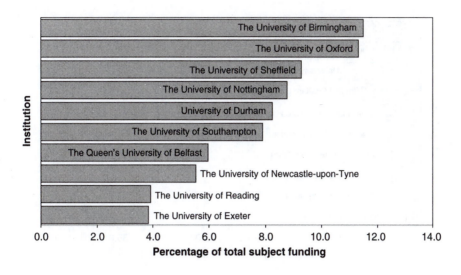

Percentage of total subject funding

Subject: (37) Archaeology	Income £(000s)	% of total
The University of Birmingham	1032	11.5
The University of Oxford	1016	11.3
The University of Sheffield	833	9.3
The University of Nottingham	788	8.8
University of Durham	740	8.2
The University of Southampton	710	7.9
The Queen's University of Belfast	536	6.0
The University of Newcastle-upon-Tyne	498	5.5
The University of Reading	352	3.9
The University of Exeter	345	3.8

Subject: (37) Archaeology

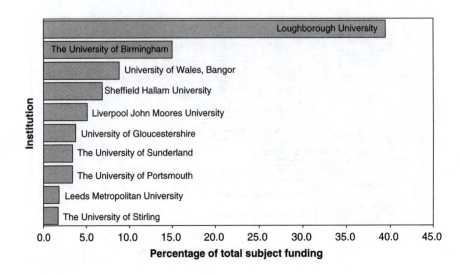

Percentage of total subject funding

Subject: (38) Sports Science and Leisure Studies	Income £(000s)	% of total
Loughborough University	1302	39.5
The University of Birmingham	494	15.0
University of Wales, Bangor	291	8.8
Sheffield Hallam University	227	6.9
Liverpool John Moores University	168	5.1
University of Gloucestershire	124	3.8
The University of Sunderland	112	3.4
The University of Portsmouth	112	3.4
Leeds Metropolitan University	62	1.9
The University of Stirling	59	1.8

Subject: (38) Sports Science and Leisure Studies

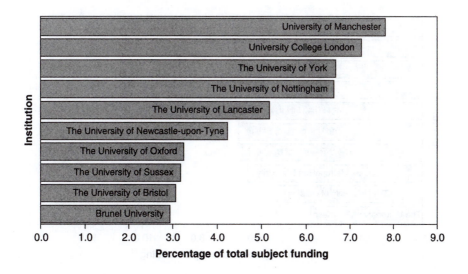

Percentage of total subject funding

Subject: (39) Computer Software Engineering	Income £(000s)	% of total
University of Manchester	3426	7.8
University College London	3185	7.3
The University of York	2927	6.7
The University of Nottingham	2910	6.6
The University of Lancaster	2271	5.2
The University of Newcastle-upon-Tyne	1856	4.2
The University of Oxford	1421	3.2
The University of Sussex	1391	3.2
The University of Bristol	1344	3.1
Brunel University	1286	2.9

Subject: (39) Computer Software Engineering

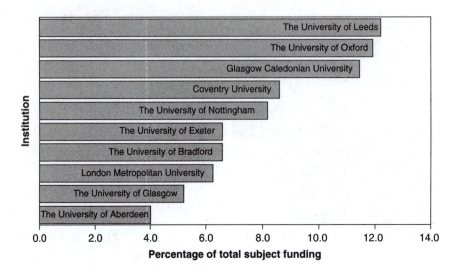

Percentage of total subject funding

Subject: (41) Continuing Education	Income £(000s)	% of total
The University of Leeds	176	12.2
The University of Oxford	172	11.9
Glasgow Caledonian University	165	11.4
Coventry University	124	8.6
The University of Nottingham	118	8.2
The University of Exeter	95	6.6
The University of Bradford	95	6.6
London Metropolitan University	90	6.2
The University of Glasgow	75	5.2
The University of Aberdeen	58	4.0

Subject: (41) Continuing Education

Index